PHP/MySQL Programming

for the absolute beginner

ANDY HARRIS

ISBN: 1-931841-32-2

Library of Congress Catalog Card Number: 2003104019
Printed in the United States of America

03 04 05 06 07 BH 10 9 8 7 6 5 4 3 2 1

Premier Press, a division of Course Technology
25 Thomson Place
Boston, MA 02210

Publisher:
Stacy L. Hiquet

Senior Marketing Manager:
Martine Edwards

Marketing Manager:
Heather Hurley

Manager of Editorial Services:
Heather Talbot

Associate Marketing Manager:
Kristin Eisenzopf

Acquisitions Editor:
Todd Jensen

Project Editor:
Sandy Doell

Technical Reviewer:
Jason Wynia

Retail Market Coordinator:
Sarah Dubois

Interior Layout:
Danielle Foster

Cover Designer:
Mike Tanamachi

CD-ROM Producer:
Keith Davenport

Indexer:
Kelly Talbot

Proofreader:
Margaret Bauer

To Heather, Elizabeth, Matthew, and Jacob

Acknowledgments

First I thank Him from whom all flows.

Heather, you always work harder on these books than I do. Thank you for your love and your support. Thank you Elizabeth, Matthew, and Jacob for understanding why Daddy was typing all the time.

Thanks to the Open Source community for creating great free software like PHP and MySQL.

Thank you, Stacy Hiquet, for your continued support and encouragement on this and other projects.

Thanks, Todd Jensen, for holding this thing together.

Special thanks to Sandy Doell for turning my drivel into something readable.

Thanks to J Wynia (www.phpgeek.com) for technical editing. Thanks also to Jason for use of PHPTriad on the CD-ROM.

Thank you to the webyog development team (http://www.webyog.com/sqlyog/) for use of the SQLyog tool.

A big thanks to Keith Davenport for putting together the CD-ROM. It's a big job, and you did it well.

Thank you to the many members of the Premier/Course team who worked on this book.

A *huge* thanks to my CSCI N399 Server Side Web Development class in Spring 2003. Thank you for being patient with my manuscript, for helping me spot many errors, and for providing invaluable advice. I learned as much from you as you did from me.

About the Author

Andy Harris began his teaching career as a high school special education teacher. During that time, he taught himself enough computing to do part-time computer consulting and database work. He began teaching computing at the university level in the late 1980s as a part-time job. Since 1995 he has been a full-time lecturer in the Computer Science Department of Indiana University/Purdue University–Indianapolis, where he manages the Streaming Media Lab and teaches classes in several programming languages. His primary interests are Java, Microsoft languages, Perl, JavaScript, PHP, Web Data, virtual reality, portable devices, and streaming media.

Contents at a Glance

Contents

Using Variables and Input 39

Controlling Your Code with Conditions and Functions 77

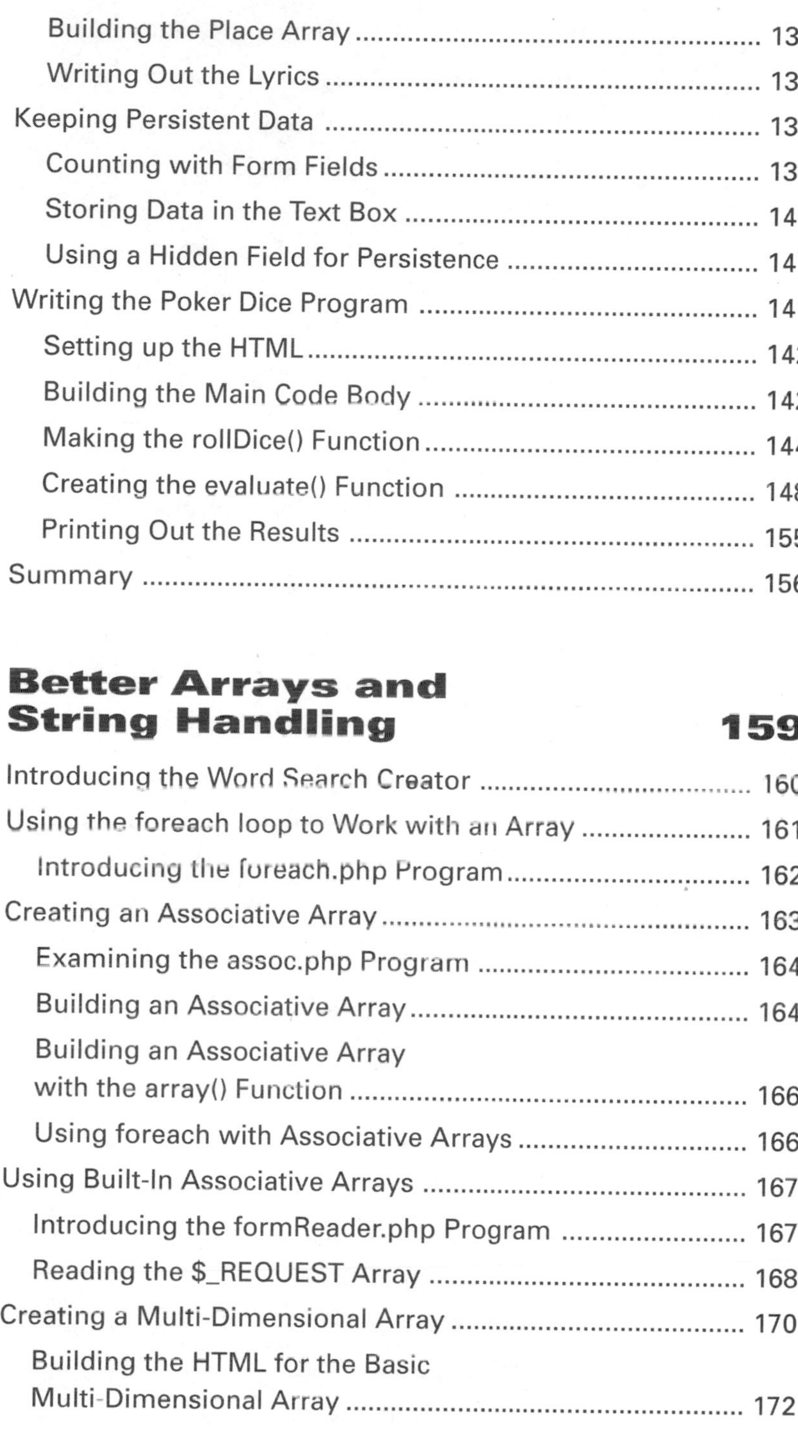

Working with Files 211

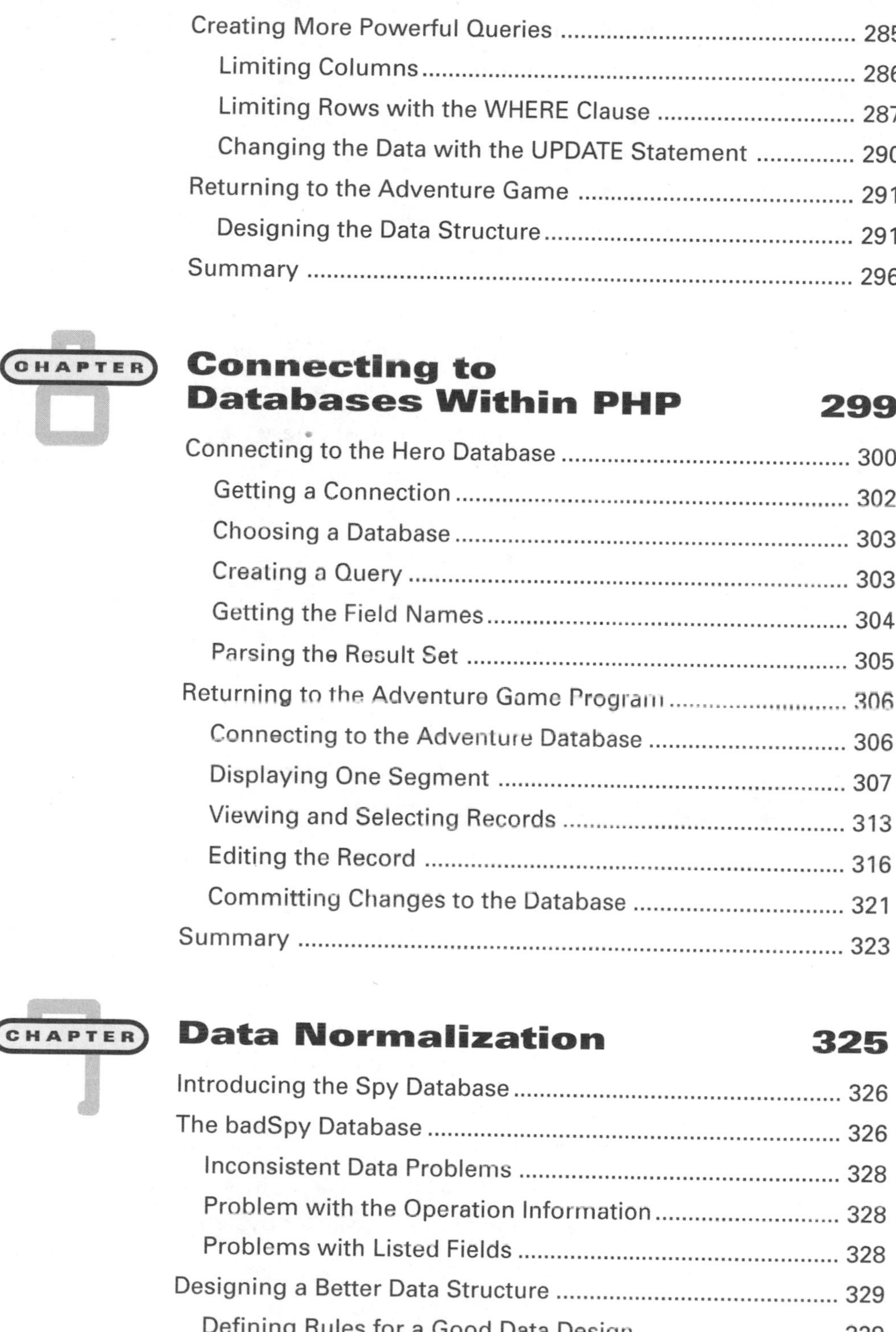

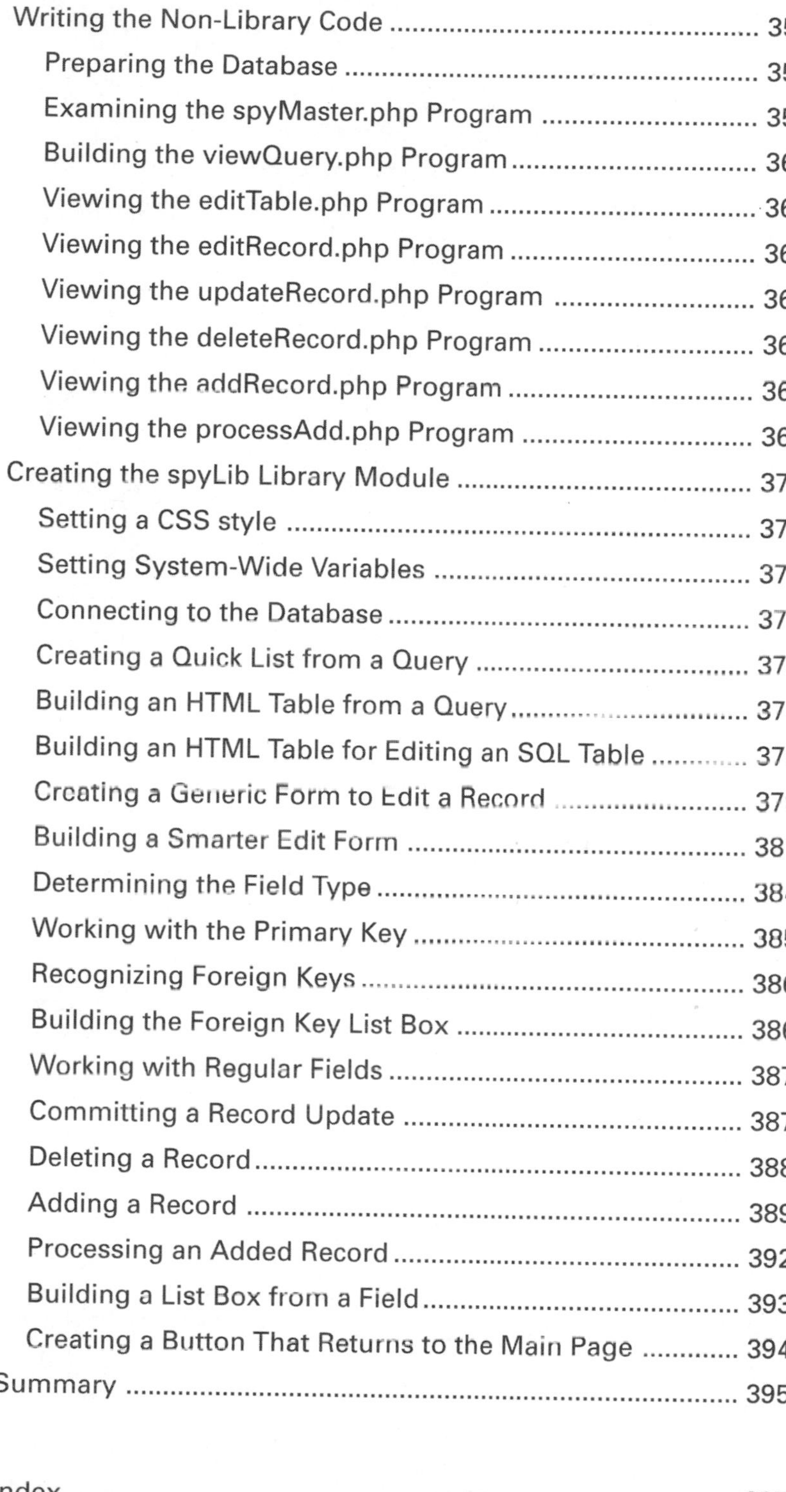

Introduction

If you've been watching the Web for a while you've probably noticed it is changing. When the Web first entered into the public consciousness, it was a way to distribute documents. These documents were pretty easy to make. Anybody with a weekend and a text editor could get a Web page up and running. Building a Web site in the early days was about making documents.

Today the Internet is much more than that. Interesting Web sites are not simply *documents*; they are *applications*. They have much more complexity and power. You might think the Web is no longer a place for individuals or beginning programmers. Many of the software development tools available are expensive and complicated.

To me, the most exciting thing about the Internet is its social implications. There is a large community that believes in powerful, easy-to-use, free software. That community has produced a number of exceptional programs, including PHP and MySQL.

PHP is a powerful programming language that lets you build dynamic Web sites. It works well on a variety of platforms, and it's reasonably easy to understand. MySQL is an impressive relational data management system used to build commercial quality databases. PHP and MySQL are such powerful and easy-to-use platforms that they make Web programming accessible even for beginners.

In this book, I will teach you about programming. Specifically, you will learn how to write programs on Web servers. You'll learn all the main concepts of programming languages. You'll also learn about how data works in the modern environment. You'll learn commands and syntax, but you'll also learn the process of programming.

If you've never written a computer program before, this book will be a good introduction. If you're an experienced programmer wanting to learn PHP and MySQL, you'll find this book to be a gentle introduction.

Programming is hard work, but it's also a lot of fun. I had a great time writing this book, and I hope you enjoy learning from it. I'm looking forward to hearing about what you can do after you learn from this book.

—Andy

Exploring the PHP Environment

Web pages are interesting, but on their own they are simply documents. You can use PHP to add code to your Web pages so they can do more. A scripting language like PHP can convert your Web site from static documents to an interactive application. In this chapter, you'll learn how to add basic PHP functionality to your Web pages. Specifically, you'll:

- Review HTML commands.
- Use Cascading Style Sheets to enhance your Web pages.
- Build HTML forms.
- Ensure PHP is on your system.
- Run a basic diagnostic of your PHP installation.
- Add PHP code to a Web page.

Introducing the "Tip of the Day" Program

Your first program probably won't win any Web awards, but it will take you beyond what you can do with regular HTML. Figure 1.1 illustrates the "Tip of the day" page, which offers friendly, helpful advice.

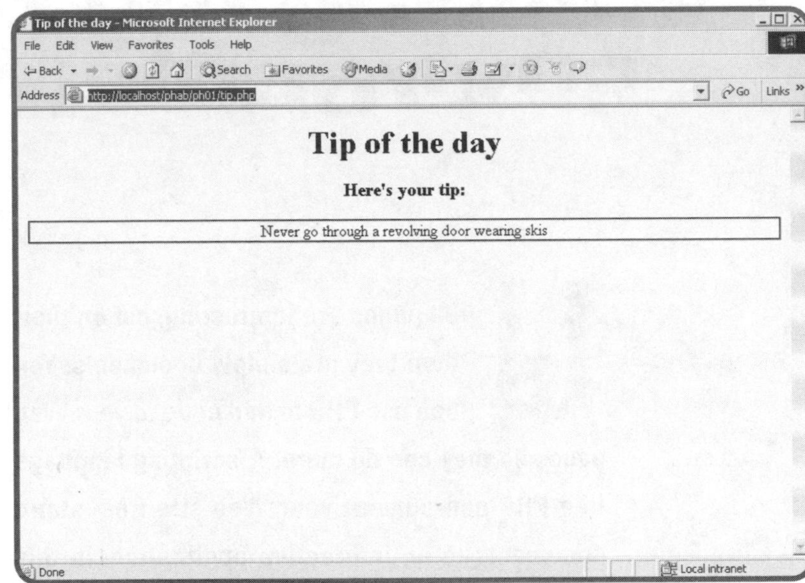

FIGURE 1.1

The tip of the day might look simple, but it is a technological marvel, because it features html, cascading style sheets, and PHP code.

Of course, you could write this kind of page without using a technology like PHP, but the program is a little more sophisticated than it might look on the surface. The tip isn't actually embedded in the Web page at all, but it is stored in a completely separate file. The program integrates this separate file into the HTML page. The page owner can change the tip of the day very easily by editing the text file that contains the tips.

You'll start by reviewing your HTML skills. Soon enough, you're going to be writing programs that write Web pages, so you need to be very secure with your HTML coding. If you usually write all your Web pages with a plain-text editor, you should be fine. If you tend to rely on higher end tools like Microsoft FrontPage or Macromedia Dreamweaver, you should put those tools aside for a while and make sure you can write solid HTML by hand.

IN THE REAL WORLD

The Tip of the day page illustrates one of the hottest concepts in Web programming today— the content management system. This kind of structure allows programmers to design the general layout of a Web site, but isolates the contents from the page design. The page owners (who might or might not know how to modify a Web page directly) can easily change a text file without risk of exposing the code that holds the site together. As you progress through this book, you'll learn how to develop powerful content management systems, as well as a lot of other cool things.

Programming on the Web Server

The Internet is all about various computers communicating with each other. The prevailing model of the Internet is the notion of clients and servers. You can understand this better by imagining a drive-through restaurant. As you drive to the little speaker, a barely intelligible voice asks for your order. You ask for your "cholesto-burger supreme," and the bored teenager packages your food. You drive up, exchange money for the combo meal, and drive away. Meanwhile, the teenager waits for another customer to appear. The Internet works much like this model. Large permanent computers called *Web servers* permanently host Web pages and other information. They are much like the drive-through restaurant. Users "drive up" to the Web server using a Web browser. The data is exchanged, and the user can read the information on the Web browser.

What's interesting about this model is the interaction doesn't have to stop there. Since the client (user's) machine is a computer, it can be given instructions. Commonly, the JavaScript language is used to store special instructions in a Web page. These instructions (like the HTML code itself) don't mean anything on the server. Once the page gets to the client machine, the browser interprets the HTML code and any other JavaScript instructions. While much of the work is passed to the client, there are some disadvantages to this client-side approach. Programs designed to work inside a Web browser are usually greatly restricted in the kinds of things they can do. A client-side Web program usually cannot access the user's printer or disk drives. This limitation alone prevents such programs from doing much of the most useful work of the Internet, such as database connectivity and user tracking.

The server is also a computer, and it's possible to write programs designed to operate on the server rather than the client. There are a number of advantages to this arrangement:

- Server-side programs run on powerful Web server computers.
- The server can freely work with files and databases.
- The code returned to the user is plain HTML, which can be displayed on any Web browser.

Building Basic HTML Pages

The basic unit of web development is the HTML page. This is simply a text document containing special tags to describe the data in the page. Although you might already be familiar with HTML, it makes sense to review these skills because PHP programming is closely tied to HTML.

As you are beginning, I strongly urge you to use a plain text editor. You can use Notepad, or one of the many free editors available. There are some exceptional free editors available on the CD-ROM that accompanies this book. Word processors usually do not save files in plain text format (which PHP and HTML require) and many of the fancy Web editors (such as FrontPage or Dreamweaver) tend to write clunky code that will really get in your way once you start to add programming functionality to it.

Creating the HTML "Hello" Page

HTML is mainly text. The Web author adds special markups to a text document to indicate the meaning of various elements. When a user requests a Web page, the text document is pulled from the Web server, and the browser interprets the various tags to determine how the document is displayed on the screen. Figure 1.2 illustrates a very simple Web page.

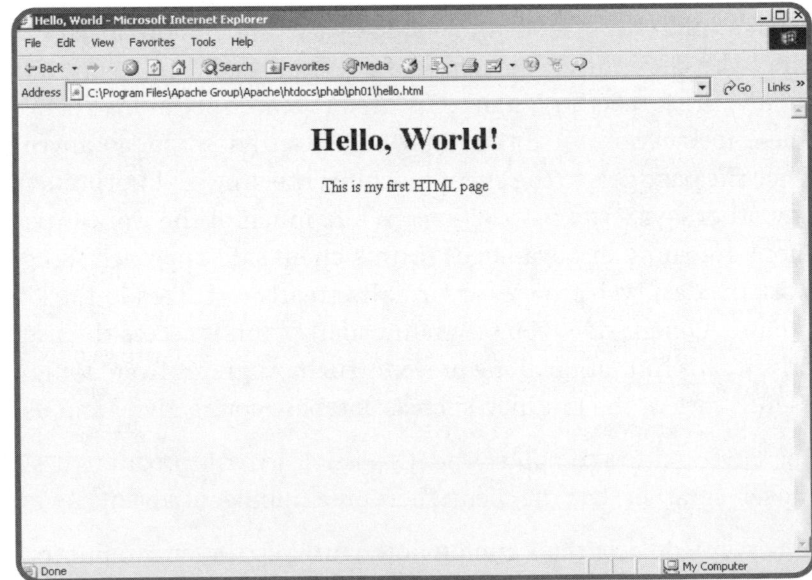

FIGURE 1.2

A very basic Web page.

If you look at the code for this page, you will see that it's pretty easy to understand, even if you aren't terribly familiar with HTML code.

```
<html>

<head>

<title>Hello, World</title>

</head>


<body>

<center>

<h1>Hello, World!</h1>

This is my first HTML page

</center>

</body>

</html>
```

As you can see, many words are encased in angle braces(<>). These words are called `tags`, and they are meant to be interpreted as instructions for the Web browser. Most tags come in pairs. For example, the entire document begins with `<html>` and ends with `</html>` The slash (/) indicates an ending tag.

Each HTML document contains a head area surrounded with a `<head></head>` pair. The header area contains information about the document in general. It almost always contains a title, which is often displayed in the title bar of the Web browser. However, there are no guarantees. HTML tags describe the *meaning* of an element, not necessarily how it is to be displayed. It's up to each browser to determine how something will be displayed.

The bulk of an HTML document is contained in the body, indicated with the `<body></body>` tags.

Within the body of the HTML document, you can use tags to define various characteristics of the page. Usually you can guess at the meanings of most of the tags. For example, the `<center></center>` pair causes all the text between the tags to be centered (if the browser can support this feature).

It's vital to understand that HTML tags are not *commands* to the browser as much as suggestions. This is because there are so many different types of computers and Web browsers available. It's possible that somebody might look at your Web page on a palm-sized computer or a cell phone. These devices will not be able to display information in the same way as full-size computers. The Web browser will try to follow your instructions, but ultimately, the way the page looks to the end user is not under your direct control.

The `<h1></h1>` tags are used to designate that the text contained between the tags is a level-one (highest priority) heading. HTML supports six levels of heading, from `<h1>` to `<h6>`. You can't be exactly sure how these headings will appear in a user's browser, but any text in an `<h1>` pair will be strongly emphasized, and each descending head level causes the text designated by that code to have less and less emphasis.

Basic Tags

There are a number of tags associated with HTML. Most of these tags are used to determine the meaning of a particular chunk of text. Table 1.1 illustrates some of these tags.

Of course, there are many other HTML tags, but those featured in Table 1.1 are the most commonly used. Figure 1.3 illustrates several of the tags featured in Table 1.1.

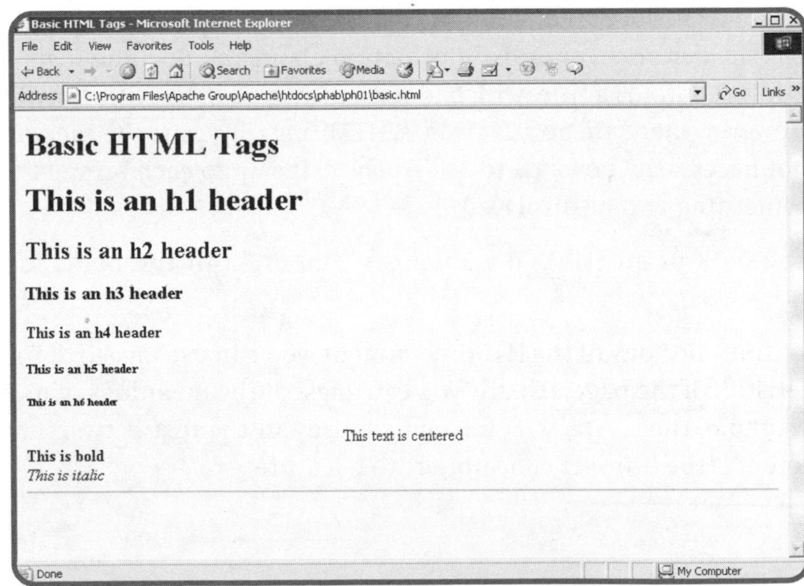

FIGURE 1.3

An HTML page containing the most common HTML tags.

Table 1.1 Basic HTML Tags

Tag	Meaning	Discussion
<b></b>	Bold	Won't work on all browsers.
<i></i>	Italic	Won't work on all browsers.
<h1></h1>	Level 1 header	Strongest headline emphasis.
<h6></h6>	Level 6 header	Weakest headline level (levels 2-5 also supported).
<ul> <li></li> </ul>	Un-numbered list	Must contain list items (<li></li>). Used for bulleted lists. Add as many list items as you wish.
<ol> <li></li> </ol>	Ordered list	Must contain list items (<li></li>). Used for numbered list. Add as many list items as you wish.
<a href = "anotherPage.html"> go to another page</a>	Anchor (hyperlink)	Places a link on the page. Text between <a> and </a> will be visible on page as a link. When user clicks on link, browser will go to the specified address.
<img src = "imgName.gif">	image	Adds the specified image to the page. Images should be in GIF, JPG, or PNG formats.
<font color = "red" size = 5> this text is red </font>	Modify font	Will not work in all browsers. It's possible to modify font color, size, and face (typeface), although typeface will often not transfer to client machine.
 	Break	Causes a carriage return in the output. Does not have an ending tag.
<hr>	Horizontal rule	Add a horizontal line to the page. Does not have an ending tag.

The source code for the basic.html document illustrates how the page was designed.

```
<html>
<head>
<title>Basic HTML Tags</title>
</head>
<body>
<h1>Basic HTML Tags</h1>

<h1>This is an h1 header</h1>
<h2>This is an h2 header</h2>
<h3>This is an h3 header</h3>
<h4>This is an h4 header</h4>
<h5>This is an h5 header</h5>
<h6>This is an h6 header</h6>

<center>
This text is centered
</center>

<b>This is bold</b>
<br>
<i>This is italic</i>
<hr>

</body>
</html>
```

The `H1` through `H6` headers create headlines of varying size and emphasis. The `<b>` tag causes text to be bold, and `<i>` formats text in italics. Finally, the `<hr>` tag is used to draw a horizontal line on the page.

More HTML Tags

The rest of the tags shown in Table 1.1 are featured in Figure 1.4.

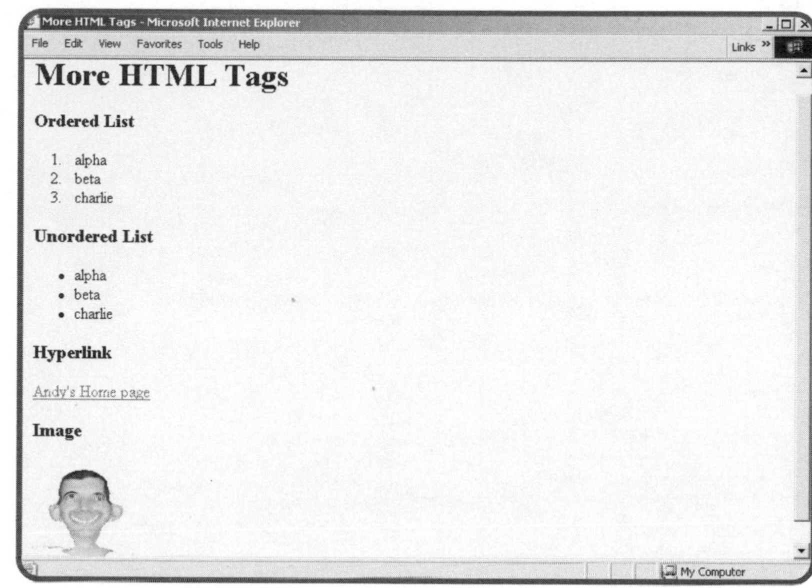

FIGURE 1.4

Examples of several other basic HTML tags.

The tags in more.html are used to add lists, links, and images to a Web page. The code used to produce this page looks like this:

```
<html>
<head>
<title>More HTML Tags</title>
</head>
<body>
<h1>More HTML Tags</h1>

<h3>Ordered List</h3>
<ol>
  <li>alpha</li>
  <li>beta</li>
  <li>charlie</li>
</ol>

<h3>Unordered List</h3>
<ul>
  <li>alpha</li>
```

```
  <li>beta</li>
  <li>charlie</li>
</ul>

<h3>Hyperlink</h3>

<a href="http://www.cs.iupui.edu/~aharris">Andy's Home page</a>

<h3>Image</h3>
<img src="silly.gif"
     height = 100
     width = 100>

</body>
</html>
```

HTML supports two types of lists. The `<ol></ol>` set creates `ordered` (or numbered) lists. Each element in the list set (specified by an `<li></li>` pair) is automatically numbered. The `<ul></ul>` tags are used to produce unnumbered lists. Each `<li></li>` element is automatically given a bullet.

Hyperlinks are the elements that allow your user to move around on the Web by clicking on specially designated text. The `<a></a>` tag is used to designate a hyperlink. The `<a>` tag almost always includes an `href` attribute, which indicates an address. The user will be redirected to whichever address is indicated in this address when he or she clicks on the link. The text (or other html) between the `<a>` and `</a>` tags will be designated as the hyperlink. That text will appear on the page as a link (usually blue and underlined). In the `more.html` example, I created a link to one of my home pages (http://www.cs.iupui.edu). When the user clicks on the "Andy's Home Page" link in the browser, he or she will be transported to that page.

The other feature illustrated in `more.html` is the `<img>` tag. This tag is used to include images into a Web page. Most browsers readily support `.gif` and `.jpg` files, and many now can support the newer `.png` format.

If you have an image in some other format, or an image that needs to be modified in some way before using it in your Web page, you can use free software such as irfanView or the Gimp (both included on the CD-ROM that accompanies this book).

Tables

There are many times you might be working with large amounts of information that could benefit from table-style organization. HTML supports a set of tags that can be used to build tables. These tags are illustrated in Figure 1.5.

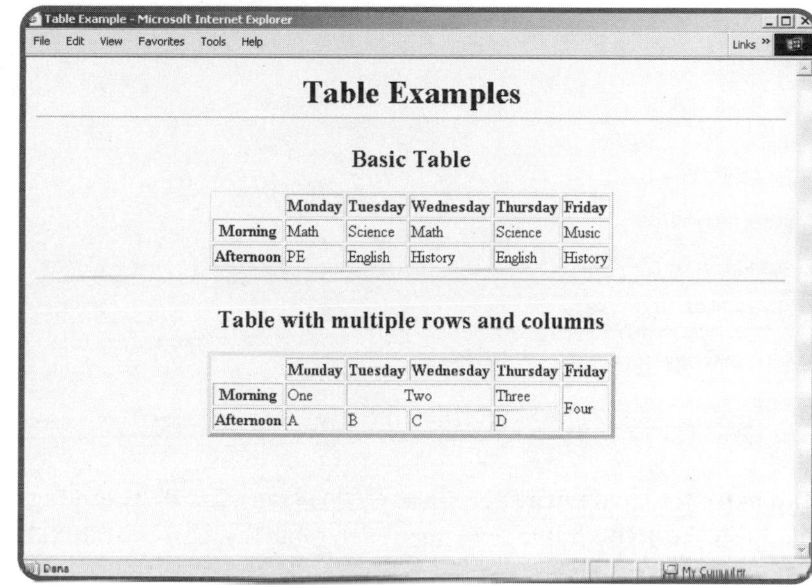

FIGURE 1.5

Tables can be basic, or cells can occupy multiple rows and columns.

The code for the simpler table looks like this:

```
<table border = "1">

<tr>

  <th></th>

  <th>Monday</th>

  <th>Tuesday</th>

  <th>Wednesday</th>

  <th>Thursday</th>

  <th>Friday</th>

</tr>


<tr>

  <th>Morning</th>

  <td>Math</td>
```

```
  <td>Science</td>
  <td>Math</td>
  <td>Science</td>
  <td>Music</td>
</tr>

<tr>
  <th>Afternoon</th>
  <td>PE</td>
  <td>English</td>
  <td>History</td>
  <td>English</td>
  <td>History</td>
</tr>
</table>
```

Tables are created with the `<table></table>` tags. Inside these tags, you create rows using the `<tr></tr>` (table row) tags. Each table row can contain table heading (`<th></th>`) or table data (`<td></td>`) elements.

The Web browser ignores spaces and indentation, but it's very smart to use white space in your HTML code to make it easier to read. Notice how I indented all elements inside each table row. This makes it much easier to see that all the information within the `<tr></tr>` set is part of one group.

In the `<table>` tag, you can use the border attribute to indicate how thick the border will be around the table.

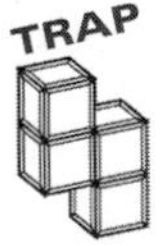

Note that browsers are not consistent in their default values. If you don't specify the border width, some browsers will show a border, and some will show no border at all. It's best to specify a border width every time. If you don't want a border, set the width to 0.

Sometimes you will find you need table cells to take up more than one row or column. The code for the second table in `table.html` shows how to accomplish this.

```
<table border = "4">

<tr>
  <th></th>
  <th>Monday</th>
  <th>Tuesday</th>
  <th>Wednesday</th>
  <th>Thursday</th>
  <th>Friday</th>

</tr>

<tr>
  <th>Morning</th>
  <td>One</td>
  <td colspan = "2"><center>Two</center></td>
  <td>Three</td>
  <td rowspan = "2">Four</td>
</tr>

<tr>
  <th>Afternoon</th>
  <td>A</td>
  <td>B</td>
  <td>C</td>
  <td>D</td>
</tr>

</table>
```

Notice that the cell containing the value "Two" has its `colspan` attribute set to 2. This tells the cell to take up two cell widths. Since this cell is twice as wide as normal, it is only necessary to define five <td> or <th> elements for this row instead of the six elements used for each row of the simpler table.

Look also at the cell containing the value "Four." This cell takes up two rows. I used the `rowspan` attribute to set up this behavior. Notice that I needed fewer elements in the next row, because one of the columns is taken by this expanded element.

Using CSS to Enhance Your Pages

Basic HTML is easy to write, but it creates pages that are dull. Modern browsers support cascading style sheets (CSS) elements, which allow you to specify how to display a particular tag. Entire books have been written about CSS, but the basic ideas are reasonably simple. You can define a `style`, which is a set of formatting rules, and attach it to various elements in your pages. An example will help clear things up.

Creating a Local Style

Figure 1.6 illustrates a Web page with some features that are not available in normal HTML.

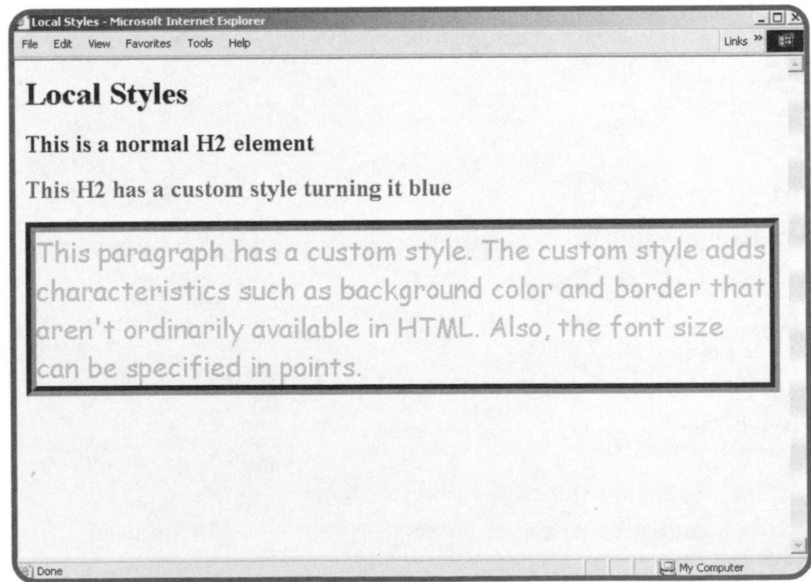

FIGURE 1.6

I used CSS to define the special styles shown on this page.

The H2 tag does not normally generate blue text, but I added a style to the text to make it blue. The code for the blue headline looks like this:

```
<h2 style = "color:blue">

This H2 has a custom style turning it blue

</h2>
```

I added a `style` attribute to the `<h2>` tag. This style attribute has a number of options that can be set. The `color` option allows you to assign a color to a style. The object which uses that style will appear in that color.

There are many other style options available. The larger paragraph in Figure 1.6 uses a number of other style elements. The code for that paragraph appears below:

```
<p style = "color:red;

           background-color: yellow;

           font-family: 'comic sans ms';

           font-size: 20pt;

           border-width: 10px;

           border-style: groove;

           border-color: green">


This paragraph has a custom style. The custom style adds

characteristics such as background color and border that aren't

ordinarily available in HTML. Also, the font size can be specified in points by specifying pt in

the font size.

</p>
```

You can see that this paragraph tag has a more complex style attribute with a number of elements. Each element has a name and a value separated by a colon; the elements are separated by semicolons. A list of the most commonly used style elements is shown in Table 1.2.

Page-Level Styles

Although it is sometimes convenient to attach a style directly to an HTML element, sometimes you wish to modify a number of elements in a particular page. You can specify the default styles of several of your elements by adding a style to your document. Figure 1.7 shows a page using a page-level style.

Table 1.2 Common CSS Elements

Element	Description	Possible values
Color	Foreground color	Valid color names (blue), hex color values (0000FF)
Background-color	Background color	Valid color names, hex color values
Font-family	Font to show	Font name must be installed on client computer
Font size	Size of font	Can be described in pixels (px), points (pt), centimeters (cm), or inches (in)
Border-width	Size of border	Usually measured in pixels (px), centimeters(cm) or inches (in)
Border-style	How border will be drawn	Some choices are groove, double, ridge, solid, inset, outset
Border-color	Color of border	Valid color names (blue), hex color values (0000FF)

Using div and span Elements in CSS

You can apply CSS styles to any HTML entity you wish. In practice, many Web authors prefer to use the `span` and `div` elements for custom CSS work. The `span` tag has basically no characteristics of its own. This makes it very predictable, because the CSS style will define essentially everything about the text within the span element. The `div` element is similar. It is sometimes used in place of `span` as a "generic" element suitable for adding CSS to. The `div` element acts like a paragraph in most instances, and the `span` element can work inside a paragraph.

With page-level styles, you use a `<style></style>` segment in your document header to specify how each listed tag should be displayed. The code for the pageStyle.html page illustrates how a page-level style sheet can be created.

```
<html>

<head>

<style type = "text/css">

h1 {

  text-align:center;

  color:green;
```

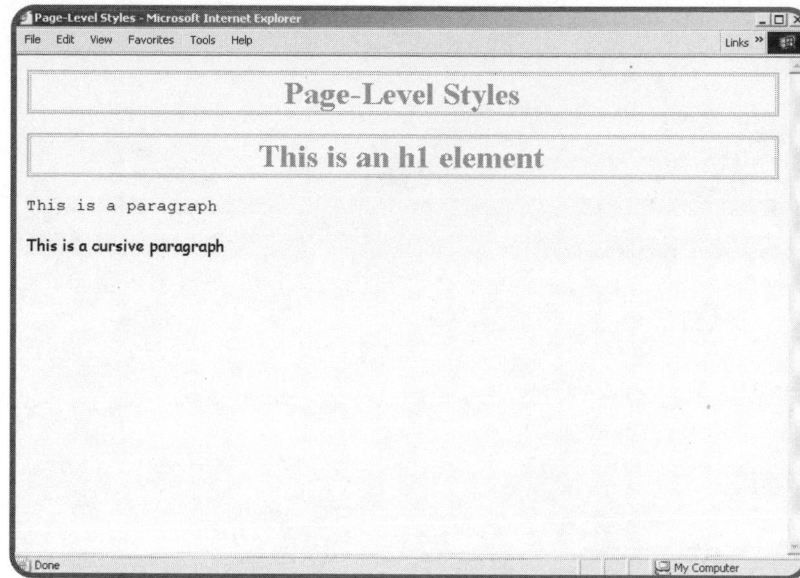

FIGURE 1.7

The H1 style has been defined for the entire page, as well as two kinds of paragraph styles.

```
  border-color:red;
  border-style:double;
  border-size: 3px
}

p {
  background-color: yellow;
  font-family: monospace
}

p.cursive {
  background-color: yellow;
  font-family: cursive
}

</style>

<title>Page-Level Styles</title>
```

```
</head>
<body>
<h1>Page-Level Styles</h1>
<h1>This is an h1 element</h1>

<p>This is a paragraph</p>

<p class = cursive>
This is a cursive paragraph
</p>
</body>
</html>
```

If you look at the main body of the page, you'll see that it looks pretty much like normal HTML code (because it is). The interesting part of this page is the code between the `<style>` and `</style>` tags. This code describes how the various tags should be displayed. Your opening tag should read `<style type = "text/css">` to specify you're using an ordinary style sheet. Inside the style element, you list each tag you wish to define. After the tag name, encase the various stylistic elements in a pair of braces ({ }). The style elements are listed just like in the style attribute. Each element consists of a name/value pair. A colon(:) separates the name and value, and each pair is separated by a semicolon(;).

Like most HTML programming, the style element is not picky about where you have spaces or carriage returns. However, judicious use of these "white space" elements can make your code much easier to read and modify. Notice how I lined up each element so they were easy to read, and how I lined up the closing brace(}) directly under the HTML element's name, so I could easily see how the various parts of code are related. You'll see the same kind of attention to indentation throughout your programming career.

Notice the second paragraph element, which looks like this:

```
p.cursive {
  background-color: yellow;
  font-family: cursive
}
```

By adding a period and another name (in this case, `.cursive`) to the HTML element's name, I was able to create a second type of paragraph tag. You can create as many variations of a tag as you wish. This is especially handy if you want to have varying text styles. You might want to have one kind of paragraph for quotes, for example, and another type for ordinary text. To use the special form of the tag, just use the `class` attribute in the HTML, as I did in the following text:

```
<p class = cursive>

This is a cursive paragraph

</p>
```

External Style Sheets

Most Web browsers support a third kind of style sheet, called the `external style sheet`. Figure 1.8 illustrates a page using an external style sheet.

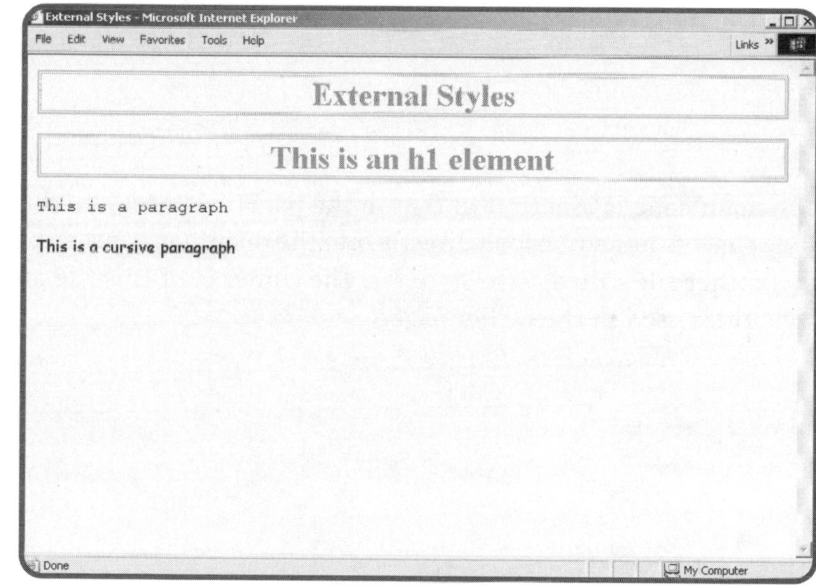

FIGURE 1.8

External style sheets look just like other styles to the user, but they have advantages for the programmer.

The user cannot tell what type of style sheet was used without looking at the code. Although the external style example looks much like the page-level style sheet program, the underlying code is different. Here is the code for `externStyle.html`:

```
<html>

<head>

<link rel="stylesheet"
```

```
     type="text/css"
     href = "externStyle.css">



<title>External Styles</title>
</head>
<body>
<h1>External Styles</h1>
<h1>This is an h1 element</h1>

<p>This is a paragraph</p>

<p class = cursive>
This is a cursive paragraph
</p>
</body>
</html>
```

The main code is identical to that in the pageLevel program, but notice that the style sheet is not embedded directly into the document. Instead, the style is stored in another file called `externStyle.css`. The contents of this file are the exact same style rules used in the earlier page.

```
h1 {
  text-align:center;
  color:green;
  border-color:red;
  border-style:double;
  border-size: 3px
}

p {
  background-color: yellow;
  font-family: monospace
```

```
}

p.cursive {
  background-color: yellow;
  font-family: cursive
}
```

When you have the CSS rules stored in a separate file, you can use the `link` tag to import the CSS rules. The advantage of this approach is you can re-use one set of CSS rules for many pages.

> **IN THE REAL WORLD**
>
> External style sheets are very useful when you are working on a project that must be consistent across many pages. Most sites go through several iterations, and it could be a real pain to change the font color in 20 pages every time the client wants to try some new variation. If all your style rules are stored in one CSS document and all your pages refer to that document, you only have to change the style rules one time, and you've automatically changed the appearance of every page that uses that set of rules.

Using Form Elements

HTML pages often utilize form elements for user input. These elements include basic tools for user input. These form elements are not useful in plain HTML. Although they are rather easy to put on a page, they don't do much unless there is some kind of program attached. Much of what you do as a PHP author will involve getting information from Web-based forms, so it's important to be familiar with the most common form elements. You'll start to write programs that retrieve values from forms in the very next chapter, so it'll be good to learn how they work.

The Text-Based Elements

Most of the form elements are really about getting some sort of text information from the user to a program. The first set of such elements are those that simply allow the user to enter some kind of text. There are four such elements, illustrated in Figure 1.9.

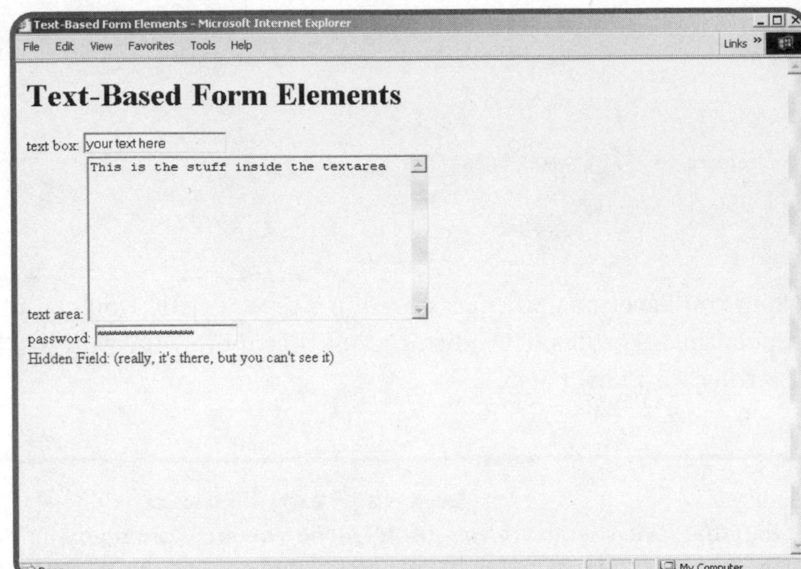

FIGURE 1.9

You can add text boxes, text areas, password boxes, and hidden fields (which do not appear to the user) to your Web pages.

The code used to generate `textForm.html` is reproduced here:

```
<html>

<head>

<title>Text-Based Form Elements</title>

</head>

<body>

<h1>Text-Based Form Elements</h1>


<form>


text box:

<input type = "text"

       name = "txtInput"

       value = "your text here">

<br>


text area:

<textarea name = "txtBigInput"

          rows = 10
```

```
          cols = 40>
This is the stuff inside the textarea
</textarea>
<br>

password:
<input type = "password"
       name = "secret"
       value = "you can't read this">
<br>

Hidden Field:  (really, it's there, but you can't see it)
<input type = "hidden"
       name = "mystery"
       value = "secret formula">

</form>
</body>
</html>
```

All the elements that will allow user interaction are placed inside a `<form></form>` pair. The most common form element is the `<input>` element, which comes in several flavors, designated by the `type` attribute.

Creating a Text Box

The most common input element of all is the humble text box. To make a plain vanilla text box, I used the following code:

```
<input type = "text"
       name = "txtInput"
       value = "your text here">
```

The element is a basic `input` element. By setting the type to `"text"`, I'm signifying how the element is to be displayed on the screen— as something that the user can type text into. An input element using the `text` type is usually called a text box. Text boxes cannot include multiple lines of text, but you can specify the length of the text box with the `size` attribute. (If you set the size to 20, you are allowing for roughly 20 characters.) It is important to add a `name` attribute to your text boxes (and indeed to all form elements) because later you are going to be writing programs that try to retrieve information from the form. These programs will use the various form element names to refer to what the user typed in.

Naming an input element is something of an art form. The name should be reasonably descriptive (`r` or `albert` are usually not good input object names, because they don't explain what kind of information is expected to be in the object). Object names should not have spaces in them, because this will cause confusion later. You'll learn more about this in the next chapter when you begin working with variables, which have a very close relationship to form elements in PHP.

The `value` attribute is used to set a default value for the text area. This is the value that will appear in the text area when the user first sees your form. It's a good idea to put default values in forms when you can, because this gives you a chance to show the user what kind of information you're expecting.

Creating a Text Area

Text boxes are very handy, but sometimes you will want to let the user type in more than one line's worth of information. For example, you might want to have a feedback page where the user can type in some comments to be e-mailed back to you. For this kind of situation, you will usually want to use an object called the `text area`. The code to create such an element looks like this:

```
<textarea name = "txtBigInput"
          rows = 10
          cols = 40>
This is the stuff inside the textarea
</textarea>
```

The text area is created using a pair of `<textarea></textarea>` tags. The text area has a name attribute, as well as attributes for determining the size of the text box in rows and columns. Text areas should also be named using the `name` attribute, but the `textarea` object does not have a `value` attribute. Instead, anything between the `<textarea>` and `</textarea>` tags is considered the contents of the text area object.

Don't forget to close the textarea with a </textarea> tag. If you don't, everything in the page after the <textarea> tag will appear inside the text area if the page renders at all!

Building a Password Field

Password fields are almost identical to text boxes. The code for creating a password is very much like the text field:

```
<input type = "password"
       name = "secret"
       value = "you can't read this">
```

The only real difference between the password field and the text box is that the value typed into a password field is shown as asterisks on the screen. Presumably this will keep the KGB from peering over the shoulders of your users while they type passwords into your pages.

It's critical to note that the password field offers virtually no real security. As you will learn in the next chapter, the information that is sent to the server via a password field is transmitted entirely in the clear, so it is only nominally secret.

Making a Hidden Field

Believe it or not, the text box has an even more secretive cousin than the password field. The hidden field is much like the text box in code, but it doesn't appear on the page at all. Here's how the code looks:

```
<input type = "hidden"
       name = "mystery"
       value = "secret formula">
```

The uses for such a field that are hidden from the user might not be obvious now, but it does come in handy when you want your page to communicate with a server-side program but you don't need the user to know all the details. (I'll show you an example soon, I promise.)

Creating the Selection Elements

It's very easy to add text elements to your Web pages, but requiring users to enter text can interrupt the flow of the program. Whenever possible, experienced programmers like to give the user choices that do not involve typing. HTML forms have a number of simple elements for allowing the user to choose from a list of options using the mouse.

Making the user's life easy is a good reason to use some of these other input features, but there's another reason. You never know what a user will enter into a text box. It can be very difficult to write code that anticipates all the possible wrong things a user can type in. If you use the various selection elements described below, you pre-determine all possible values your program will need to deal with (at least in most circumstances).

Figure 1.10 shows a number of these selection-style elements on a Web page.

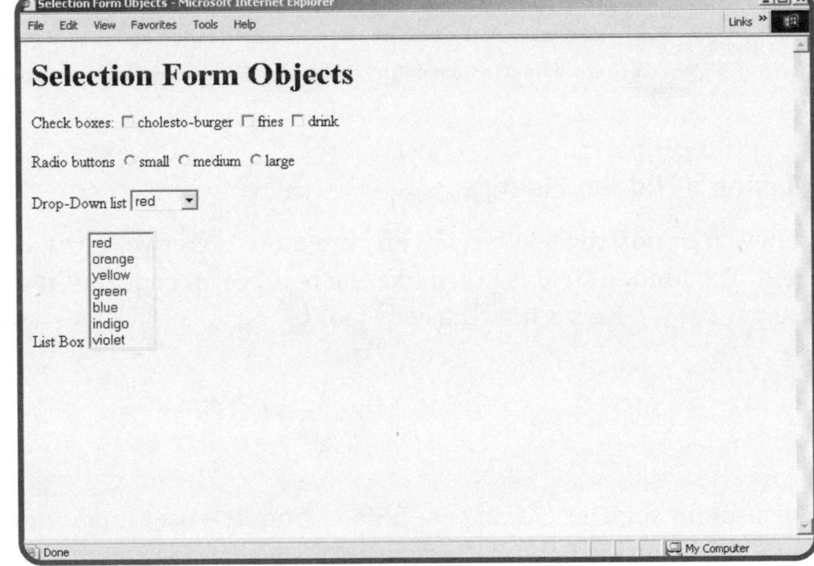

FIGURE 1.10

Several HTML elements allow the user to enter information without having to type anything.

Creating Checkboxes

The first type of input to consider is the checkbox. Checkboxes usually look like, well, boxes that can be checked. Usually there is some kind of text near the checkbox.

The box can be checked or not checked. Here's the code used to create the checkboxes in the `selectForm.html` page:

```
<input type = "checkbox"
       name = "chkBurger">cholesto-burger
<input type = "checkbox"
       name = "chkFries">fries
<input type = "checkbox"
       name = "chkDrink">drink
```

A checkbox is simply an input element of type `checkbox`. Although you can specify the `value` attribute of a checkbox, it isn't usually necessary as it is with other `input` elements. Note that the caption next to the checkbox is plain html text. Each checkbox is a completely independent entity. Even though several checkboxes appear together in the HTML document, the value of one checkbox has no bearing on the value of any other checkboxes.

Checkboxes are appropriate when any combination of the various elements is appropriate. For example, the user might want the burger, fries, and a drink. The user might want none of these things, or any combination. Checkboxes are not as appropriate when the options are mutually exclusive. For example, if asking what size a drink should be, only one size should be allowed per drink. That kind of situation is a perfect place to use another feature called `radio buttons`.

Selecting with Radio Buttons

You can use radio buttons (sometimes called option buttons) to let the user choose an item from several options. Radio buttons get their name from the radios on cars (at least when I was a kid) that had several buttons sticking out. To select a station, you pressed the corresponding button in, which caused all the other buttons to pop out. HTML radio buttons have similar behavior. Radio buttons are grouped so that when you select one button, all the others in the group are automatically deselected.

Look at the code for the radio buttons, and see if you can spot how the radio elements are grouped.

```
<input type = "radio"
       name = "size"
       value = "small">small
```

```
<input type = "radio"
       name = "size"
       value = "medium">medium
<input type = "radio"
       name = "size"
       value = "large">large
```

The interesting thing about radio buttons is the way they are named. There are three radio buttons, but they all have the same name. This little trick groups the radio buttons so they act as expected. As soon as the user selects one item in a radio group, all other radio elements on the page with the same name are automatically selected. Each of the radio objects has a distinct value. Your programs will be able to determine the value of whichever radio button in the group was selected.

Building Drop-Down List Boxes

Another common user interface trick is to use some kind of drop-down list. These devices allow the user to choose from a list of options, but the various options only appear when the user is choosing from the list. This is especially useful when screen real estate is an issue or you want to keep the interface clean. Drop-down lists are made with two different elements. The main object is the `select` object. It contains a series of `option` objects. (This is analogous to the way `li` objects appear inside a `ul` or `ol` object.) The code for building a drop-down list box will make it all clear.

```
<select name = "selColor">
  <option value = "red">red</option>
  <option value = "orange">orange</option>
  <option value = "yellow">yellow</option>
  <option value = "green">green</option>
  <option value = "blue">blue</option>
  <option value = "indigo">indigo</option>
  <option value = "violet">violet</option>
</select>
```

The `select` object has a `name` attribute. Each option has its own `value` attribute. Your program will use the `value` attribute of whichever element is returned. The `value` property of an option button doesn't display anywhere. Place the text you want to have visible on the page between the `<option>` and `</option>` tags.

Creating a Multi-Select List Box

One more selection element can be useful in certain situations. This isn't really a new object at all, but a variation of the drop-down list. The code for the last element in selectForm.html is shown below:

```
<select name = "lstColor"
        size = 7
        multiple>
  <option value = "red">red</option>
  <option value = "orange">orange</option>
  <option value = "yellow">yellow</option>
  <option value = "green">green</option>
  <option value = "blue">blue</option>
  <option value = "indigo">indigo</option>
  <option value = "violet">violet</option>
</select>
```

The code looks identical to the previous (drop-down) list except for a few differences in the select tag itself. By setting the size attribute to a value of 7, I indicated that seven lines of the list should be shown at any time. This is useful when you want the user to be able to see all (or many) of the choices all the time. The other interesting thing about this type of list box is it can allow for multiple selections if the multiple attribute is included. A multi-selection list box lets the user choose more than one element using standard multiple selection rules (for example, Shift+Click to select a range of contiguous options or Ctrl+Click to add or remove a particular element from the range of selections).

Adding Buttons to Your Programs

The last major form element is the button. Buttons are important because the user is accustomed to clicking on them to make things happen. Your programs will take advantage of this conditioning. Figure 1.11 shows a page containing three distinct buttons.

All three button types are variants of the basic input tag you've used so much in this chapter. The code for the buttonForm.html page illustrates this clearly:

```
<html>
<head>
<title>Button Demo</title>
```

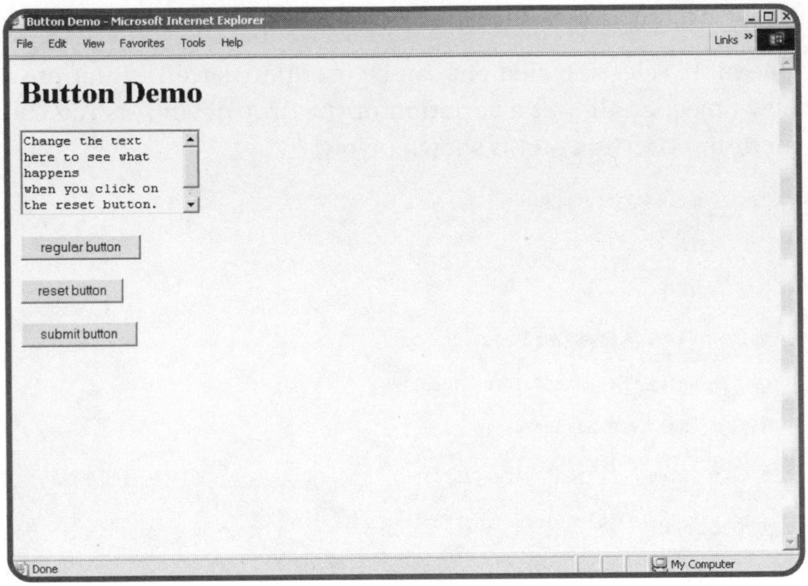

FIGURE 1.11

Although these buttons all look very similar to the user, they are different, and have distinctive behaviors.

```
</head>
<body>
<h1>Button Demo</h1>
<form>
<textarea rows = 5>
Change the text here to see what happens
when you click on the reset button.
</textarea>
<br><br>

<input type = "button"
       value = "regular button">

<br><br>
<input type = "reset"
       value = "reset button">
<br><br>

<input type = "submit"
```

```
      value = "submit button">

<br><br>

</form>

</body>
</html>
```

The three different types of buttons look the same but behave differently. When you set the `type` attribute of an input element to `button`, you are creating a generic button. These buttons are frequently used in client-side programming. To make something happen when the user clicks on such a button, you'll need to embed code in your Web page using a language such as JavaScript or VBScript. (Of course, there are exceptional books in the *Absolute Beginners'* series describing exactly how to do this.) Server-side programming (which is the focus of this book) rarely involves the ordinary button object.

The `reset` button is used to let the user reset the page to its default condition. This is a handy feature to add to a program, because it lets the user back up if the page got messed up. It isn't necessary to write any code for the `reset` button, because the browser automatically handles the resetting behavior.

The Submit button style is by far the most important kind of button for server-side programming that we will do in this book. The Submit button provides the link between Web pages and your programs. Most interactions in server-side programming involve sending an HTML page with a form to the user. When the user has finished making selections and typing values into the various form elements, he or she presses the Submit button, which essentially bundles up all the data in the form elements and sends them to a program. In the next chapter, you'll learn how to make this actually work, but for now it's important to know how to add a Submit button to your forms, because many pages will use this type of element.

Adding PHP to Your Pages

All this HTML is nice, but presumably you're here to learn PHP, so it's high time to add PHP code to a page. PHP can be used to add characteristics to your page that aren't typically possible with normal HTML and CSS.

Ensuring That Your Server Supports PHP

A page written in PHP can be identical to an HTML page. Both are written with a plain text editor, and stored on a Web server. A PHP program can have `<script>` elements embedded in the page. When the user requests a PHP page, the server first examines the page and executes any script elements before it sends the resulting HTML to the user. This will only work if the Web server has been configured to use the PHP language. You might need to check with your server administrator to see if this support is available. On a home computer, you can use the PHP Tripod software included on the CD-ROM that accompanies this book to set up all the necessary components.

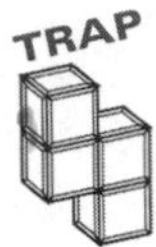

To run all the programs in this book, your server needs to have three different components installed. First, you will need a Web server such as Microsoft IIS or Apache. Secondly, you'll need the PHP interpreter, which is a program that reads PHP files and converts them into HTML pages. Finally, you'll need a database management program to handle data. PHP Triad integrates all these features into one installation. It includes the Apache (free and very powerful) Web server, the PHP interpreter, and the mySQL database management system. This package is very typical of most servers that use PHP. If the Web host you are using does not yet support PHP, you can still install the programs and practice on your own machine (although nobody outside your computer will be able to get to your programs).

Adding PHP Commands to an HTML Page

The easiest way to determine if PHP exists on your server is to write a simple PHP program and see if it works. Here's a very simple PHP program.

```
<html>
<head>
<title>Hello in PHP</title>
</head>
<body>
<h1>Hello in PHP</h1>

<?
print "Hello, world!";
```

```
phpInfo();
?>


</body>
</html>
```

The <? ?> sequence is the easiest way to indicate PHP code, but it isn't always the best way. You can also indicate PHP code with a longer version like this: <?php ?>. This version works better when your code will be interpreted as XML. You can also specify your code with normal HTML tags just like JavaScript <script language = "php"></script>. Some PHP servers are configured to prefer one type of script tag over another so you may need to be flexible. However, all these variations work in exactly the same way.

A PHP program looks a lot like a typical HTML page. The only thing that's different is the special `<?    ?>` tag. This tag specifies the existence of PHP code. Any code inside the tag will be read by the PHP interpreter, then converted into HTML code. The code written between the <? and ?> symbols is PHP code. I added two commands to the page. Look at the output of the program shown in Figure 1.12, and you might be surprised:

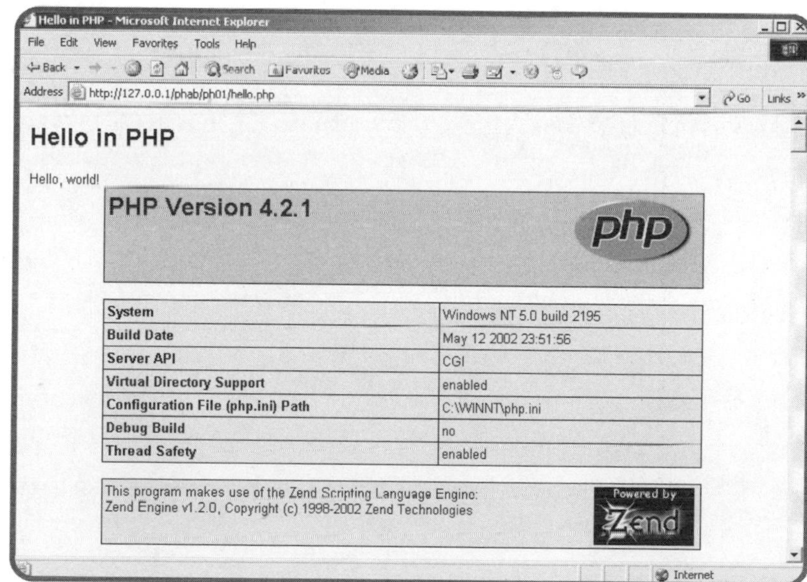

FIGURE 1.12

The page mixes HTML with some other things.

Examining the Results

There are three distinct types of text on this page. First, the "Hello in PHP" line is ordinary HTML. I wrote it just like a regular HTML page, and it was displayed just like regular HTML. The "Hello world" line is a little different though, because it was written by the PHP program embedded in the page. The rest of the page is a bit mysterious. It contains a lot of information about the particular PHP engine being used. It actually stretches on for several pages. All that code was generated by the `phpInfo()` command. This command is used to display information about the PHP installation. It isn't that important to understand all the information displayed by the `phpInfo()` command. It's much more critical to appreciate that when the user requests the `hello.html` Web page, the text of the page is first run through the PHP interpreter. This program scans for any PHP commands, executes the commands, and prints HTML code in place of the original commands. By the time a page gets to the user, all the PHP code is gone, because the server used the PHP to generate HTML code. For proof of this, point your browser at `hello.php` and then view the source code. It will look something like this:

```
<html>
<head>
<title>Hello in PHP</title>
</head>
<body>
<h1>Hello in PHP</h1>

Hello, world!<!DOCTYPE HTML PUBLIC "-//W3C//DTD HTML 4.01 Transitional//EN">
<html>
<head><style type="text/css"><!--
a { text-decoration: none; }
a:hover { text-decoration: underline; }
h1 { font-family: arial, helvetica, sans-serif; font-size: 18pt; font-weight: bold;}
h2 { font-family: arial, helvetica, sans-serif; font-size: 14pt; font-weight: bold;}
body, td { font-family: arial, helvetica, sans-serif; font-size: 10pt; }
th { font-family: arial, helvetica, sans-serif; font-size: 11pt; font-weight: bold; }
//--></style>
<title>phpinfo()</title></head><body><table border="0" cellpadding="3" cellspacing="1"
width="600" bgcolor="#000000" align="center">
```

```
<tr valign="middle" bgcolor="#9999cc"><td align="left">
<a href="http://www.php.net/"><img src="/phab/ph01/hello.php?=PHPE9568F34-D428-11d2-A769-
00AA001ACF42" border=0 align="right" alt="PHP Logo"></a><h1>PHP Version 4.2.1</h1>
```

Note that I showed only a small part of the code generated by the `phpInfo()` command, and that the details of the code might be different when you run the program on your own machine. The key point here is the PHP code to write "Hello World!" (`print "Hello World!"`) is replaced with the actual text "Hello World!" More significantly, the very simple `phpInfo()` command is replaced by a huge amount of HTML code.

A small amount of PHP code can very efficiently generate large and complex HTML documents. This is one significant advantage of PHP. Also, by the time the document gets to the Web browser, it's plain vanilla HTML code, which can be read easily by any browser. These two features are important benefits of server-side programming in general, and of PHP programming in particular. As you progress through this book, you'll learn about many more commands for producing interesting HTML, but the basic concept is always the same. Your PHP program is simply an HTML page that contains special PHP markup. The PHP code is examined by a special program on the server, and the results are embedded into the Web page before it is sent to the user.

Creating the "Tip of the Day" Program

Way back at the beginning of the chapter I promised you would be able to write the "Tip of the day" program featured at the beginning of the chapter. This program requires HTML, Cascading Style Sheets, and one line of PHP code. The code shows a reasonably basic page.

```
<html>
<head>
<title>Tip of the day</title>
</head>

<body>
<center>

<h1>Tip of the day</h1>

<div style = "border-color:green; border-style:groove; border-width:2px">
```

```
<?
readfile("tips.txt");
?>
</div>



</center>
</body>
</html>
```

The page is basic HTML. It contains one div element with a custom style setting up a border around the tip of the day. Inside the div element, I added PHP code with the <? and ?> devices. This code calls one PHP function called readFile(). The readFile() command takes as an argument the name of some file. It reads the contents of that file and displays it onto the page as if it were HTML. As soon as that line of code stops executing (that is, the text in the tips.txt file has been printed to the Web browser) the ?> symbol indicates that the PHP coding is finished and the rest of the page will be typical HTML.

Summary

You've already come a very long way. You've learned or reviewed all the main HTML objects. You've investigated cascading style sheets and how they are used to modify an HTML attribute. You experimented with the main form elements and learned how to add various kinds of text boxes and selection devices to your Web pages. You saw how PHP code can be integrated into an HTML document. Finally, you created your first page that includes all these elements. You should be proud of your efforts already. In the next chapter, you'll explore more fully the relationship between PHP and HTML, and learn how to use variables and input to make your pages do interesting things.

CHALLENGES

1. Create a Web-based version of your resume incorporating headings, lists, and varying text styles.
2. Modify one of your existing pages so it incorporates CSS styles.
3. Install a practice configuration of Apache, PHP, and mySQL (or some other package) Use a tool like PHP Tripod if possible to make the configuration simpler.
4. Build a page that calls the `phpInfo()` command and run it from your Web server. Ensure that you have a reasonably recent version of PHP installed on the server.

Using Variables and Input

In Chapter 1, "Exploring the PHP Environment," you learned the foundations of all PHP programming. Now that you have reviewed your HTML and CSS skills, you're ready to start seeing the real power of programming in general, and PHP in particular. Computer programs are ultimately about data. In this chapter, you'll begin looking at the way programs store and manipulate data in variables. Specifically, you'll learn how to:

- Create a variable in PHP.,
- Recognize the main types of variables.
- Name variables appropriately.
- Output the values of variables in your scripts.
- Perform basic operations on variables.
- Read variables from an HTML form.

Introducing the Story Program

By the end of this chapter, you'll be able to write the program featured in Figures 2.1 and 2.2.

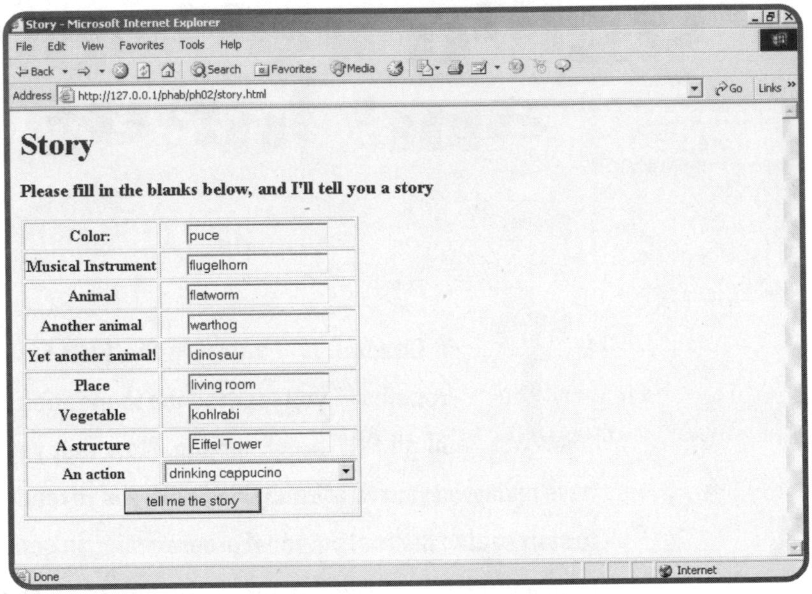

FIGURE 2.1

The program begins by asking the user to enter some information.

The program asks the user to enter some values into an HTML form, and then uses those values to build a custom version of a classic nursery rhyme. The story program works like most server-side programs. It has two distinctive parts. First, the user enters information into a plain HTML form and hits the submit button. The PHP program doesn't execute until after the user has submitted a form. The program takes the information from the form and does something to it. Usually the PHP program also returns an HTML page to the user.

Using Variables in Your Scripts

The most important new idea in this chapter is the notion of a *variable*. A variable is a container for holding information in the computer's memory. To make things easier for the programmer, every variable has a name. You can store information into a variable and get information out of a variable.

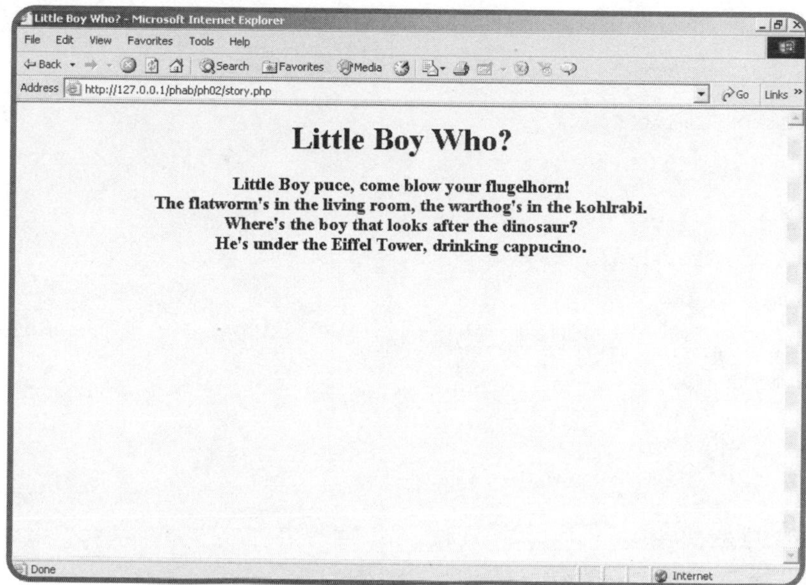

FIGURE 2.2

I hate it when the warthog's in the kohlrabi.

Introducing the "Hi Jacob" program

The program featured in Figure 2.3 uses a variable, although you might not be able to tell simply by looking at the output.

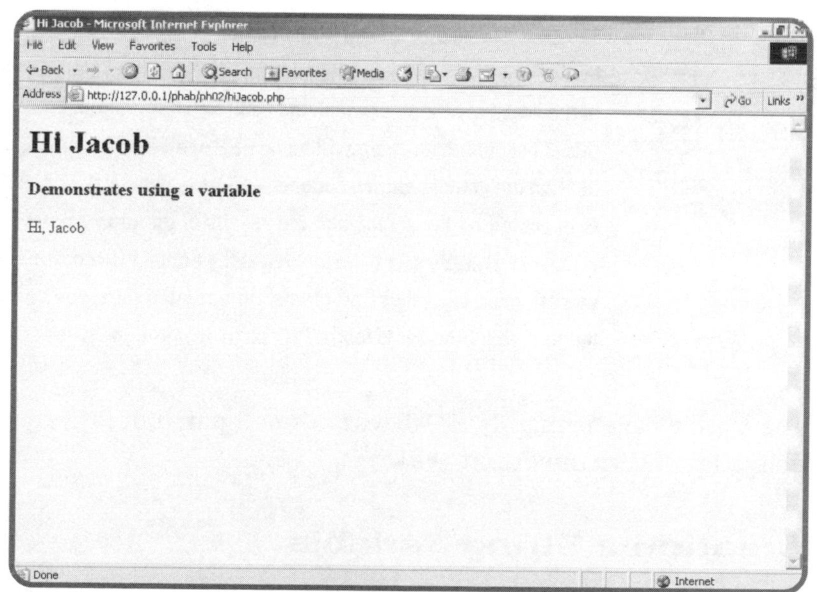

FIGURE 2.3

The word "Jacob" is stored in a variable in this page. You can't really see anything special about this program from the Web page itself (even if you look at the HTML source). To see what's new, look at the source code of `hiJacob.php`.

```
<html>
<head>
<title>Hi Jacob</title>
</head>
<body>
<h1>Hi Jacob</h1>

<h3>Demonstrates using a variable</h3>

<?

$userName = "Jacob";

print "Hi, $userName";

?>
</body>
</html>
```

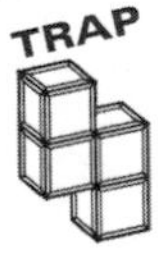

In regular HTML and JavaScript programming, you can use the "view source" command of the Web browser to examine the code for your programs. For server-side languages, this is not sufficient. There will be no PHP at all in the view source document. Remember that the actual program code never gets to your Web browser. Instead, the program is executed on the server, and the *results* of the program are sent to the browser as ordinary HTML. Be sure to be looking at the actual PHP source code on the server when you are examining these programs. On a related note, you cannot simply use the File menu of your browser to load a PHP page. Instead, you'll need to run it through a server.

The `hiJacob` page is mainly HTML with a small patch of PHP code in it. That code does a lot of very important work.

Creating a String Variable

The line `$userName = "Jacob";` does a number of things. First, it creates a variable named `$userName`. In PHP, all variables begin with a dollar sign to distinguish them from other program elements. The variable's name is significant.

Naming Your Variables

As a programmer, you will frequently get to name things. Experienced programmers have learned some tricks about naming variables and other elements.

- Make the name descriptive. It's much easier to figure out what $userName means than something like $myVariable or $r. When possible, make sure your variable names describe the kind of information they contain.
- Use an appropriate length. Your variable name should be long enough to be descriptive, but not so long that it becomes tedious to type.
- Don't use spaces. Most languages (including PHP) don't allow spaces in variable names.
- Don't use punctuation. Most of the special characters such as #, *, and / already have meaning in programming languages, so they can't be used in variable names. Of course, every variable in PHP begins with the $ character, but otherwise you should avoid using punctuation. One exception to this rule is the underscore (_) character, which is allowed in most languages, including PHP.
- Be careful about case. PHP is a case-sensitive language, which means that it considers $userName, $USERNAME, and $UserName to be three different variables. The convention in PHP is to use all lowercase except when separating words (note the uppercase "N" in $userName.) This is a good convention to follow, and it's the one I use throughout this book.
- Watch your spelling! Every time you refer to a variable, PHP checks to see if that variable already exists somewhere in your program. If so, it uses that variable. If not, it quietly makes a new variable for you. If you misspell a variable name, PHP will not catch it. Instead, it will make a whole new variable, and your program probably won't work correctly.

It isn't necessary to explicitly create a variable. When you refer to a variable, it is automatically created by PHP.

Assigning a Value to a Variable

The equals sign (=) is special in PHP. It does *not* mean "equals" (at least in the present context.) The equals sign is used for assignment. If you read the equals sign as the word "gets," you'll be closer to the meaning PHP uses for this symbol. For example, the line

```
$userName = "Jacob"
```

should be read

"The variable `$userName` gets the value "Jacob."

Usually when you create a variable in PHP, you'll also be assigning some value to it. Assignment flows from right to left.

The `$userName` variable has been assigned the value "Jacob." Computers are picky about what type of information goes into a variable, but PHP automates this process for you. Still, it's important to recognize that "Jacob" is a text value, because text is stored and processed a little bit differently in computer memory than numeric data.

Computer programmers almost never refer to text as *text*. Instead, they prefer the more esoteric term *string*. The word string actually has a somewhat poetic origin, because the underlying mechanism for storing text in a computer's memory reminded early programmers of making a chain of beads on a string.

Printing the Value of a Variable

The next line of code prints a message to the screen. You can print any text to the screen you wish. Text (also called string data) is usually encased in quotes. If you wish to print the value of a variable, simply place the variable name in the text you want printed. The line

```
print "Hi, $userName";
```

actually produces the output

```
Hi, Jacob
```

because when the server encounters the variable `$userName`, it replaces it with the value of that variable, which is `"Jacob."` The output of the PHP program will be sent directly to the Web browser, so you can even include HTML tags in your output if you wish, simply by including them inside the quotes.

The ability to print the value of a variable inside other text is called `string interpolation`. That's not critical to know, but it could be useful information on a trivia show or something.

Using the Semicolon to End a Line

If you look back at the complete code for the `hiJacob` program, you can see that it has two lines of code inside the PHP block. Each line of PHP code ends with a semicolon. PHP is a more formal language than HTML and, like most programming languages, has some strict rules about the syntax used when writing a page.

Each unique instruction is expected to end with a semicolon. You'll end most lines of PHP code with a semicolon. If you forget to do this, you'll get an error that looks like Figure 2.4.

If you see this particular message, look back at your code to ensure you've remembered to add a semicolon at the end of the line.

There will be times when an instruction is longer than a single line on the editor. The semicolon goes at the end of the *instruction*, which often (but not always) corresponds with the end of the *line*.

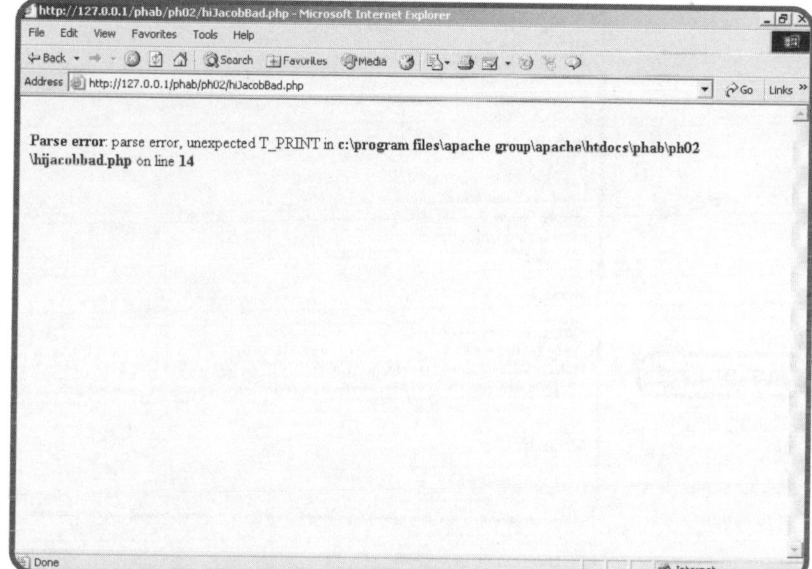

FIGURE 2.4

This error will occur if you forget to add a semicolon to the end of every line.

Don't panic if you get an error message or two. They are a completely normal part of programming. Even experienced programmers expect to see many error messages while building and testing programs. Usually the resulting error code gives you important clues about what went wrong. Make sure you look carefully at whatever line of code the error message reports. Although the error isn't always on that line, you can often get a hint what went wrong by examining that line closely. In many cases (particularly a missing semicolon), a syntax error will indicate an error on the line that actually follows the real problem. If you get a syntax error on line 14, and the problem is a missing semicolon, the problem line is actually line 13.

Using Variables for More Complex Pages

While the `HiJacob` program was interesting, there was no real advantage to using a variable. Now you will see another use of variables that shows how useful they can be.

Building the "Row Your Boat" Page

Figure 2.5 shows the "Row Your Boat" page.

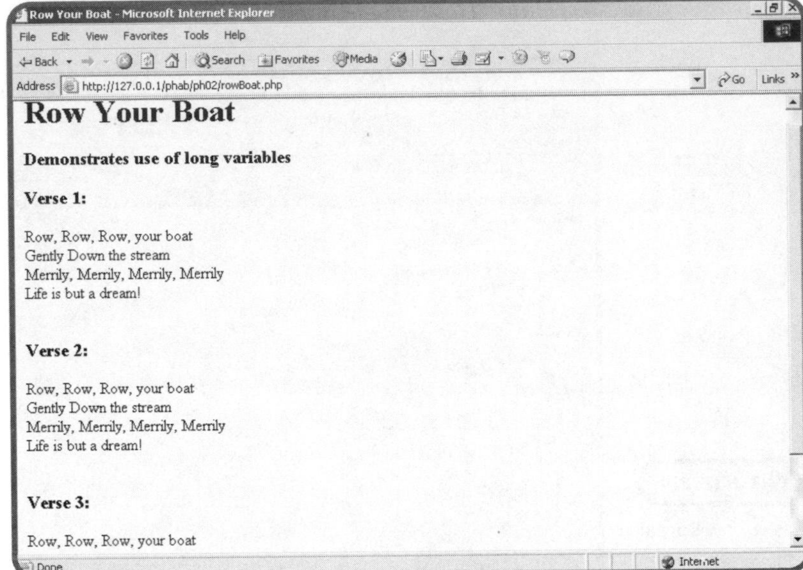

FIGURE 2.5

This program shows the words to a popular song. They sure repeat a lot.

I chose this song in particular because it repeats the same verse three times. If you look at the original code for the `rowBoat.php` program, you'll see I used a special trick to save some typing.

```
<html>

<head>

<title>Row Your Boat</title>

</head>

<body>

<h1>Row Your Boat</h1>
```

```
<h3>Demonstrates use of long variables</h3>

<?

$verse = <<<HERE
Row, Row, Row, your boat<br>
Gently down the stream<br>
Merrily, merrily, merrily, merrily<br>
Life is but a dream!<br>
<br><br>
HERE;

print "<h3>Verse 1:</h3>";
print $verse;

print "<h3>Verse 2:</h3>";
print $verse;
print "<h3>Verse 3:</h3>";
print $verse;

?>

</body>
</html>
```

Creating Multi-Line Strings

You'll frequently find yourself wanting to print several lines of HTML code at once. It can be very tedious to use quote signs to indicate such strings (especially because HTML also often uses the quote symbol). PHP provides a special quoting mechanism, which is perfect for this type of situation. The line

```
$verse = <<<HERE
```

begins assigning a value to the `$verse` variable. The `<<<HERE` segment indicates this will be a special multi-line string that will end with the symbol "`HERE`." You can use

any phrase you wish, but I generally use the word `HERE` because I think of the three less than symbols as "up to." In other words, you can think of

```
$verse = <<<HERE
```

as meaning "verse gets everything up to HERE."

You can also think of `<<<HERE` as a special quote sign, which is ended with the value `HERE`.

You can write as much text as you wish between `<<<HERE` and `HERE`. You can put variables inside the special text, and PHP will replace the variable with its value, just like in ordinary (quoted) strings. The ending phrase (`HERE`) must be on a line by itself, and there must be no leading spaces in front of it.

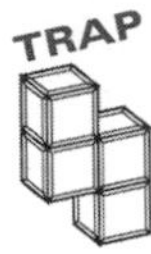

You might wonder why the `$verse = <<<HERE` line doesn't have a semicolon after it. Although this is one line in the editor, it begins a multi-line structure. Technically, everything from that line to the end of the `HERE;` line is part of the same logical line, even though the code takes up several lines in the editor. Everything between `<<<HERE` and `HERE` is a string value. The semicolon doesn't have any special meaning inside a string. If this doesn't make sense to you, don't worry about it for now, as you'll get some other chances to think about this concept later. As a minimum, you should know that a line beginning a multi-line quote doesn't need a semicolon, but the line at the end of the quote does.

Once the multi-line string is built, it is very easy to use. It's actually harder to write the captions for the three verses than the verses themselves. The `print` statement simply places the value of the `$verse` variable in the appropriate spots of the output HTML.

Working with Numeric Variables

Computers ultimately store information in on/off impulses. These very simple data values can be converted into a number of more convenient kinds of information. The PHP language makes most of this invisible to you, but it's still important to know that string (text) is handled differently in memory than numeric values, and there are two main types of numeric values.

Making the ThreePlusFive Program

As an example of how PHP works with numbers, consider the `ThreePlusFive.php` program illustrated in Figure 2.6.

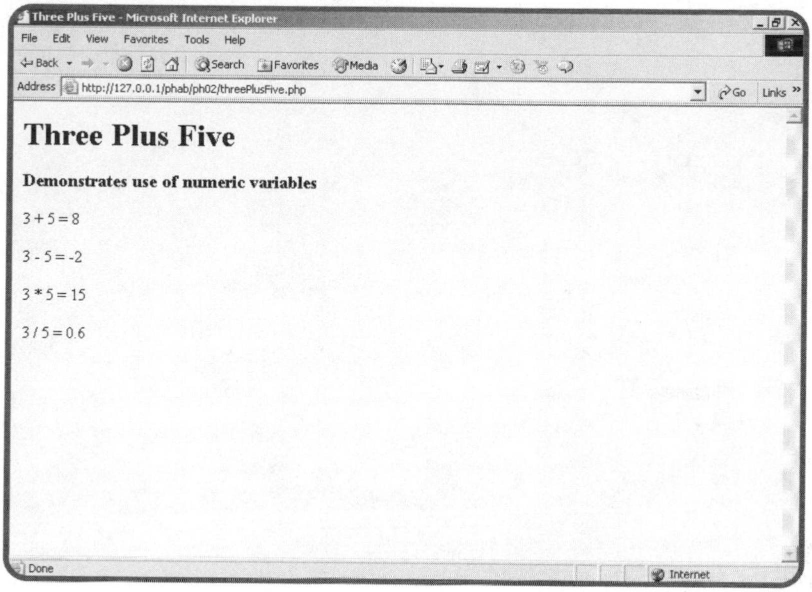

FIGURE 2.6

This program does basic math on variables containing the values 3 and 5.

All the work in the `ThreePlusFive` program is done with two variables called `$x` and `$y`. (I know, I recommended that you assign variables longer, descriptive names, but these variables are commonly used in arithmetic problems, so these very short variable names are OK in this instance.) The code for the program looks like this:

```
<html>

<head>

<title>Three Plus Five</title>

</head>

<body>

<h1>Three Plus Five</h1>

<h3>Demonstrates use of numeric variables</h3>


<?

$x = 3;

$y = 5;


print "$x + $y = ";

print $x + $y;
```

```
print "<br><br>";

print "$x - $y = ";
print $x - $y;
print "<br><br>";

print "$x * $y = ";
print $x * $y;
print "<br><br>";

print "$x / $y = ";
print $x / $y;
print "<br><br>";

?>

</body>
</html>
```

Assigning Numeric Values

You create a numeric variable like any other variable in PHP. Simply assign a value to a variable, and the variable is created. Notice that numeric values do not require quotes. I created variables called `$x` and `$y` and assigned appropriate values to these variables.

Using Mathematical Operators

For each calculation, I wanted to print the problem as well as its solution. The line that says

```
print "$x + $y = ";
```

prints out the values of the $x and $y variables with the plus sign between them. In this particular case (since `$x` is 3 and `$y` is 5), it prints out the literal value

```
3 + 5 =
```

Because the plus sign and the equals sign are inside quotes, they are treated as ordinary text elements and PHP doesn't do any calculation (such as addition or assignment) with them.

The next line

```
print $x + $y;
```

does not contain any quotes. It calculates the value of `$x + $y` and prints the result of this calculation (8) to the Web page.

Most of the math symbols you are familiar with also work with numeric variables. The plus sign (+) is used for addition, the minus sign (-) indicates subtraction, the asterisk (*) is used for multiplication, and the forward slash (/) is used for division. The remainder of the program illustrates how PHP does subtraction, multiplication, and division.

IN THE REAL WORLD

Those numbers without any decimal point are called `integers` and the numbers with decimal values (like 1.5, 0.333, and so on) are called `real numbers`. These two types of numbers are stored differently in computers, and this distinction sometimes leads to problems. PHP does its best to shield you from this type of issue. For example, since the values 3 and 5 are both integers, the results of the addition, subtraction, and multiplication problems are also guaranteed to be integers. However, the quotient of two integers is often a real number. Many languages would either refuse to solve this problem or would not give a complete result. They might say that 3 / 5 = 0 rather than 0.6. PHP tries to convert things to the appropriate type whenever possible, and it usually does a pretty good job. There are times, however, that you will need to control this behavior. The `setType()` function lets you force a particular variable into a particular type. You can look up the details in the online help for PHP (included in the CD-ROM that accompanies this book).

Creating a Form to Ask a Question

It's very typical for PHP programs to be made of two or more separate documents. An ordinary HTML page contains a form, which the user fills out. When the user presses the `submit` button, the information in all the form elements is sent to a program specified by a special attribute of the form. This program processes the information from the form and returns a result, which looks to the user like an ordinary Web page. To illustrate, look at the `whatsName.html` page illustrated in Figure 2.7.

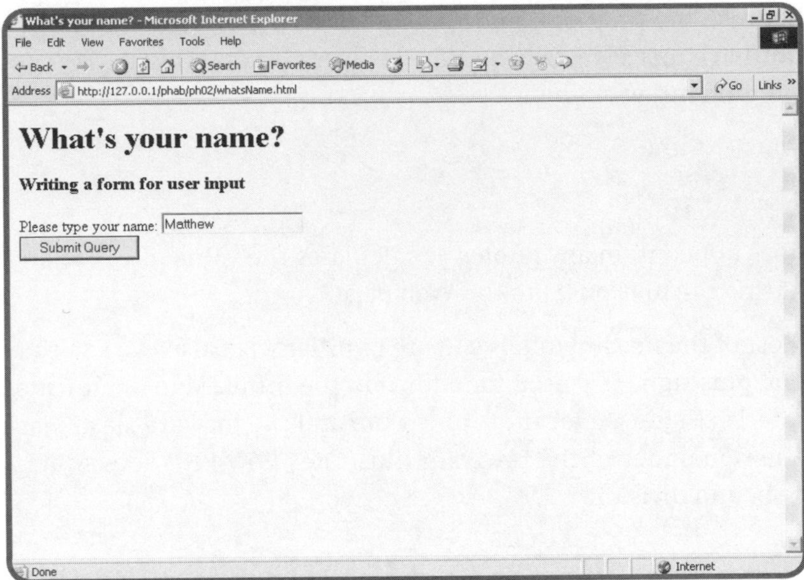

FIGURE 2.7

This is an ordinary HTML page containing a form.

The `whatsName.html` page does not contain any PHP at all. It's simply an HTML page with a form on it. When the user clicks on the Submit Query button, the page sends the value in the text area to a PHP program called `hiUser.php`. Figure 2.8 shows what happens when the `hiUser.php` program runs:

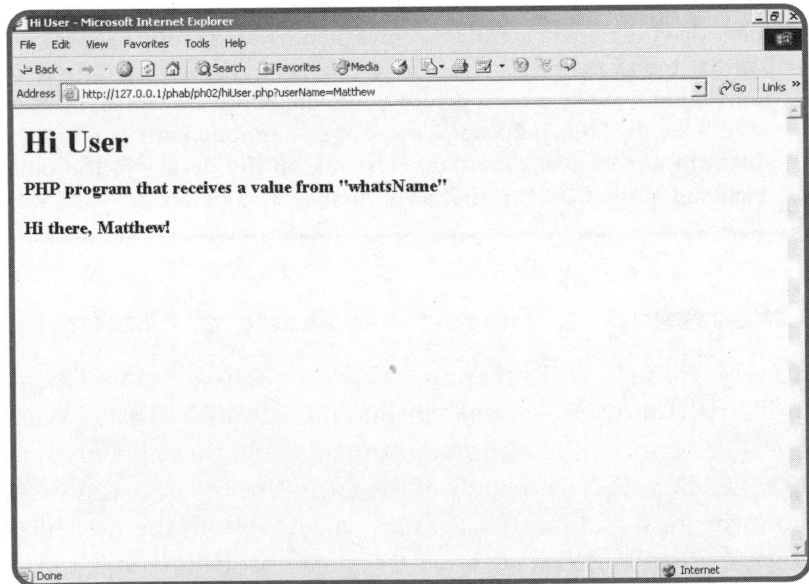

FIGURE 2.8

The resulting page uses the value from the original HTML form.

It's important to recognize that two different pages are involved in the transaction. In this section, you'll learn how to link an HTML page to a particular script, and how to write a script that expects certain form information.

Building an HTML Page with a Form

Forms are very useful when you want to get information from the user. To illustrate how this is done, look at the code for the `whatsName.html` file.

```
<html>
<head>
<title>What's your name?</title>
</head>
<body>
<h1>What's your name?</h1>
<h3>Writing a form for user input</h3>
<form method = "post"
      action = "hiUser.php">
Please type your name:
<input type = "text"
       name = "userName"
       value = "">
<br>
<input type = "submit">

</form>
</body>
</html>
```

There is only one element of this page that may not be familiar to you. Take a careful look at the `form` tag. It contains two new attributes. The `method` attribute indicates how the data will be sent to the browser. There are two primary methods, `get` and `post`. The `post` method is the most powerful and flexible, so it is the one I use most often in this book. However, you'll see some interesting ways to use the `get` method later in this chapter in the section called "Sending Data without a Form."

Setting the Action Attribute to a Script File

The other attribute of the `form` tag is the `action` attribute. This is used to determine the URL of a program that will interpret the form. This attribute is used to connect a Web page to a program to read the page and respond with another page. The URL can be an absolute reference (which begins with `http://` and contains the entire domain name of the response program), or they can be relative references (meaning the program will be in the same directory as the original Web page).

The `whatsName.html` page contains a form with its `action` attribute set to `hiUser.php`. Whenever the user clicks on the submit button, the values of all the fields (there's only one in this case) will be packed up and sent to a program called `hiUser.php`, which is expected to be in the same directory as the original `whatsName.html` page.

Writing a Script to Retrieve the Data

The code for `hiUser.php` is specially built. The form that called the hiUser.php code is expected to have an element called `userName`. Take a look at the code for `hiUser.php` and you'll see what I mean.

In the Real World

Some PHP servers have turned off the ability to automatically create a variable from a form. You might be able to convince your server administrator to turn `register_globals` on in the PHP.INI file. If not, here's a workaround: If your form has a field called `userName`, add this code to the beginning of the program that needs the value of that field:

```
$userName = $_REQUEST["userName"];
```

Repeat this code for every variable you wish to pull from the original form.

For a complete explanation of this code, you'll need to skip ahead to Chapter 5, "Better Arrays and String Handling." In that chapter, you'll also find a routine for automatically extracting all the fields of a form even if you don't know the names of the fields.

```
<html>

<head>

<title>Hi User</title>

</head>

<body>
```

```
<h1>Hi User</h1>

<h3>PHP program that receives a value from "whatsName"</h3>


<?


  print "<h3>Hi there, $userName!</h3>";


?>


</body>

</html>
```

Like many PHP pages, `hiUser.php` is mainly HTML. The only thing that's different is the one print statement. This statement incorporates the variable `$userName`. The puzzling thing is there is no other mention of the variable anywhere in the code.

When a user submits a form to a PHP program, the PHP processor automatically creates a variable with the same name as every form element on the original HTML page. Since the `whatsName.html` page has a form element called `userName`, any PHP program that `whatsName.html` activates will automatically have access to a variable called `$userName`. The value of that variable will be whatever the user has entered into the field before pressing the Submit button.

Sending Data without a Form

Sometimes it can be very handy to send data to a server-side program without necessarily using a form. This is a little-known trick that can really enhance your Web pages without requiring a lick of PHP programming. The Link Demo page (`linkDemo.html`) shown in Figures 2.9 and 2.10 illustrate this phenomenon.

Understanding the get Method

All the links in the `linkDemo.html` page use a similar trick. As you recall from earlier in the chapter, form data can be sent to a program through two different methods. The `post` method is the technique you'll usually use in your forms, but you've actually been using the `get` method all along, because normal HTML requests actually are `get` requests. The interesting thing about that is that you can send form data to

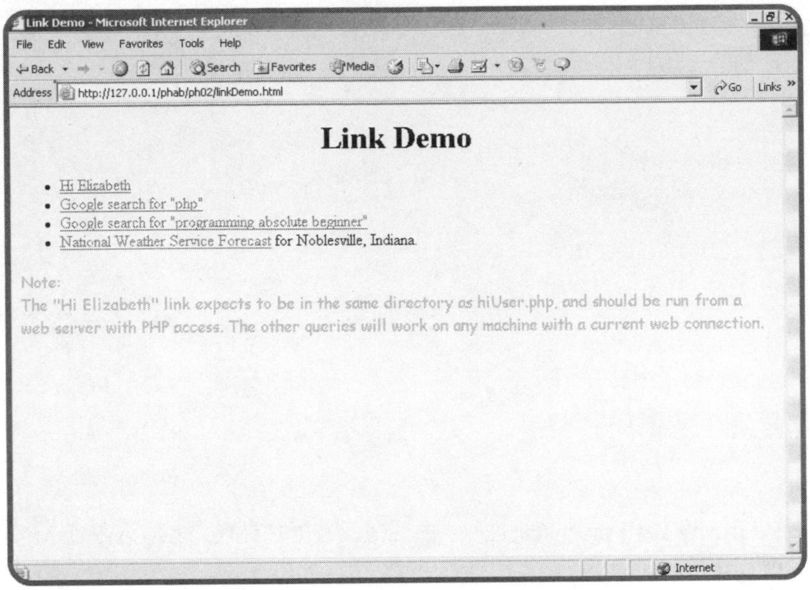

FIGURE 2.9

The links on this page appear ordinary, but they are unusually powerful.

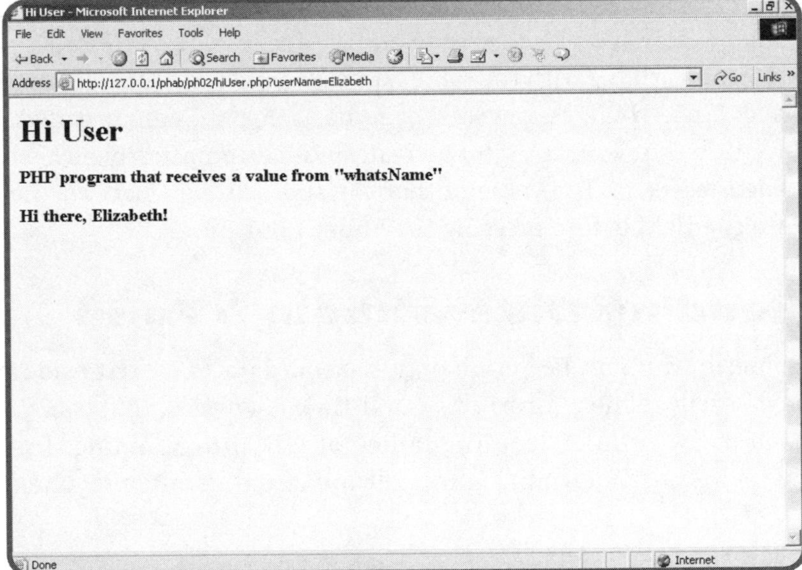

FIGURE 2.10

When I clicked on the "`Hi Elizabeth`" link, I was taken to the `HiUser` program with the value "Elizabeth" automatically sent to the program!

any program that knows how to read `get` requests by embedding the request in your URL. As an experiment, switch the `method` attribute of `whatsName.html` so the form looks like this:

```
<form method = "get"
      action = "hiUser.php">
```

Then run the page again. It will work the same as before, but the URL of the resulting page will look like this (presuming you said the user's name is "Andy"):

```
http://127.0.0.1/phab/ph02/hiUser.php?userName=Andy
```

The `get` method stashes all the form information into the URL using a special code. If you go back to the `whatsName` page and put in "Andy Harris," you'll get a slightly different result:

```
http://127.0.0.1/phab/ph02/hiUser.php?userName=Andy+Harris
```

The space between "Andy" and "Harris" was converted to a plus sign because space characters cause a lot of confusion. When form data is transmitted, it often undergoes a number of similar transformations. In PHP programming, all the translation is automatic, so you don't have to worry about it.

Using a URL to Embed Form Data

If you understand how this works, you can use a similar technique to harness any server-side program on the Internet. (Presuming it's set up to take `get`-method data—some are not.) When I examined the URLs of Google searches, I could see my search data in a field named `"q"` (for query, I suppose). I took a gamble that all the other fields would have default values, and wrote a hyperlink that incorporates a query. My link looked like this:

```
<li><a href = "http://www.google.com/search?q=php">
     Google search for "php"</a></li>
```

Whenever the user clicks on this link, it sets up a `get`-method query to google's search program. The result is a nifty Google search. One fun thing you might want to do is figure out how to set up "canned" versions of your most common queries in various search engines so you can get updated results with one click. Figure 2.11 illustrates what happens when the user clicks on the "google php" link in the `linkDemo` page.

Figure 2.12 shows the results of this slightly more complex search.

```
<li><a href =
     "http://www.google.com/search?q=programming for the absolute beginner">
      Google search for "programming absolute beginner"</a></li>
```

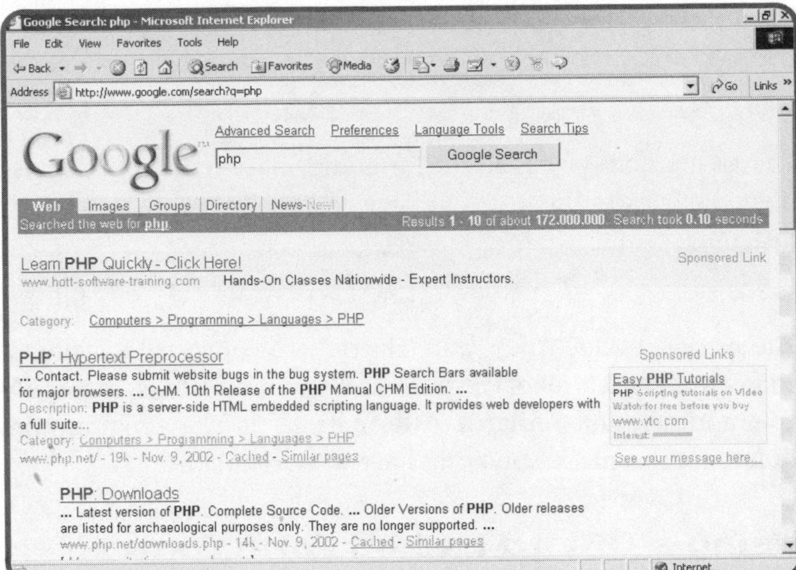

FIGURE 2.11

The Google PHP runs a search on www.google.com for the term "PHP".

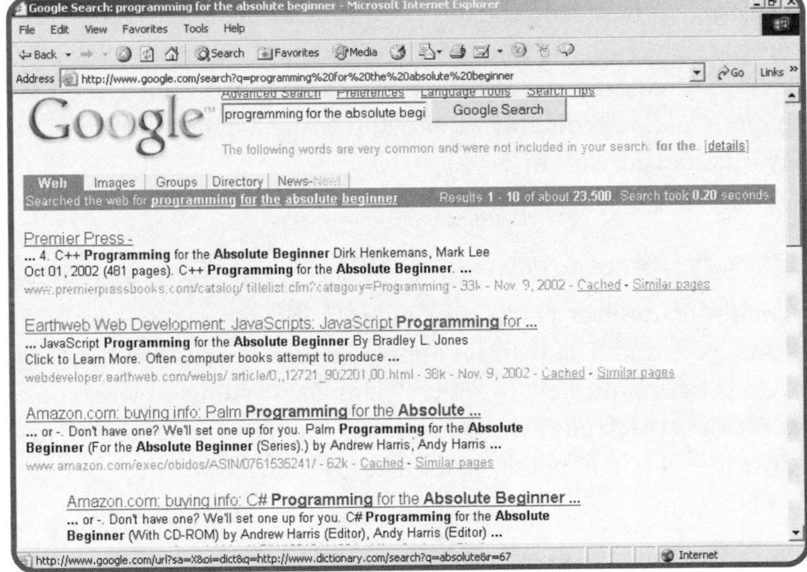

FIGURE 2.12

The Google search for "Absolute Beginners Programming" shows some really intriguing book offerings!

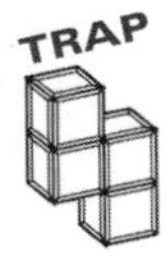

There's a down side to this approach. The owner of the program can change the program without telling you, and your link will no longer work correctly. Most Web programmers assume that their programs will be called only by the forms that they originally built.

The other thing to consider is people can do this with your programs. Just because you *intend* for your program to be called only by a form doesn't mean that's how it will always work. Such is the vibrant nature of the free-form Internet.

Working with Multiple Field Queries

As one more practical example, the code for the National Weather service link looks like this:

```
<li><a href =     "http://www.crh.noaa.gov/data/forecasts/
INZ039.php?warncounty=INC057&city=Noblesville">
National Weather Service Forecast</a>
for Noblesville, Indiana.
```

While this link looks a little more complex, it didn't require any special knowledge. I simply searched the National Weather Service Web site until I found the automatically generated page for my hometown. When I looked at the URL that resulted, I was pleased (but not surprised) to see that the page was generated by a PHP script. (Note the `.php` extension in the URL.) I copied the link from my browser and incorporated it into `linkDemo.html`. The weather page is automatically created by a PHP program based on two inputs (the county and city name). Any time I want to see the local weather, I can re-call the same query even though the request doesn't come directly from the National Weather Service. This is a really easy way to customize your Web page.

In the last paragraph I mentioned that the PHP program requires two fields. I've never actually seen the program, but I know this because I looked carefully at the URL. The part that says `warncounty=INC057` indicates the state and county (at least that's a reasonable guess), and the `city=Noblesville` indicates which city within the county I'm interested in. When a form has two or more input elements, they are attached to each other with the ampersand (&) as you can see in the National Weather Service example.

Reading Input from Other Form Elements

A PHP program can read the input from any type of HTML form element. In all cases, the `name` attribute of the HTML form object becomes a variable name in PHP. In general, the value of the PHP variable comes from the `value` property of the form object.

Introducing the borderMaker program

To examine most of the various form elements, I built a simple page to demonstrate various attributes of Cascading Style Sheet borders. The HTML program is shown in Figure 2.13.

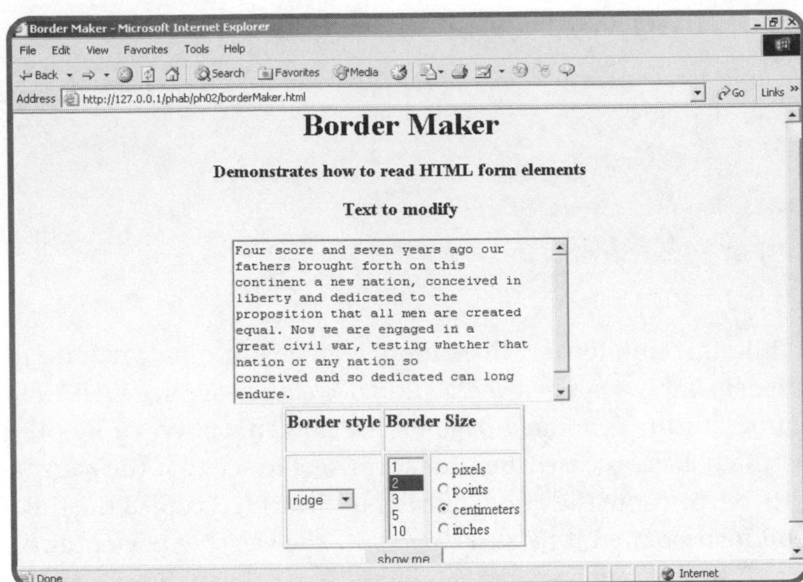

FIGURE 2.13

The borderMaker HTML page uses a text area, two list boxes, and a select group.

Building the borderMaker.html Page

The `borderMaker.html` page contains a very typical form with most of the major input elements in it. The code for this form is

```
<html>
<head>
<title>Font Choices</title>
</head>
<body>
<center>
<h1>Font Choices</h1>
<h3>Demonstrates how to read HTML form elements</h3>

<form method = "post"
      action = "borderMaker.php">


<h3>Text to modify</h3>
<textarea name = "basicText"
          rows = "10"
```

```
          cols = "40">
Four score and seven years ago our fathers brought forth on this
continent a new nation, conceived in liberty and dedicated to the
proposition that all men are created equal. Now we are engaged in a
great civil war, testing whether that nation or any nation so
conceived and so dedicated can long endure.
</textarea>

<table border = 2>
<tr>
  <td><h3>Border style</h3></td>
  <td colspan = 2><h3>Border Size</h3></td>
</tr>

<tr>
<td>
<select name = borderStyle>
  <option value = "ridge">ridge</option>
  <option value = "groove">groove</option>
  <option value = "double">double</option>
  <option value = "inset">inset</option>
  <option value = "outset">outset</option>
</select>
</td>
<td>

<select size = 5
        name = borderSize>
  <option value = "1">1</option>
  <option value = "2">2</option>
  <option value = "3">3</option>
  <option value = "5">5</option>
  <option value = "10">10</option>
```

```
</select>
</td>

<td>
<input type = "radio"
       name = "sizeType"
       value = "px">pixels<br>
<input type = "radio"
       name = "sizeType"
       value = "pt">points<br>
<input type = "radio"
       name = "sizeType"
       value = "cm">centimeters<br>
<input type = "radio"
       name = "sizeType"
       value = "in">inches<br>
</td>
</tr>
</table>

<input type = "submit"
       value = "show me">

</form>

</center>
</body>
</html>
```

The `borderMaker.html` page is designed to interact with a PHP program called `borderMaker.php`, as you can see by inspection of the `action` attribute. Note that I added a `value` attribute for each `option` element, and the radio buttons all have the same name but different values. The `value` attribute becomes very important when your program is destined to be read by a program, as you shall see very shortly. Finally, the Submit button is critical, because nothing interesting will happen until the user submits the form.

You might have noticed I didn't include checkboxes in this particular example. Checkboxes work much like the other `form` elements, but in practice they are more useful when you understand conditional statements, which will be the major topic of the next chapter. You'll get plenty of opportunity to practice these elements when we get there.

Reading the Form Elements

The `borderMaker.php` program expects input from `borderMaker.html`. When the user submits the HTML form, the PHP program produces results like those shown in Figure 2.14.

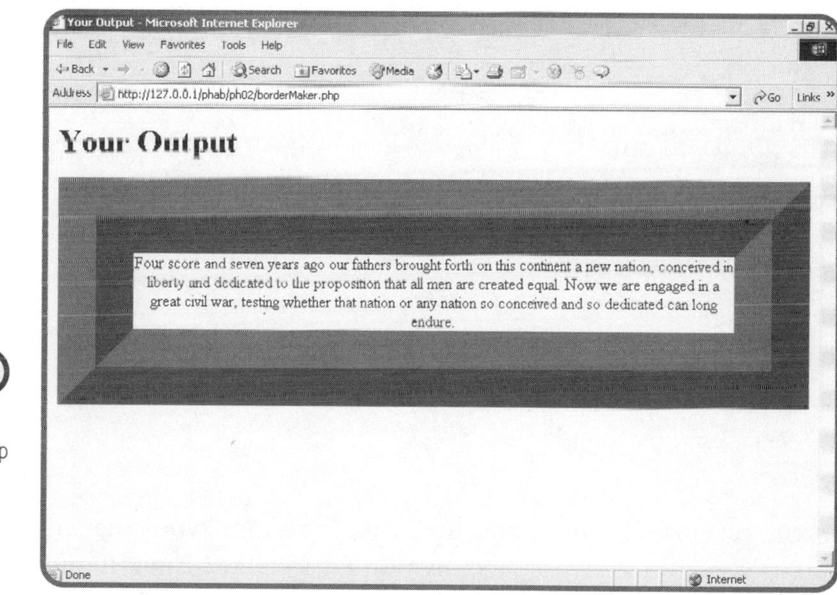

FIGURE 2.14

The `borderMaker.php` code reacts to all the various input elements on the form.

In general, it doesn't matter what type of element is used on an HTML form. The PHP interpreter simply looks at the name of each element and the value. By the time the information gets to the server, it doesn't really matter what type of input element was used. PHP automatically creates a variable corresponding to each form element. The value of that variable will be the value of the element. The code used in borderMaker.php illustrates:

```
<html>
<head>
<title>Your Output</title>
</head>
<body>
<h1>Your Output</h1>
<center>
<?
$theStyle = <<<HERE
"border-width:$borderSize$sizeType;
border-style:$borderStyle;
border-color:green"
HERE;

print "<div style = $theStyle>";
print $basicText;
print "</span>";


?>
</center>


</body>
</html>
```

In the case of text boxes and text areas, the user types the value directly in. In borderMaker.html, there is a text area called basicText. The PHP interpreter creates a variable called $basicText. Anything typed into that text box (as a default the first few lines of the Gettysburg Address) becomes the value of the $basicText variable.

Reading Select Elements

Recall that both drop-down lists and list boxes are created with the select object. That object has a name attribute. Each of the possible choices in the list box is an option object. Each option object has a value attribute.

The name of the `select` object will become the name of the variable. For example, `borderMaker.html` has two select objects, `borderSize` and `borderStyle`. The PHP program can expect to find two corresponding variables, `$borderSize` and `$borderStyle`. Because there is no place for the user to type a value into a `select` object, the values it can return must be encoded into the structure of the form itself. The `value` of whichever `option` the user selected will be sent to the PHP program as the value of the corresponding variable. For example, if the user chose `groove` as the border style, the `$borderStyle` variable will have the value `groove` in it.

IN THE REAL WORLD

Note that the value of the options doesn't necessarily have to be what the user sees on the form. This is handy if you want to show the user one thing, but send something else to the server. For example, you might want to let the user choose from several colors. In this case you might want to create a list box that shows the user several color names, but the `value` property corresponding to each of the `option` objects might have the actual hexidecimal values used to generate the color. Similar tricks are used in online shopping environments where you might let the user choose an item by its name, but the value associated with that item might be its catalog number, which is easier to work with in a database environment.

You might recall that it is possible to have multiple selections enabled in a list box. In that case, the variable will contain a *list* of responses. While managing this list is not difficult, it is a topic for another chapter (To be specific, Chapter 4, "Loops and Arrays." For now, concentrate on the singular style of list box.

Reading Radio Groups

CSS allows the developer to indicate sizes with a variety of measurements. This is an ideal place for a group of radio buttons because only one unit of measure is appropriate at a time. Even though there are four different radio buttons on the `borderDemo.html` page with the name `sizeType`, the PHP program will only see one `$sizeType` variable. The `value` associated with whichever option is selected will become the value of the `$sizeType` variable. Note that like option elements, it is possible for the value of a radio button to be different than the text displayed beside it.

IN THE REAL WORLD

How do you decide what type of form element to use?

You might wonder if all these different form elements are necessary, since they all boil down to a name and value by the time they get to the PHP interpreter. The various kinds of user interface elements do make a difference in a few ways:

- **First, it's easier (for many users) to use a mouse than to type. Whenever possible, it is nice to add lists, checks, and options so the user can navigate your forms more quickly. Typing is often much slower than the kinds of input afforded by the other elements.**
- **Secondly, interface elements (especially the drop-down list box) are extremely efficient in terms of screen space. You can pack a lot of choices on a small screen by using drop-downs effectively. While you might not think this is an issue any more, take a look at how many people are now surfing the Web with PDAs and cell phones.**
- **Third, your life as a programmer is much easier if you can predict what the user will be sending you. When users type things, they make spelling and grammar mistakes, use odd abbreviations, and are just unpredictable. If you limit the user's choices whenever possible, you are less likely to frustrate your users because your program should be able to anticipate all the possible choices.**

Returning to the Story Program

The story program introduced at the beginning of this chapter is an opportunity to bring together all the new elements you've learned. It doesn't introduce anything new, but it helps you see a larger context.

Designing the Story

Even though this is not an especially difficult program to write, you'll run into problems if you simply open up your text editor and start blasting away. It really pays to plan ahead. The most important thinking happens before you write a single line of code.

In this situation, start by thinking about your story. You can write your own story, or you can modify some existing text for humorous effect. I raided a nursery rhyme book for my story. Regardless of how you come up with a story, you need to have it in place *before* you start to write code. I wrote the original unmodified version of "Little Boy Blue" in my text editor first so I could admire its artistic genius—and then mangle it beyond recognition. As you look over the original prose, look for key words you can take out, and try to find a description that will hint at the original word without giving anything away. For example, I printed out my story, circled the word "blue" in the original poem, and wrote "color" on another piece of paper. Keep doing this until you've found several words you can take out of the original story. You should have a document with a bunch of holes in it, and a list of hints. Mine looked like Figure 2.15.

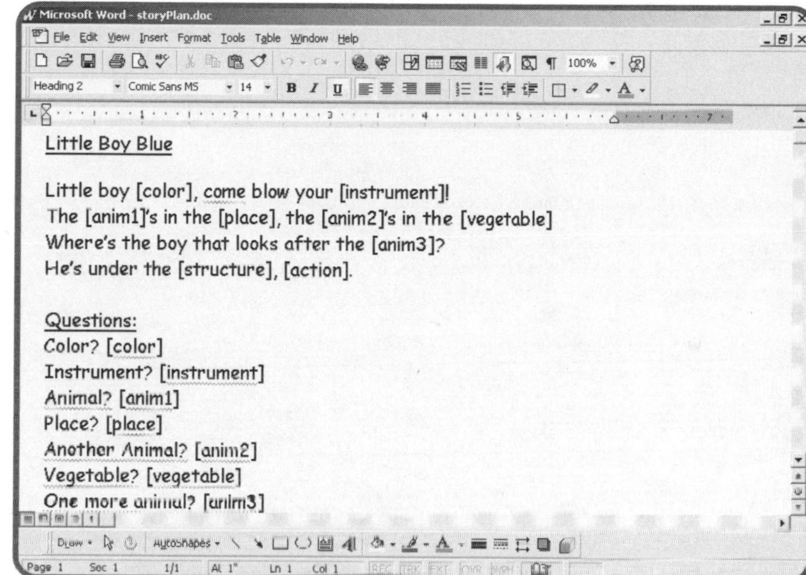

FIGURE 2.15

My plan for the story game. I thought through the story and the word list *before* writing any code.

In the Real World

Figure 2.15 shows the plan written as a MS Word document. Although things are sometimes done this way (especially in a professional programming environment) I *really* wrote the plan on paper. I reproduced it in a cleaner format because you don't deserve to be subjected to my handwriting. I usually plan my programs on paper, chalkboard, or dry erase board. I avoid planning programs on the computer, because it's too tempting to start programming immediately. It's really important to make your plan describe what you wish to do in *English* before you worry about how exactly you'll implement the plan. Most beginners (and a lot of pros) start programming way too early, and get stuck as a result. You'll see throughout the rest of this chapter how this plan evolves into a working program.

Building the HTML Page

With the basic outline from Figure 2.15, it becomes clear how the story program should be created. It should have two parts. The first is an HTML page that prompts the user for all the various words. Here's the code for my version:

```
<html>
<head>
<title>Story</title>
</head>
<body>
<h1>Story</h1>
<h3>Please fill in the blanks below, and I'll tell
    you a story</h3>
<form method = "post"
      action = "story.php">

<table border = 1>
<tr>
  <th>Color:</th>
  <th>
    <input type = "text"
           name = "color"
           value = "">
  </th>
</tr>

<tr>
  <th>Musical Instrument</th>
  <th>
    <input type = "text"
           name = "instrument"
           value = "">
  </th>
```

```
</tr>

<tr>
  <th>Animal</th>
  <th>
    <input type = "text"
           name = "anim1"
           value = "">
  </th>
</tr>

<tr>
  <th>Another animal</th>
  <th>
    <input type = "text"
           name = "anim2"
           value = "">
  </th>
</tr>

<tr>
  <th>Yet another animal!</th>
  <th>
    <input type = "text"
           name = "anim3"
           value = "">
  </th>
</tr>

<tr>
  <th>Place</th>
  <th>
    <input type = "text"
```

```
          name = "place"
          value = "">
  </th>
</tr>

<tr>
  <th>Vegetable</th>
  <th>
    <input type = "text"
           name = "vegetable"
           value = "">
  </th>
</tr>

<tr>
  <th>A structure</th>
  <th>
    <input type = "text"
           name = "structure"
           value = "">
  </th>
</tr>

<tr>
  <th>An action</th>
  <th>
    <select name = "action">
      <option value = "fast asleep">fast asleep</option>
      <option value = "drinking cappuccino">drinking cappuccino</option>
      <option value = "wandering around aimlessly">wandering around aimlessly</option>
      <option value = "doing nothing in particular">doing nothing in particular</option>
    </select>
  </th>
```

```
</tr>

<tr>
  <td colspan = 2>
    <center>
      <input type = "submit"
             value = "tell me the story">
    </center>
  </td>
</tr>
</table>

</form>
</body>
</html>
```

There's nothing terribly exciting about the HTML. In fact, since I had the plan, I knew exactly what kinds of things I was asking for and created form elements to ask each question. I used a list box for the last question so I could put in some interesting suggestions. Note that I changed the order a little bit just to throw the user off.

There are a few things to check when you're writing a page that will connect to a script. First, ensure you've got the correct `action` attribute in the `form` tag. (for that matter, make sure you've added an `action` attribute.) Make sure each form element has an appropriate `name` attribute. If you have radio or option objects, make sure each one has an appropriate value. Finally, be sure there is a Submit button somewhere in your form.

Checking the Form

I actually wrote two different scripts to read this form. The first one I wrote simply checked each element to make sure it received the value I expected. Here's the first program, called `storySimple.php`.

```
<html>
<head>
<title>Little Boy Who?</title>
</head>
```

```
<body>
<h1>Little Boy Who?</h1>

<h3>Values from the story page</h3>

<table border = 1>
<tr>
  <th>Variable</th>
  <th>Value</th>
</tr>

<tr>
  <th>color</th>
  <td><? print $color ?></td>
</tr>

<tr>
  <th>instrument</th>
  <td><? print $instrument ?></td>
</tr>

<tr>
  <th>anim1</th>
  <td><? print $anim1 ?></td>
</tr>

<tr>
  <th>anim2</th>
  <td><? print $anim2 ?></td>
</tr>

<tr>
  <th>anim3</th>
```

```
    <td><? print $anim3 ?></td>
  </tr>

  <tr>
    <th>place</th>
    <td><? print $place ?></td>
  </tr>

  <tr>
    <th>vegetable</th>
    <td><? print $vegetable ?></td>
  </tr>

  <tr>
    <th>structure</th>
    <td><? print $structure ?></td>
  </tr>

  <tr>
    <th>action</th>
    <td><? print $action ?></td>
  </tr>

</table>
<form>
</html>
```

I made this program as simple as possible, because I didn't expect to need it for long. It's simply a table with the name of each variable and its associated value. I did it this way to ensure that I get all the variables exactly the way I want them. There's no point in building the story if you don't have the variables working.

Building the Final Story

The story itself is very simple to build if you've made a plan and ensured that the variables are working right. All I had to do was write out the story as it was written in the plan, with the variables incorporated in the appropriate places. Here's the code for the finished `story.php` page:

```
<html>
<head>
<title>Little Boy Who?</title>
</head>
<body>
<center>

<h1>Little Boy Who?</h1>

<?

print <<<HERE
<h3>
Little Boy $color, come blow your $instrument!<br>
The $anim1's in the $place, the $anim2's in the $vegetable.<br>
Where's the boy that looks after the $anim3?<br>
He's under the $structure, $action.
</h3>
HERE;
?>

</center>

</body>
</html>
```

It might astonish you that the final program is quite a bit simpler than the test program. Neither is very complicated, but once you have created the story, set up the variables, and tested that all the variables are being sent correctly, the story program itself turns out to be almost trivial. Most of the `story.php` code is plain HTML. The only part that's in `PHP` is one long `print` statement. This uses the `print <<<HERE` syntax to print out a long line of HTML text with PHP variables embedded inside. The story itself is this text.

Summary

In this chapter you have learned some incredibly important concepts. You learned what variables are, and how to create them in PHP. You've learned how to connect a form to a PHP program with modifications to the form's `method` and `action` attributes. You learned how to write normal links to send values to server-side scripts. You've built programs that respond to various kinds of input elements, including drop-down lists, radio buttons, and list boxes. You've gone through the process of writing a program from beginning to end, including the critical planning stage, creating a form for user input, and using that input to generate interesting output.

CHALLENGES

1. Write a Web page that asks the user for first and last name, then uses a PHP script to write a form letter to that person. Inform the user he or she might be a millionaire.
2. Write a custom Web page that uses the "embedded data" tricks described in this chapter to generate custom links for your favorite Web searches, local news and weather, and other elements of interest to you.
3. Write your own story game. Find or write some text to modify, create an appropriate input form, and output the story with a PHP script.

Controlling your Code with Conditions and Functions

So far you've written some PHP programs that get information from the user, store things in variables, and do some simple operations on those variables. Most of the really interesting things you can do with a computer involve letting it make decisions. Actually, the computer only appears able to decide things. The programmer generates code that tells the computer exactly what to do in different circumstances. In this chapter, you'll learn how to control the flow of a program. Specifically, you'll learn how to:

- Create a random integer.
- Use the `if` structure to change the program's behavior.
- Write conditions to evaluate variables.
- Work with the `else` clause to provide instructions when a condition is not met.
- Use the `switch` statement to work with multiple choices.
- Build functions to better manage your code.
- Write programs that can create their own forms.

Examining the "Petals Around the Rose" Game

The Petals Around the Rose game, featured in Figure 3.1 illustrates all the new skills you will learn in this chapter.

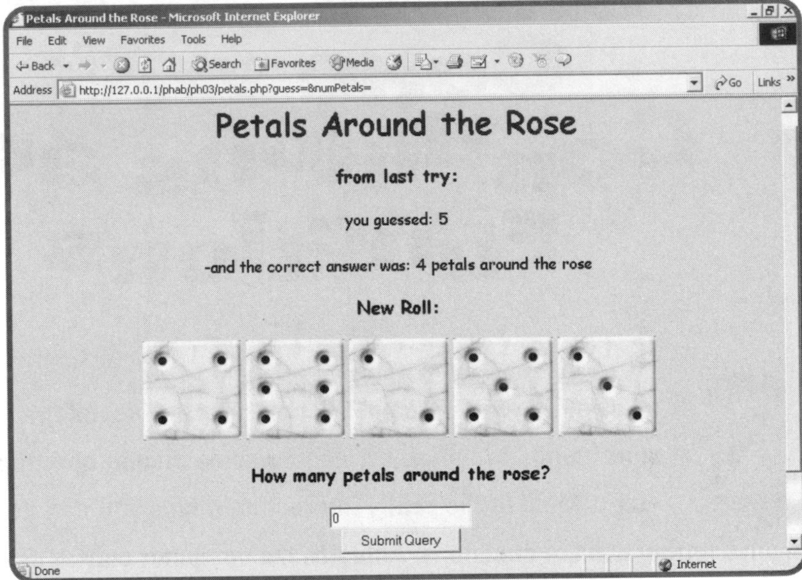

FIGURE 3.1

This is a new twist on an old dice puzzle.

The premise of the Petals game is very simple. The computer rolls a set of five dice and asks the user to guess the number of "petals around the rose." The user enters a number and presses the button. The computer then indicates whether this value was correct, and provides a new set of dice. Once the user understands the secret, it's a very easy game, but it can take a long time to figure out how it works. When you look at the code towards the end of this chapter, you'll learn the secret, but for now you should try the game yourself before you know how it's done.

Creating a Random Number

The dice game, like many other games, relies on random number generation to make things interesting. Most languages have at least one way to create random numbers. PHP makes it very easy to create random numbers with the `rand` function.

Viewing the "Roll 'em" Program

The `roll' em` program shown in Figure 3.2 demonstrates how the `rand` function can be used to generate virtual dice.

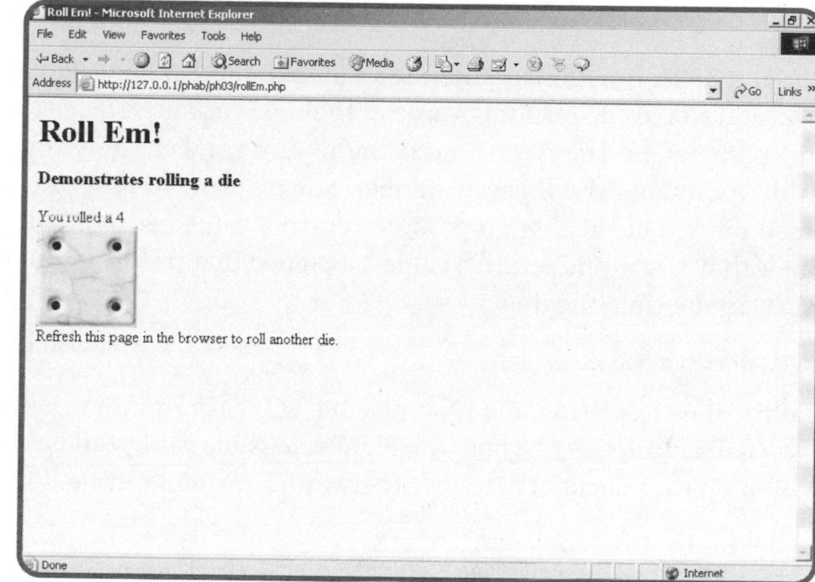

FIGURE 3.2

The die roll is randomly generated by PHP.

The code for the `rollEm` program shows how easy random number generation is.

```
<html>

<head>

<title>Roll Em!</title>

</head>

<body>

<h1>Roll Em!</h1>

<h3>Demonstrates rolling a die</h3>


<?

$roll = rand(1,6);

print "You rolled a $roll";

print "<br>";

print "<img src = die$roll.jpg>";

?>
```

```
<br>
Refresh this page in the browser to roll another die.

</body>
</html>
```

I used the `rand` function to generate a random number between one and six (inclusive) and stored the resulting value in the `$roll` variable. The `rand` function expects two parameters. The first value is the lowest number you wish, and the second value represents the highest number. Since I want to replicate an ordinary six-sided die, I told the `rand` function to return a value between one and six. Since I knew that `rand` would return a value, I assigned that resulting value to the variable `$roll`. By the time the line

```
$roll = rand(1,6);
```

has finished executing, the `$roll` variable will have a random value in it. The lowest possible value will be one, the highest possible value will be six, and the value will not have a decimal part. (In other words, it will never be 1.5.)

If you're coming from another programming language, you might be a little surprised at the way random numbers are generated in PHP. Most languages allow you to create a random floating point value between zero and one, and then require you to transform that value to whatever range you wish. PHP allows (in fact requires) you to create random integers within a range, which is usually what you want anyway. If you really want a value between zero and one, you can generate a random number between zero and 1000 and then divide that value by 1000.

Printing a Corresponding Image

Notice the sneaky way I used variable interpolation. I carefully named my first image die1.jpg, the second die2.jpg, and so on. When I was ready to print an image to the screen, I used an ordinary HTML image tag, but the source is set to die$roll.jpg. If `$roll` is three, the image will show die3.jpg. You'll see some other ways to let the computer respond to random numbers shortly, but variable interpolation can be a wonderful trick if you know how the file names are structured.

You might recall from Chapter 2, "Using Variables and Input" that *interpolation* is the technique that allows you to embed a variable in a quoted string by simply using its name.

ACQUIRING IMAGES

The dice games in this chapter demonstrate the power of graphical images to make your programs more interesting and fun. There are a number of ways to get graphics for your programs. The easiest is to find an existing image on the Web. Although this is technically very simple, many of the images on the Web are owned by somebody, so you should try to respect the intellectual property rights of the original owners. Try to get permission for any images you use.

Another alternative is to create the graphics yourself. Even if you don't have any artistic talent at all, modern software and technology make it quite easy to generate passable graphics. You can do a lot with a digital camera and a freeware graphics editor. Even if you will hire a professional artist to do graphics for your program, you might still need to be able to sketch what you are looking for. We've added a couple of very powerful freeware image editing programs to the CD-Rom that accompanies this book.

Using the if Statement to Control Program Flow

One of the most interesting things computers do is appear to make decisions. The decision-making ability of the computer is really an illusion. The programmer stores very specific instructions inside a computer, and it acts only on those instructions. The simplest form of this behavior is a structure called the `if` statement.

Introducing the Ace Program

I'll slightly modify the "roll-em" program to illustrate how it can be improved with an `if` structure. Figure 3.3 shows the program when the program rolls any value except one.

However, this program does something exciting (okay, moderately exciting) when it rolls a one, as you can see from Figure 3.4.

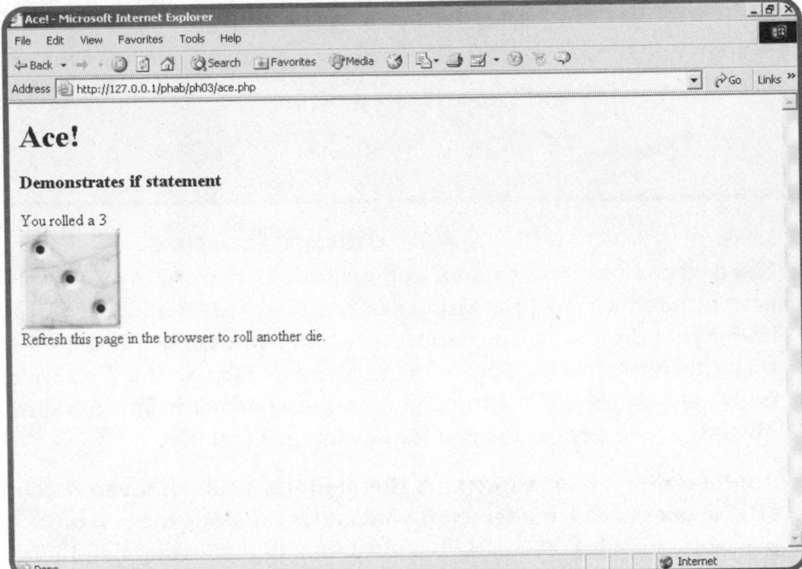

FIGURE 3.3

When the roll is not a one, nothing interesting happens.

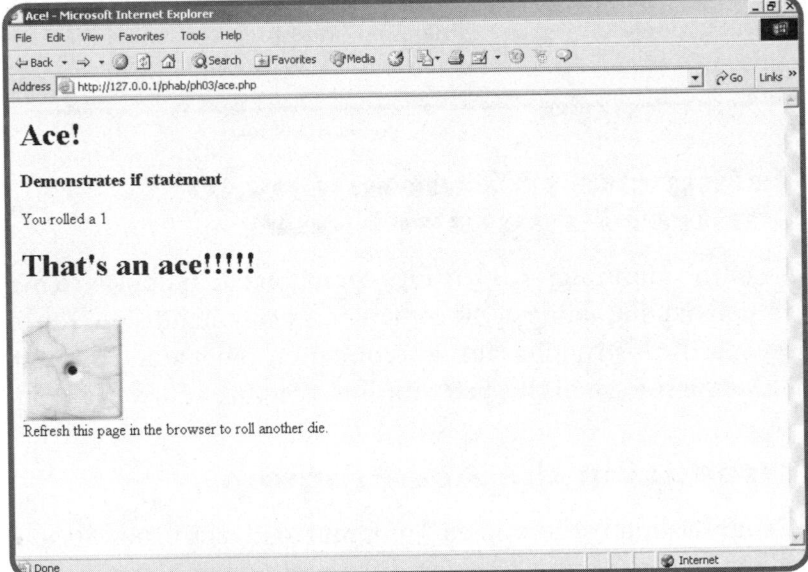

FIGURE 3.4

When a one appears, the user is treated to a lavish multimedia display.

Creating a Condition

On the surface, the behavior of the Ace program is very straightforward: it does something interesting only if the die roll is one, and it doesn't do that interesting thing in any other case. While it is a simple idea, the implications are profound.

The same simple mechanism used in the Ace program is the foundation of all complicated computer behavior, from flight simulators to heart monitors. Take a look at the code for the Ace program and see if you can spot the new element:

```
<html>
<head>
<title>Ace!</title>
</head>
<body>
<h1>Ace!</h1>
<h3>Demonstrates if statement</h3>

<?
$roll = rand(1,6);
print "You rolled a $roll";

if ($roll == 1){
  print "<h1>That's an ace!!!!!</h1>";
} // end if

print "<br>";
print "<img src = die$roll.jpg>";
?>
<br>
Refresh this page in the browser to roll another die.

</body>
</html>
```

The secret to this program is the segment that looks like this:

```
if ($roll == 1){
  print "<h1>That's an ace!!!!!</h1>";
} // end if
```

The line that prints "That's an ace!" will not happen every time the program is run. It will only happen if a certain condition is true. The `if` statement sets up a *condition* for evaluation. In this case, the condition is read "`$roll` is equal to one." If that condition is true, all the code between the left brace ({) and the right brace (}) will evaluate. If the condition is not true, the code between the braces will be skipped altogether.

A condition can be thought of as an expression that can be evaluated as true or false. Any expression that can return a true or false value can be used as a condition. Most conditions look much like the one in the Ace program. This condition checks the variable `$roll` to see if it is equal to the value `1`.

Note that equality is indicated by two equals signs (==).

This is important, because computer programs are not nearly as flexible as humans. We humans often use the same symbol for different purposes. While computer languages can do this, it often leads to problems. The single equals sign is reserved for *assignment*. You should read this line

```
$x = 5;
```

as `x gets five`, indicating that the value five is being assigned to the variable `$x`. The code fragment

```
$x == 5;
```

should be read as `x is equal to five`, as it is *testing equality*. It is essentially asking whether x is equal to five. A condition such as `$x == 5` does not stand on its own. Instead, it is used inside some sort of other structure, such as an `if` statement.

Exploring Comparison Operators

Equality (==) is not the only type of comparison PHP allows. There are several other ways to compare a variable and a value or two variables. These comparison operators are described in table 3.1

These comparison operators work on any type of data, although the results might be a little strange. For example, if you have a condition like

```
"a" < "b"
```

you would get the result `true` because alphabetically, the letter "a" is earlier than "b," so it has a "smaller" value.

Table 3.1 Comparison Operators

Operator	Description
==	equal to
<	less than
>	greater than
<=	less than or equal to
>=	greater than or equal to
!=	not equal to

Creating an if Statement

An `if` statement begins with the keyword `if` followed by a condition inside parentheses. After the parentheses is a left brace ({). You can put as many lines of code between the left brace and the right brace(}) as you wish. Any code between the braces will only be executed if the condition is true. If the condition is false, program control flows to the next line after the right brace. It is not necessary to put a semicolon on a line ending with a brace. It is customary to indent all the code between the left brace and the right brace.

Code Style

You might be aware that the PHP processor actually ignores the spaces and carriage returns in your PHP code, so you might wonder if it matters to pay such attention to how code is indented, where the braces go, and so on. While the PHP processor doesn't care how you format your code, human readers do. Programmers have passionate arguments about how you should format your code. If you are writing code with a group (for instance in a large project or for a class), you will often be given a style guide you are expected to follow. When you're working on your own, the specific style you adopt is not as important as staying with it and being consistent in your coding. The particular stylistic conventions I have adopted for this book are reasonably common, relatively readable (especially for beginners), and easily adapted to a number of languages. If you don't have your own programming style, the one presented in this book is a good starting place. However, if your team leader or teacher requires another style, you will need to adapt to it. Regardless of the specific style guidelines you use, it makes lots of sense to indent your code, place comments liberally throughout your program, and use white space to make your programs easier to read and debug.

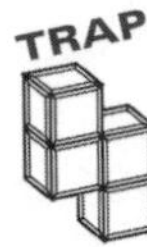

Do not put a semicolon at the end of the `if` line. The following code

```
if ("day" == "night") ; {
  print "we must be near a black hole";
} // end if
```

will print "we must be near a black hole." When the processor sees the semicolon following ("day" == "night"), it thinks there is no code at all to evaluate if the condition is true, so the condition is effectively ignored. Essentially, the braces are used to indicate that an entire group of lines are to be treated as one structure, and that structure is part of the current logical line.

Working with Negative Results

The Ace program shows how to write code that handles a condition. Much of the time, you'll want the program to do one thing if the condition is true, and something else if the condition is false. Most languages include a special variant of the `if` statement to handle exactly this type of contingency.

Demonstrating the Ace or Not Program

The Ace or Not program is built from the Ace program, but it has an important difference, as you can see from Figures 3.5 and 3.6.

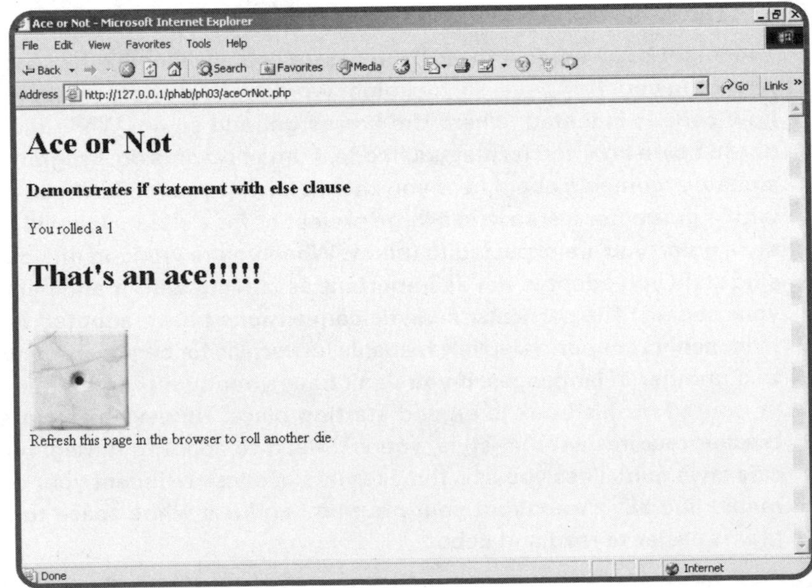

FIGURE 3.5

If the program rolls a "one," it still hollers out "Ace!"

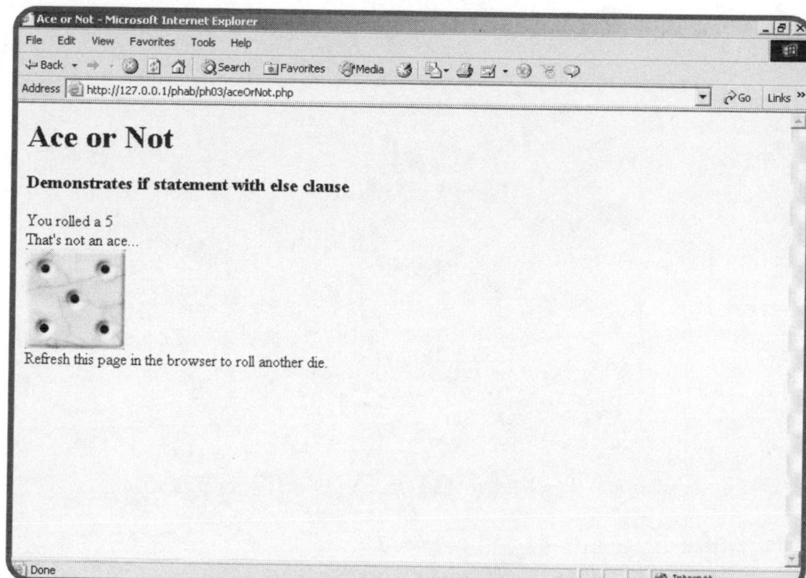

FIGURE 3.6

If the program rolls anything but a one, it still has a message for the user.

In other words, the program does one thing when the condition is true and something else when the condition is false.

Using the else Clause

The code for the `aceOrNot` program shows how the `else` clause can be used to allow for multiple behavior.

```
<html>
<head>
<title>Ace or Not</title>
</head>
<body>
<h1>Ace or Not</h1>
<h3>Demonstrates if statement with else clause</h3>

<?
$roll = rand(1,6);
print "You rolled a $roll";
```

```
print "<br>";

if ($roll == 1){
  print "<h1>That's an ace!!!!!</h1>";
} else {
  print "That's not an ace...";
} // end if

print "<br>";
print "<img src = die$roll.jpg>";
?>
<br>
Refresh this page in the browser to roll another die.

</body>
</html>
```

The interesting part of this code comes near the if statement:

```
if ($roll == 1){
  print "<h1>That's an ace!!!!!</h1>";
} else {
  print "That's not an ace...";
} // end if
```

If the condition `$roll == 1` is true, the program prints "That's an ace!!!!!" If the condition is *not* true, the code between `else` and the end of the `if` structure is executed instead. Notice the structure and indentation. One chunk of code (between the condition and the `else` statement, encased in braces) occurs if the condition is true. If the condition is false, the code between `else` and the end of the `if` structure (also in braces) is executed. You can put as much code in either segment as you wish. Only one of the segments will run (based on the condition), but you are guaranteed that one *will* execute.

Working with Multiple Values

Often you will find yourself working with more complex data. For example, you might want to respond differently to each of the six possible rolls of a die. The Binary Dice program illustrated in Figures 3.7 and 3.8 demonstrates just such a situation.

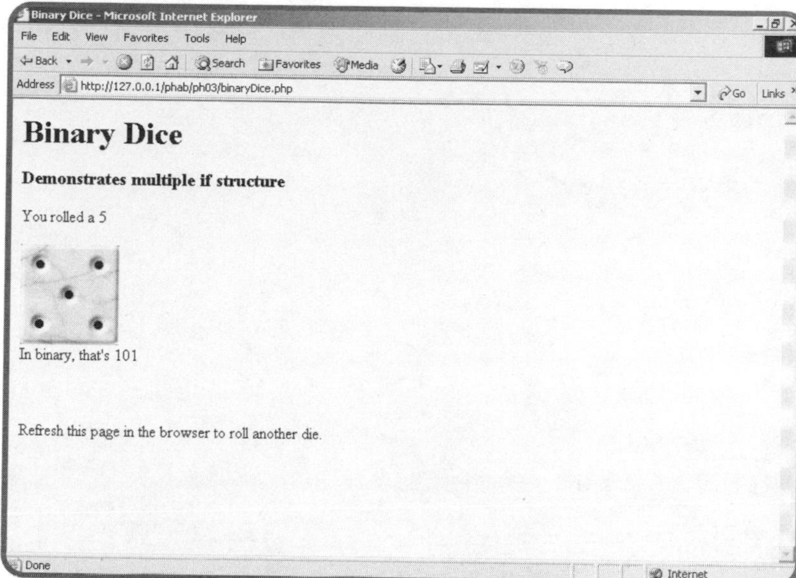

FIGURE 3.7

The roll is a 5, and the program shows the binary representation of that value.

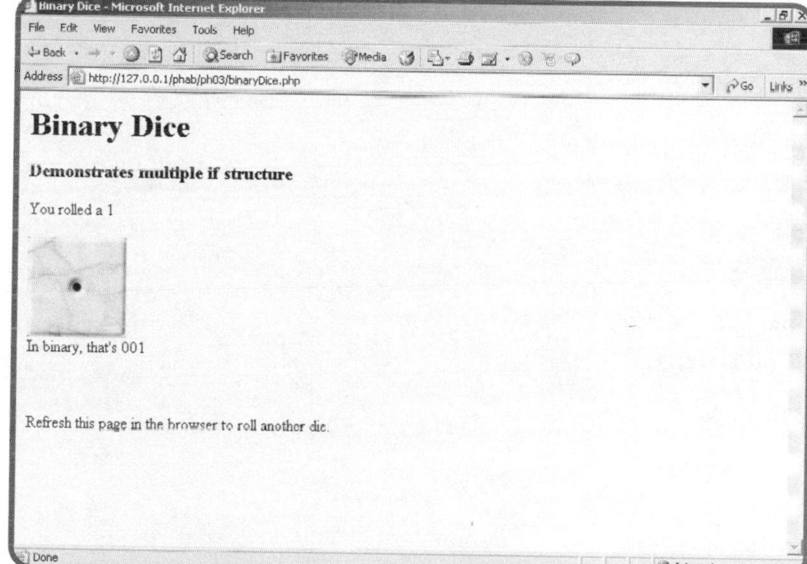

FIGURE 3.8

After rolling again, the program again reports the binary representation of the new roll.

Writing the Binary Dice Program

This program has a slightly more complex `if` structure than the others, because the binary value should be different for each of six possible outcomes. An ordinary `if` structure would not be sufficient, but it is possible to put several `if` structures together to solve this kind of dilemma.

```
<html>
<head>
<title>Binary Dice</title>
</head>
<body>
<h1>Binary Dice</h1>
<h3>Demonstrates multiple if structure</h3>

<?
$roll = rand(1,6);
print "You rolled a $roll";
print "<br>";

if ($roll == 1){
  $binValue = "001";
} else if ($roll == 2){
  $binValue = "010";
} else if ($roll == 3){
  $binValue = "011";
} else if ($roll == 4){
  $binValue = "100";
} else if ($roll == 5){
  $binValue = "101";
} else if ($roll == 6){
  $binValue = "110";
} else {
  print "I don't know that one...";
} // end if

print "<br>";
print "<img src = die$roll.jpg>";
print "<br>";
print "In binary, that's $binValue";
```

```
print "<br>";

print "<br>";

print "<br>";


?>

<br>

Refresh this page in the browser to roll another die.


</body>

</html>
```

Using Multiple else if Clauses

The `binaryDice` program still has only one `if` structure, but that structure has multiple `else` clauses. The first condition simply checks to see if `$roll` is equal to one. If it is, the appropriate code runs (assigning the binary representation of 1 to the `$binValue` variable.) If the first condition is false, the program looks at all the successive `if else` clauses until it finds a condition that evaluates to true. If none of the conditions is true, the code in the `else` clause will be executed.

You may be surprised that I even put an `else` clause in this code. Since you know the value of `$roll` must be between one and six, and we've checked each of those values, the program should never need to evaluate the `else` clause. Things in programming don't always work out the way you expect, so it's a great idea to have some code in an `else` clause even if you don't expect to ever need it. It's much better to get a message from your program explaining that something unexpected occurred than to have your program blow up inexplicably while your users are using it.

The indentation for a multiple-condition `if` statement is useful so you can tell which parts of the code are part of the `if` structure, and which parts are meant to be executed if a particular condition turns out to be true.

Using the switch Structure to Simplify Programming

The situation in the Binary Dice program happens often enough that another structure is designed for exactly this kind of case, when you are comparing one variable to a number of possible values. The Switch Dice program shown in Figure 3.9 looks identical to the Binary Dice program as far as the user is concerned, except it shows the Roman numeral representation of the die roll instead of the binary version.

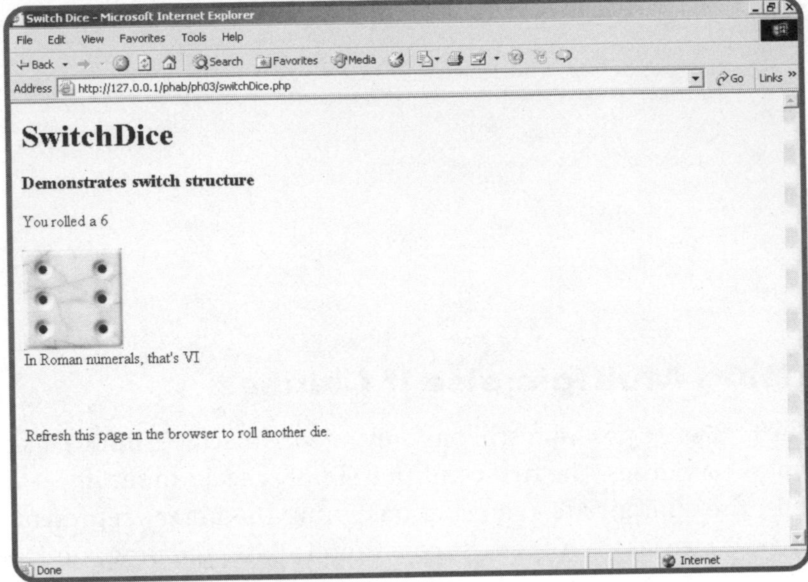

FIGURE 3.9

This version shows a die roll in Roman numerals.

While the outward appearance of the last two programs is extremely similar, the underlying structure of the code is changed to illustrate a very handy device called the `switch` structure.

Building the Switch Dice Program

The code of the Switch Dice program looks different than the Binary Dice demo, but the results are the same.

```
<html>
<head>
<title>Switch Dice</title>
</head>
<body>
<h1>SwitchDice</h1>
<h3>Demonstrates switch structure</h3>

<?
```

```
$roll = rand(1,6);
print "You rolled a $roll";
print "<br>";

switch ($roll){
  case 1:
    $romValue = "I";
    break;
  case 2:
    $romValue = "II";
    break;
  case 3:
    $romValue = "III";
    break;
  case 4:
    $romValue = "IV";
    break;
  case 5:
    $romValue = "V";
    break;
  case 6:
    $romValue = "VI";
    break;
  default:
    print "This is an illegal die!";
} // end switch


print "<br>";
print "<img src = die$roll.jpg>";
print "<br>";
print "In Roman numerals, that's $romValue";
print "<br>";
```

```
print "<br>";
print "<br>";

?>
<br>
Refresh this page in the browser to roll another die.

</body>
</html>
```

Using the switch Structure

The `switch` structure is optimized for those situations where you have one variable that you want to compare against a number of possible values. To make it work, use the `switch` keyword followed by the name of the variable you wish to evaluate in parentheses. A set of braces indicates that the next block of code will be focused on evaluating the possible values of this variable.

For each possible value, use the `case` statement, followed by the value, followed by a colon. End each case with a `break` statement, which indicates the program should stop thinking about this particular case, and get ready for the next one.

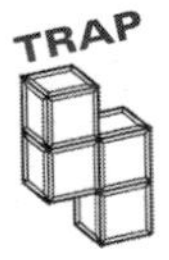

The use of the `break` statement is probably the trickiest part of using the `switch` statement, especially if you are familiar with a language, such as Visual Basic, which does not require such a construct. It's important to add the `break` statement to the end of each case, or the program flow will simply "fall through" to the next possible value, even if that value would not otherwise evaluate to true. As a beginner, you should always place the `break` statement at the end of each case.

The last case is called `default`. This works just like the `else` clause of the multi-value `if` statement. It defines code to execute if none of the other cases is active. As in multi-value `if` statements, it's smart to test for a `default` case even if you think it is impossible for the computer to get to this default option. Crazy things happen, and it's good to be prepared for them.

Combining a Form and Its Results

Most of your PHP programs up to now have had two distinct files. An HTML file has a form, which calls a PHP program. Sometimes it can be tedious to keep track of two separate files. You can use the `if` statement to combine both functions into one page. The `hiUser` program shown in Figures 3.10 and 3.11 looks much like its counterpart in Chapter 2, Using Variables and Input, but it has an important difference. Rather than being an HTML page and a separate PHP program, the entire program resides in one file on the server.

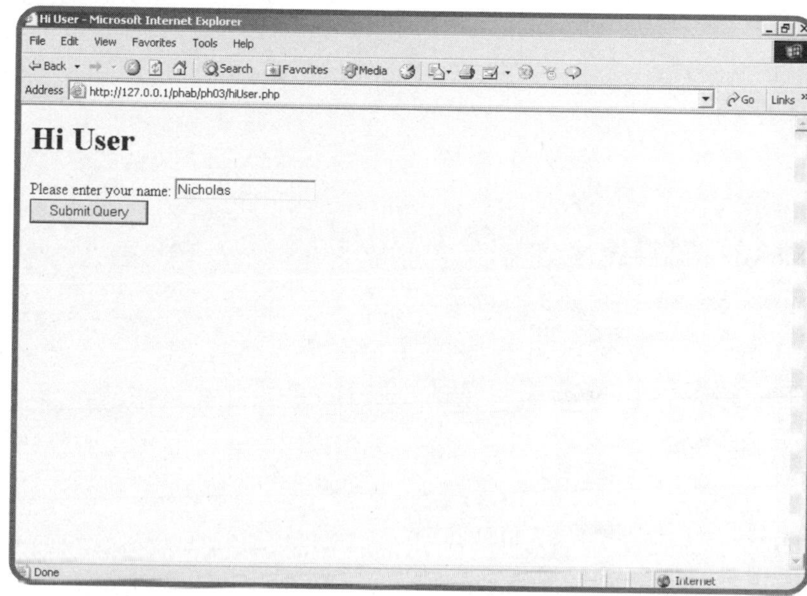

FIGURE 3.10

The HTML page is actually produced through PHP code.

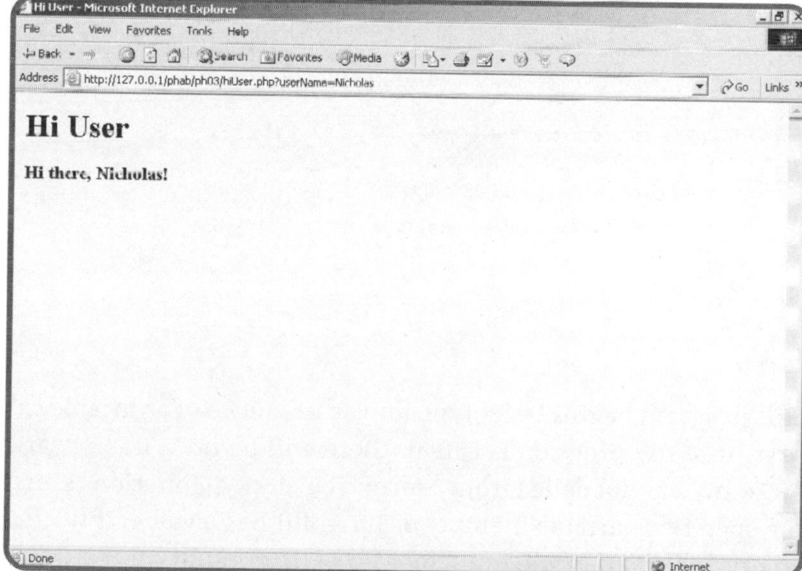

FIGURE 3.11

The result is produced by exactly the same program.

The code for the new version of `hiUser` shows how to achieve this trick.

```
<html>
<head>
<title>Hi User</title>
</head>
<body>
<h1>Hi User</h1>

<?

if (empty($userName)){
  print <<<HERE
  <form>
  Please enter your name:
  <input type = "text"
         name = "userName"><br>
  <input type = "submit">
  </form>
HERE;

} else {
  print "<h3>Hi there, $userName!</h3>";
} //end
?>

</body>
</html>
```

This program begins by looking for the existence of a variable called `$userName`. The first time the program is called, there will be no `$userName` variable, because the program was not called from a form. The empty() function returns the value `true` if the specified variable is empty or `false` if it has a value. If `$userName` does not exist, empty($userName) will evaluate as `true`. The condition `(empty($userName))` will generally be true if this is the first time this page has been called. If it's true, the program should generate a form so the user can enter his or her name. If the condition is false, that means somehow the user has entered a name (presumably through the form) so the program greets the user using that name.

The key idea here is that the program runs *more than once*. When the user first links to `hiUser.php`, the program creates a form. The user enters a value on the form, and presses the Submit button. This causes exactly the same program to be run again on the server. This time, though, the `$userName` variable is *not* empty, so rather than generating a form, the program uses the variable's value in a greeting.

Server-side programming frequently works in this way. It isn't uncommon for a user to call the same program many times in succession as part of solving a particular problem. You'll often use branching structures such as the `if` and `switch` statements to direct the flow of the program based on the user's current state of activity.

Using Functions to Encapsulate Parts of the Program

It hasn't taken long for your programs to get complex. As soon as the code gets a little bit larger than the size of a screen in your editor, it gets much harder to keep track of. Programmers like to break up code into smaller segments called `functions` to help keep everything straight. A function is like a miniature program. It should be designed to do one job well. As a silly example, look at Figure 3.12.

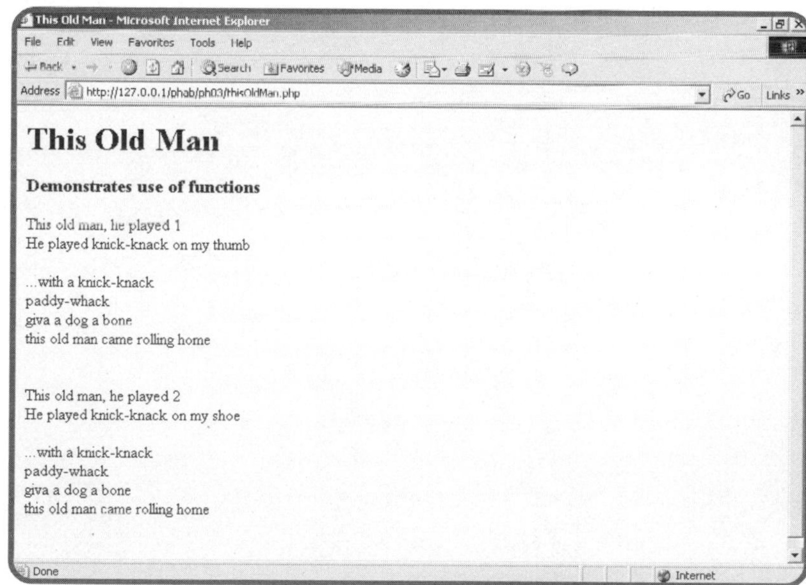

FIGURE 3.12

This song has a straightforward verse, chorus, verse, chorus pattern.

Examining the This Old Man Program

Song lyrics often have a very repetitive nature. The This Old Man song shown in Figure 3.12 is a good example. Each verse is different, but the chorus is always the same. Often when you write the lyrics to such a song, you will write out each verse, but you'll only write the chorus once. After that, you simply write "chorus" and people generally understand they are not to sing the word "chorus" but to repeat the song's chorus. This works very much like subroutines in programming language. The code for the `thisOldMan` program illustrates how it works.

```
<html>
<head>
<title>This Old Man</title>
</head>
<body>
<h1>This Old Man</h1>
<h3>Demonstrates use of functions</h3>
<?

verse1();
chorus();
verse2();
chorus();

function verse1(){
  print <<<HERE
  This old man, he played 1<br>
  He played knick-knack on my thumb<br><br>
HERE;
} // end verse1

function verse2(){
  print <<<HERE
  This old man, he played 2<br>
  He played knick-knack on my shoe<br><br>
```

```
HERE;
} // end verse1

function chorus(){
  print <<<HERE
  ...with a knick-knack<br>
  paddy-whack<br>
  giva a dog a bone<br>
  this old man came rolling home<br>
  <br><br>
} // end chorus

?>
</body>
</html>
```

Careful examination of this code will show how it works. The main part of the program is extremely simple:

```
verse1();
chorus();
verse2();
chorus();
```

Creating New Functions

There appear to be some new PHP functions. I called the `verse1()` function, then the `chorus()` function, and so on. There are some new functions, but they weren't shipped with PHP. Instead, I made them as part of the page. You can take a set of instructions and store them with a name. This essentially builds a new temporary command in PHP, so you can combine simple commands to do complex things. Building a function is simple. Use the keyword `function` followed by the function's name and a set of parentheses. Keep the parentheses empty for now. You'll learn how to use this feature in the next section. Use a pair of braces ({}) to combine a series of code lines into one function. Don't forget the right brace (}) to end the function definition. It's smart to indent everything between the beginning and end of a function.

When you look at my code, you'll note there's one line I never indent. That's the `HERE` **token used for multi-line strings. Recall that the word** `HERE` **is acting like a closing quote, and it must be all the way on the left side of the screen, so it can't be indented.**

Although you can use any function name you like, be careful. If you try to define a function that already exists, you're bound to get confused. PHP has a large number of functions already built in. If you're having strange problems with a function, you might look at the online help (it comes with PHP, or you can get it at www.php.net) to see if that function already exists.

The `chorus()` function is especially handy in this program because it can be re-used. It isn't necessary to re-write the code for the chorus each time when you can simply call a function instead.

Using Parameters and Function Values

Functions are meant to be self-contained. This is good because the entire program can be too complex to understand. If you break the complex program into smaller functions, each function can be set up to work independently. When you work inside a function, you don't have to worry about anything outside the function. If you create a variable inside a function, that variable dies as soon as you leave the function. This prevents many errors that can otherwise creep into your code. The bad side of functions being so self-contained is you often want them to work with data from the outside program. There are a couple of ways to do this. You can send a *parameter* to a function, which allows you to determine one or more values sent to the function as it starts. Each function can also have a *return* value. An example will make this more clear. The `param` program, shown in Figure 3.13 illustrates another form of the This Old Man song. Although again the user might not be aware of it, there are some important differences between this more sophisticated program and the first This Old Man program.

Examining the Param.php Program

Notice that the output of Figure 3.13 is longer than that of 3.12, but the code that generates this longer output is shorter and more efficient.

```
<html>
<head>
<title>Param Old Man</title>
</head>
<body>
```

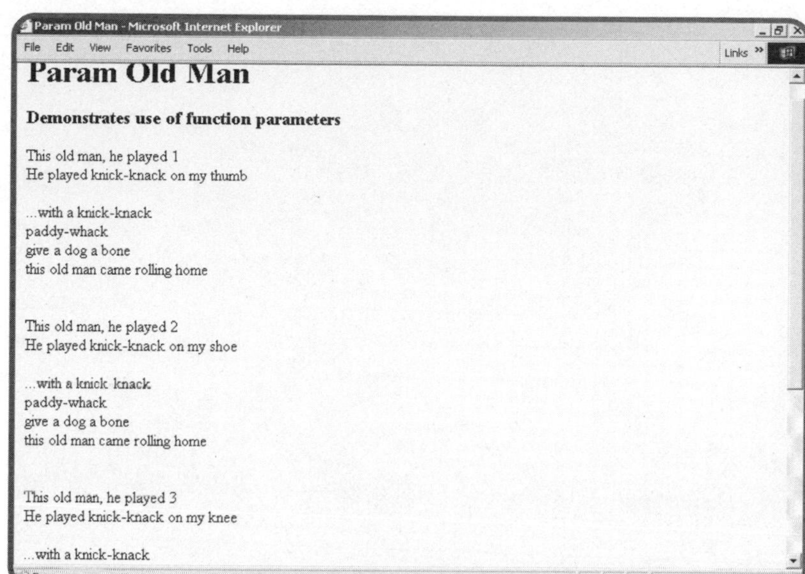

FIGURE 3.13

While the output looks similar to Figure 3.12, the program that produced this page is much more efficient.

```
<h1>Param Old Man </h1>
<h3>Demonstrates use of function parameters</h3>
<?

print verse(1);
print chorus();
print verse(2);
print chorus();
print verse(3);
print chorus();
print verse(4);
print chorus();

function verse($stanza){
  switch ($stanza){
    case 1:
      $place = "thumb";
      break;
    case 2:
```

```
      $place = "shoe";
      break;
    case 3:
      $place = "knee";
      break;
    case 4:
      $place = "door";
      break;
    default:
      $place = "I don't know where";
  } // end switch

  $output = <<<HERE
  This old man, he played $stanza<br>
  He played knick-knack on my $place<br><br>
HERE;
  return $output;
} // end verse

function chorus(){
  $output = <<<HERE
  ...with a knick-knack<br>
  paddy-whack<br>
  give a dog a bone<br>
  this old man came rolling home<br>
  <br><br>
HERE;
  return $output;
} // end chorus

?>
</body>
</html>
```

Looking at Encapsulation in the Main Code Body

This code features a number of improvements over the previous version. First, look at the main body of the code that looks like this:

```
print verse(1);
print chorus();
print verse(2);
print chorus();
print verse(3);
print chorus();
print verse(4);
print chorus();
```

The main code body is very easy to understand. The program is to print the first verse, then the chorus, then the second verse, then the chorus, and so on. The details of how all these things are to be generated is left to the individual functions. This is an example of *encapsulation*. Encapsulation is good, because it allows you to think about problems in multiple levels. At the highest level, you're interested in the main ideas (print the verses and chorus) but you're not so concerned about the exact details. You use the same technique when you talk about your day: "I drove to work, had some meetings, went to lunch, and taught a class." You don't usually describe each detail of each task. Each major task can be broken down into its component tasks later. (If somebody asks, you could really describe the meeting: "I got some coffee, appeared to be taking notes furiously on my palm pilot, got a new high score on Solitaire while appearing to take notes, scribbled on the agenda, and dozed off during a presentation.")

Returning a Value: The chorus() Function

Another interesting thing about the main section of code is the use of the `print()` function. In the last program, I simply said `chorus()` and the program printed the verse. In this program, I did it a little differently. The `chorus()` function doesn't actually print anything to the screen. Instead, it creates the chorus as a big string and sends that value back to the program, which can do whatever it wants with it. This behavior isn't really new to you. Think about the `rand()` function. It always returns a value back to the program. The functions in this program work in the same way. Take another look at the `chorus()` function to see what I mean.

```
function chorus(){
  $output = <<<HERE
```

```
  ...with a knick-knack<br>
  paddy-whack<br>
  give a dog a bone<br>
  this old man came rolling home<br>
  <br><br>
HERE;
  return $output;
} // end chorus
```

I began the function by creating a new variable called `$output`. You can create variables inside functions by mentioning them, just like you can in the main part of the program. However, a variable created inside a function loses its meaning as soon as the function is finished. This is good, because it means the variables inside a function belong only to that function. You don't have to worry about whether the variable already exists somewhere else in your program. You also don't have to worry about all the various things that can go wrong if you mistakenly modify an existing variable. I assigned a long string (the actual chorus of the song) to the `$output` variable with the `<<<HERE` construct.

The last line of the function uses the `return` statement to send the value of `$output` back to the program. Any function can end with a `return` statement. Whatever value follows the keyword `return` will be passed to the program. This is one way your functions can communicate to the main program.

Accepting a Parameter in the verse() Function

The most efficient part of this newer program is the `verse()` function. Rather than having a different function for each verse, I wrote one function that can work for all the verses. After careful analysis of the song, I noticed that each verse is remarkably similar to the others. The only thing that differentiates each verse is what the old man played (which is always the verse number) and where he played it (which is something rhyming with the verse number). If there is some way to indicate which verse to play, it should be easy enough to produce the correct verse. Notice that when the main body calls the verse function, it always indicates a verse number in parentheses. For example, it makes a reference to `verse(1)` and `verse(3)`. These commands both call the `verse` function, but they send different values (`1` and `3`) to the function. Take another look at the code for the `verse()` function to see how the function responds to these inputs.

```
function verse($stanza){
  switch ($stanza){
    case 1:
      $place = "thumb";
      break;
    case 2:
      $place = "shoe";
      break;
    case 3:
      $place = "knee";
      break;
    case 4:
      $place = "door";
      break;
    default:
      $place = "I don't know where";
  } // end switch

  $output = <<<HERE
  This old man, he played $stanza<br>
  He played knick-knack on my $place<br><br>
HERE;
  return $output;
} // end verse
```

In this function, I indicated `$stanza` as a parameter in the function definition. A parameter is simply a variable associated with the function. If you create a function with a parameter, you are required to supply some sort of value whenever you call the function. The parameter variable automatically receives the value from the main body. For example, if the program says `verse(1)`, the `verse` function will be called, and the `$stanza` variable will contain the value `1`.

I then used a `switch` statement to populate the `$place` variable based on the value of `$stanza`. Finally, I created the `$output` variable using the `$stanza` and `$place` variables and returned the value of `$output`.

You can create functions with multiple parameters if you wish. Simply declare several variables inside the parentheses of the function definition, and be sure to call the function with the appropriate number of arguments. Make sure to separate parameters with commas.

IN THE REAL WORLD

If you're an experienced programmer, you probably know there are other ways to make this code even more efficient. We'll come back to this program as you learn about loops and arrays in the coming chapters.

Managing Variable Scope

You have learned some ways to have your main program share variable information with your functions. In addition to parameter passing, sometimes you'll want your functions to have access to variables created in the main program. This is especially true because all the variables automatically created by PHP (such as those coming from forms) will be generated at the main level. You must tell PHP when you want a function to use a variable that has been created at the main level.

If you've programmed in another language, you're bound to get confused by the way PHP handles global variables. In most languages, any variable created at the main level is automatically available to every function. In PHP, you must explicitly request that a variable be global inside a function. If you don't do this, a new local variable with the same name (and no value) will be created at the function level.

Looking at the Scope Demo

To illustrate the notion of global variables, take a look at the scope demo, shown in Figure 3.14.

Take a look at the code for the Scope Demo, and you'll see how it works.

```
<html>

<head>

<title>Scope Demo</title>

</head>

<body>
```

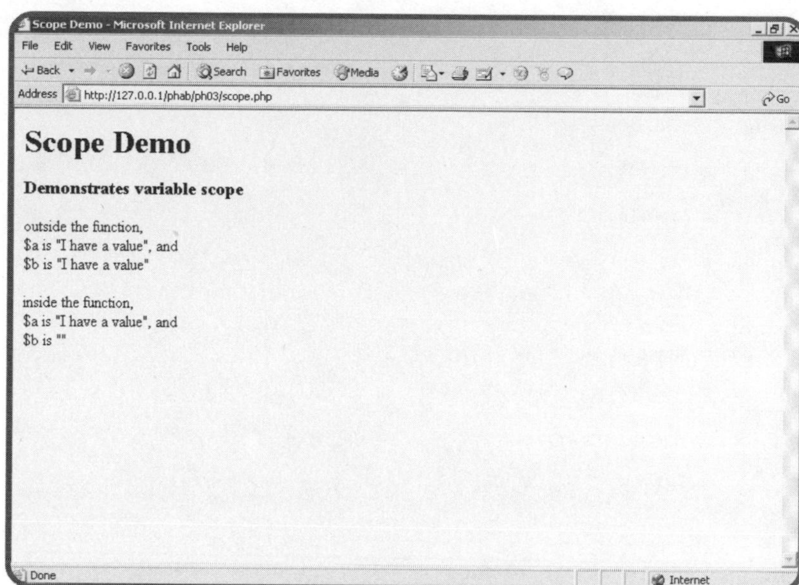

FIGURE 3.14

Variable $a keeps its value inside a function, but $b does not.

```
<h1>Scope Demo</h1>

<h3>Demonstrates variable scope</h3>


<?


$a = "I have a value";

$b = "I have a value";


print <<<HERE

  outside the function, <br>

  \$a is "$a", and<br>

  \$b is "$b"<br><br>

HERE;


myFunction();


function myFunction(){


  //make $a global, but not $b
```

```
  global $a;

  print <<<HERE
    inside the function, <br>
    \$a is "$a", and<br>
    \$b is "$b"<br><br>
HERE;
} // end myFunction

?>

</body>
</html>
```

For this demonstration, I created two variables, called `$a` and `$b`. I gave them both the value "I have a value." As a test, I printed out the values for both `$a` and `$b`.

Notice the trick I used to make the actual dollar sign show up in the quotes. When PHP sees a dollar sign inside quotes, it usually expects to be working with a variable. Sometimes (as in this case) you really want to print a dollar sign. You can precede a dollar sign with a backslash to indicate you really want the dollar sign to appear. So, `print $a` **will print the value of the variable** `$a`**, but** `print \$a` **will print out the value** `"$a"`**.**

Returning to the Petals Game

At the beginning of this chapter, I showed you the Petals Around the Rose game. This game uses all the skills you have learned so far, including the new concepts you learned in this chapter. If you haven't already done so, play the game now so you can see how it works, because it won't be as much fun once you know the secret.

Here's the basic plan of the Petals game: Each time the page is drawn, it randomly generates five dice, and calculates the correct number of petals based on a super-secret formula. The page includes a form that has a text area called `guess` for the user to guess the right answer. The form also includes a hidden field called `numPetals`, which tells the program what the correct answer was.

IN THE REAL WORLD

Can't the program simply remember the right answer?

Since the program generated the correct answer in the first place, you might be surprised to learn that the right answer must be hidden in the Web page and then retrieved by the same program that generated it. Each contact between the client and the server is *completely new*. When the user first plays the game, the page will be sent to the browser and then the connection will be completely severed until the user hits the Submit button. When the user submits the form, the petals program starts over again. It's possible the user plays the game right before he or she goes to bed, then leaves the page on the computer overnight. Meanwhile, a hundred other people might use your program. For now, you'll use hidden data to help keep track of the user's situation. Later in this book, you'll learn some other clever methods for keeping track of the users' situations.

The Petals game doesn't really introduce anything new, but it's a little longer than any of the other programs you've seen so far. I'll introduce the code in smaller chunks. Look on the CD-ROM for the program in its entirety.

Starting HTML

Like most PHP programs, the Petals game uses some HTML to set everything up. The HTML is pretty basic because most of the interesting HTML will be created by the PHP code.

```
<HTML>

<head>

<title>Petals Around the Rose</title>

</head>

<body bgcolor = "tan">

<center>

<font face = "Comic Sans MS">

<h1>Petals Around the Rose</h1>
```

I decided on a tan background with a whimsical font. This should give the program a light feel.

Main Body Code

The main PHP code segment has three main jobs to do. These jobs are (appropriately enough) stored in three different functions. One goal of encapsulation is to make the main code body as clean as possible. This goal has been achieved in the Petals game.

```
<?

printGreeting();
printDice();
printForm();
```

All the real work is passed off to the various functions, which will each be described shortly. Even before you see the functions themselves, you have a good idea what each function will do, and you also have a good sense of the overall flow of the program. If you encapsulate your code and name your functions well, it makes your code much easier to read and repair.

The printGreeting() Function

The purpose of this function is to print a greeting to the user. There are three possible greetings. If the user has never called this program before, the program should provide a welcome. If the user has been here before, he or she has guessed the number of petals. That guess might be correct (in which case a congratulatory message is appropriate) or incorrect, requiring information about what the correct answer was. The `printGreeting()` function uses a `switch` statement to handle the various options.

```
function printGreeting(){
  global $guess, $numPetals;
  if (empty($guess)){
    print "<h3>Welcome to Petals Around the Rose</h3>";
  } else if ($guess == $numPetals){
    print "<h3>You Got It!</h3>";
  } else {

    print <<<HERE

      <h3>from last try: </h3>
```

```
        you guessed: $guess<br><br>

        -and the correct answer was: $numPetals petals around the rose<br>
HERE;

  } // end if

} // end printGreeting
```

This function refers to both the `$guess` and `$numPetals` variables, which are both automatically created. You can use one `global` statement to make more than one variable global by separating the variables with commas.

The `$guess` variable will be empty if this is the first time the user has come to the program. If `$guess` is empty, I print a welcoming greeting. If `$guess` is equal to `$numPetals`, the user has guessed correctly, so I print an appropriate congratulations. If neither of these conditions is true (which will be most of the time), the function will print out a slightly more complex string indicating the user's last guess and the correct answer. This should give the user enough information to finally solve the riddle.

The `else if` structure turned out to be the easiest option here for handling the three possible conditions I wanted to check.

The printDice() Function

After the program prints out a greeting, it does the important business of generating the random dice. It's relatively easy to generate random dice, as you saw from earlier in this chapter. However, I also wanted to be efficient and calculate the correct number of petals. To make the `printDice()` function more efficient, you'll see that it calls some other custom functions.

```
function printDice(){
  global $numPetals;

  print "<h3>New Roll:</h3>";
  $numPetals = 0;

  $die1 = rand(1,6);
  $die2 = rand(1,6);
  $die3 = rand(1,6);
```

```
  $die4 = rand(1,6);
  $die5 = rand(1,6);

  showDie($die1);
  showDie($die2);
  showDie($die3);
  showDie($die4);
  showDie($die5);

  print "<br>";

  calcNumPetals($die1);
  calcNumPetals($die2);
  calcNumPetals($die3);
  calcNumPetals($die4);
  calcNumPetals($die5);

} // end printDice
```

The `printDice()` function is very concerned with the `$numPetals` variable, but doesn't need access to `$guess`. It requests access to `$numPetals` from the main program. After printing out the "New Roll" message, it resets `$numPetals` to zero. The value of `$numPetals` will be recalculated each time the dice are rolled.

I got new dice values by calling the `rand(1, 6)` function six times. I stored each result in a different variable, named `$die1` to `$die6`. To print out an appropriate graphic for each die, I called the `showDie()` function (which will be described next). I printed out a line break, then called the `calcNumPetals()` function (which will also be described soon) once for each die.

The showDie() Function

The `showDie()` function is used to simplify repetitive code. It accepts a die value as a parameter, and generates the appropriate HTML code for drawing a die with the corresponding number of dots.

```
function showDie($value){
  print <<<HERE
```

```
  <img src = "die$value.jpg"
       height = 100
       width = 100>
HERE;
} // end showDie
```

One advantage of using functions for repetitive HTML code is the ease with which you can modify large sections of code. For example, if you wish to change the image sizes, all you need to do is change the `img` tag in this one function, and all six die images will be changed.

The calcNumPetals Function

The `printDice()` function also calls `calcNumPetals()` once for each die. This function receives a die value as a parameter. It also references the `$numPetals` global variable. The function uses a `switch` statement to determine how much to add to `$numPetals` based on the current die's value.

Here's the trick. The center dot of the die is the rose. Any dots around the center dot are the petals. The value one has a rose but no petals. 2, 4, and 6 have petals, but no rose. 3 has two petals, and 5 has four. If the die roll is 3, `$numPetals` should be increased by 2, and if the roll is 5, `$numPetals` should be increased by 4.

```
function calcNumPetals($value){

  global $numPetals;

  switch ($value) {
    case 3:
      $numPetals += 2;
      break;
    case 5:
      $numPetals += 4;
      break;
  } // end switch

} // end calcNumPetals
```

The += code is a shorthand notation. The line

```
$numPetals += 2;
```

is exactly equivalent to

```
$numPetals = $numPetals + 2;
```

The first style is much shorter and easier to type, so it's the form most programmers prefer.

The printForm() Function

The purpose of the `printForm()` function is to print out the form at the bottom of the HTML page. This form is pretty straightforward except for the need to place the hidden field for `$numPetals`.

```
function printForm(){
  global $numPetals;

  print <<<HERE

  <h3>How many petals around the rose?</h3>

  <form method = "post">
  <input type = "text"
         name = "guess"
         value = "0">
  <input type = "hidden"
         name = "numPetals"
         value = "$numPetals">
  <br>
  <input type = "submit">
  </form>
  <br>
  <a href = "petalHelp.html"
```

```
      target = "helpPage">
   give me a hint</a>
HERE;

} // end printForm
```

This code places the form on the page. I could have done most of the form in plain HTML without needing PHP for anything but the hidden field, but when I start using PHP, I like to have much of my code in PHP. It helps me see the flow of things more clearly (print greeting, print dice, print form).

The Ending HTML Code

The final set of HTML code closes everything up. It completes the PHP segment, the font, the centered text, the body, and finally the HTML itself.

```
?>
</font>
</center>
</body>
</html>
```

Summary

You learned a lot in this chapter. You've learned several kinds of branching structures, including the `if` clause, `else` statements, and the `switch` structure. You know how to write functions, which make your programs much more efficient and easier to read. You know how to pass parameters to functions and return values from them. You can access global variables from inside functions. You've put all these things together to make an interesting game. You should be very proud! In the next chapter, you'll learn how to use looping structures to make your programs even more powerful.

CHALLENGES

1. Write a program that generates 4-, 10-, or 20-sided dice (sometimes used in various games).
2. Write a program that lets the user choose how many sides a die will have and print out a random roll with the appropriate maximum values (don't worry about using images to display the dice).
3. Write a "loaded dice" program that generates the value 1 half the time, and some other value the other half.
4. Modify the adventure game from the last chapter so the form and the program are all one file.
5. Create a Web page generator. Make a form for the page caption, background color, font color, and text body. Use this form to generate an HTML page.

Loops and Arrays: The Poker Dice Game

You know all the basic parts of a program now, but your programs can be much easier to write and much more efficient when you know some other things. In this chapter, you'll learn about two very important tools. Arrays are special variables that form lists. Looping structures are used to repeat certain code segments. As you might expect, arrays and loops often work together. You'll learn how to use these new elements to make more interesting programs. Specifically, you'll:

- Use the `for` loop to build basic counting structures.
- Modify the `for` loop for different kinds of counting.
- Use a `while` loop for more flexible looping.
- Identify the keys to successful loops.
- Create basic arrays.
- Write programs that use arrays and loops.
- Store information in hidden fields.

Introducing the Poker Dice Program

The main program for this chapter is a simplified dice game. In this game, you are given $100 dollars of virtual money. On each turn, you bet two dollars. The computer will roll five dice. You can elect to keep each die or roll it again. On the second roll, the computer checks for various combinations. You can earn money back for rolling pairs, triples, four and five of a kind, and straights (five numbers in a row) Figures 4.1 and 4.2 illustrate the game in action.

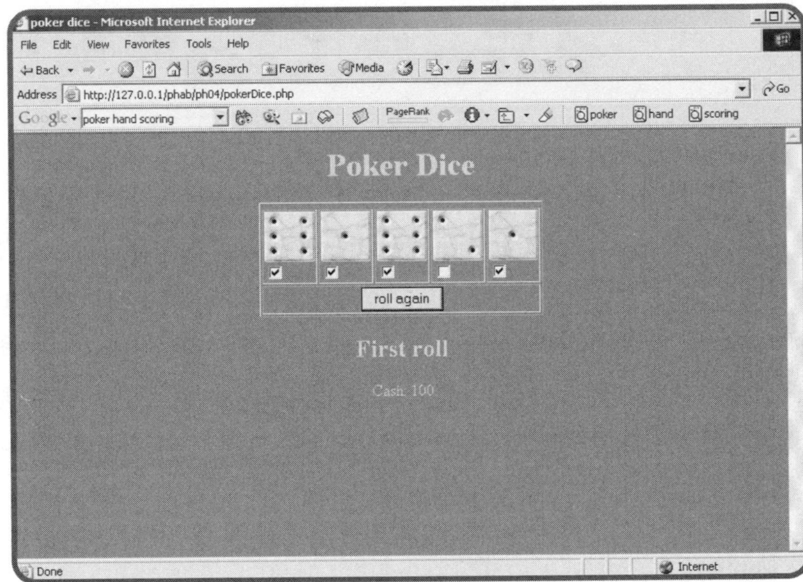

FIGURE 4.1

After the first roll, you can choose to keep some of the dice by selecting the checkboxes underneath each die.

The basic concepts of this game are much like the ones you used in the earlier programs. Keeping track of all five dice can get very complicated, so this program uses arrays and loops to manage all the information.

Counting with the for Loop

Computers are good at repetitive behavior. There are many times you might want the computer to repeat some sort of action multiple times. For example, take a look at the `simpleFor.php` program shown in Figure 4.3.

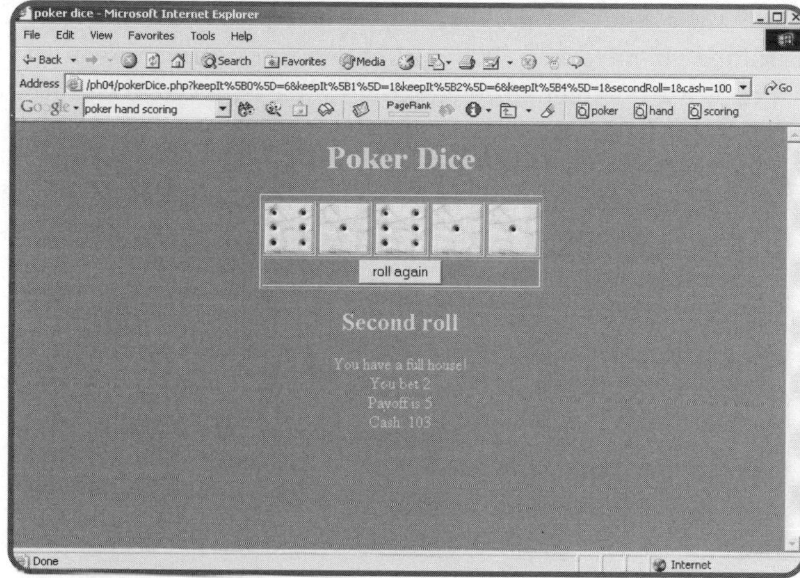

FIGURE 4.2

The player has earned back some money with a full house!

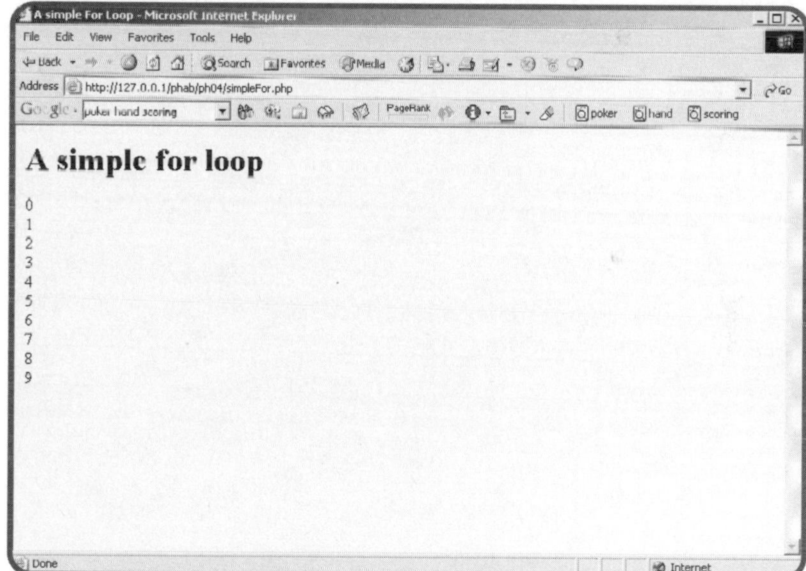

FIGURE 4.3

This program counts from zero to one using only one print statement!

While the output of the simpleFor program doesn't look all that interesting, it has a unique characteristic. It has only one print statement in the entire program, which is executed ten different times. Take a look at the source code of this program to see how it works.

```
<html>


<head>
<title>
A simple For Loop
</title>
</head>


<body>


<h1>A simple for loop</h1>


<?


for ($i = 0; $i < 10; $i++){
  print "$i <br>\n";
} // end for loop


?>




</body>
</html>
```

Each number is printed in the line that looks like this:

```
  print "$i <br>\n";
```

This line can only print one value, but it happens ten times. The key to this behavior is the for statement. The for structure has three main parts.

Initializing a Sentry Variable

`for` loops usually involve an integer variable. Sometimes the key variable in a loop is referred to as a *sentry* variable, because it acts like a gatekeeper to the loop. The first part of a for loop definition is a line of code that identifies the sentry variable and initializes it to some starting value. In the simple for loop demo, the initialization segment looks like this:

```
$i = 0;
```

It specifies that the sentry variable will be called `$i`, and its starting value will be zero.

IN THE REAL WORLD

You might wonder why the sentry variable is called `$i`. Like most variables, it's really best if sentry variables have a name that suits their purpose. Sometimes, however, a `for` loop sentry is simply an integer, and it doesn't really have any other meaning. In those situations, an old programming tradition is often called into play. In the Fortran language (one of the earliest common programming languages) all integer variables had to begin with the letters "i," "j," and a few other characters. Fortran programmers would commonly use "i" as the name of their generic sentry variables. Even though most modern programmers have never written a line of Fortran code, the tradition remains. It's amazing how much folklore exists in such a relatively new activity as computer programming.

Computer programs frequently begin counting with zero, so I initialized `$i` to zero as well.

Although the `$i = 0;` segment looks like (and is) a complete line of code, it is usually placed on the same line as the other parts of the `for` loop construct.

Setting a Condition to Finish the Loop

Getting a computer to repeat behavior is actually the easy part. The harder task comes when you try to get the computer to stop correctly. The second part of the `for` loop construct is a condition. When this condition is evaluated as true, the loop should continue. As soon as the condition is evaluated to false, the loop should exit. In this case, I set the condition as `$i < 10;` This means that as long as the variable `$i` has a value less than 10, the loop continues. As soon as the program detects that `$i` has a value equal to or larger than 10, the loop exits. Usually a for loop's condition checks the sentry variable against some terminal value.

Changing the Sentry Variable

The final critical element of a `for` loop is some mechanism for changing the value of the sentry variable. At some point the value of `$i` must become 10 or larger, or the loop will continue forever. In the `basicLoop` program, the part of the `for` structure which makes this happen looks like `$i++`. The notation `$i++` is just like saying 'add one to $i,' or `$i = $i + 1`. The `++` symbol is called an *increment operator* because it provides an easy way to increment (add one) to a variable.

Building the Loop

Once you've set up the parts of the `for` statement, the loop itself is easy to use. Place braces (`{ }`) around your code and indent all code that will be inside the loop. You can have as many lines of code as you wish inside a loop, including branching statements and other loops. The sentry variable will have special behavior inside the loop. It will begin with the initial value. Each time the loop repeats, it will be changed as specified in the `for` structure, and the interpreter will check the condition to ensure that it's still true. If so, the code in the loop will occur again. In the case of the `basicArray` program, `$i` begins as zero. The first time the `print` statement occurs, it prints out zero, because that is the current value of `$i`. When the interpreter reaches the right brace that ends the loop, it increments `$i` by one (following the `$i++` directive in the `for` structure) and checks the condition (`$i < 10`). Because 0 is less than 10, the condition is true, and the code inside the loop occurs again. Eventually, the value of `$i` becomes 10, so the condition (`$i < 10`) is no longer true. Program control then reverts to the next line of code after the end of the loop, which ends the program.

Modifying the for Loop

Once you understand the basics of the `for` loop structure, you can modify it in a couple of interesting ways. You can build a loop that counts by fives, or one that counts backwards.

Counting by Fives

The `countByFive.php` program shown in Figure 4.4 illustrates a program that counts by fives.

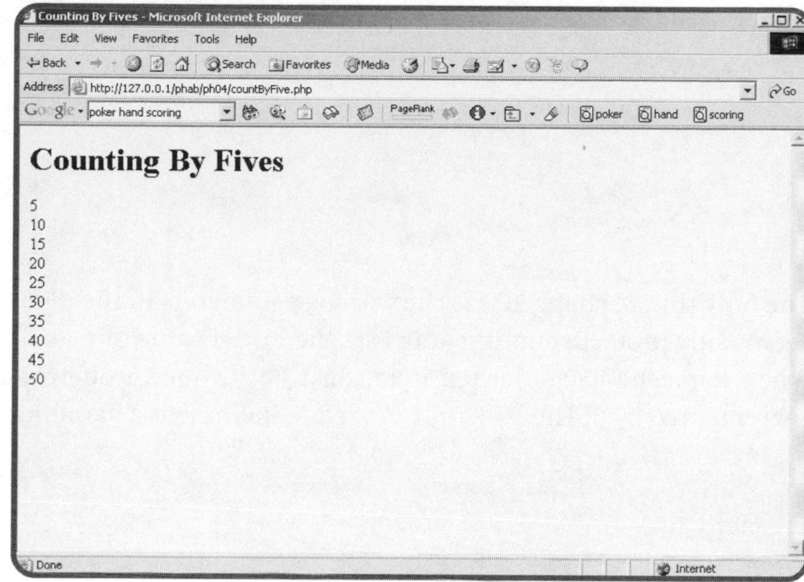

FIGURE 4.4

This program uses a `for` loop to count by five.

The program is very much like the `basicArray` program, but with a couple of twists.

```
<html>


<head>

<title>

Counting By Fives

</title>

</head>


<body>


<h1>Counting By Fives</h1>


<?


for ($i = 5; $i <= 50; $i+= 5){

  print "$i <br>\n";
```

```
} // end for loop

?>

</body>
</html>
```

The only thing I changed was the various parameters in the `for` statement. Since it seems silly to start counting at 0, I set the initial value of `$i` to 5. I decided to stop when `$i` reached 50 (after ten iterations). Each time through the loop, `$i` will be incremented by 5. The += syntax is used to increment a variable.

```
$i += 5;
```

is exactly like

```
$i = $i + 5;
```

Counting Backwards

It is fairly simple to modify a `for` loop so it counts backwards. Figure 4.5 illustrates this feat.

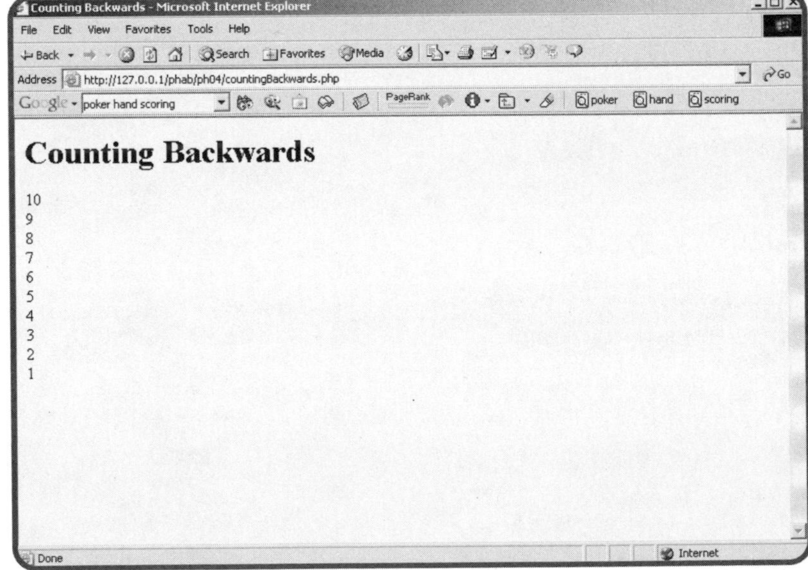

FIGURE 4.5

This program counts backwards from ten to one using a `for` loop.

Once again, the basic structure is just like the basic for loop program, but by changing the parameters of the for structure I was able to alter the behavior of the program. The code for this program shows how it is done.

```
<html>

<head>
<title>
Counting Backwards
</title>
</head>

<body>

<h1>Counting Backwards</h1>

<?

for ($i = 10; $i > 0; $i--){
  print "$i <br>\n";
} // end for loop

?>


</body>
</html>
```

If you understand how for loops work, the changes will all make sense. I'm counting backwards this time, so $i begins with a large value (in this case 10.) The condition for continuing the loop is now $i > 0, which means the loop will continue as long as $i is greater than zero. As soon as $i is zero or less, the loop will end. Note that rather than adding a value to $i, this time I decrement by one each time through the loop. If you're counting backwards, you must be very careful that the sentry variable has a mechanism for getting smaller, or the loop will never end. Recall that $i++ adds one to $i. $i-- subtracts one from $i.

Using a while Loop

PHP, like most languages, provides another kind of looping structure that is even more flexible than the `for` loop. The `while` loop can be used when you know how many times something will happen, just like the `for` loop. Figure 4.6 shows how a `while` loop can work much like a `for` loop:

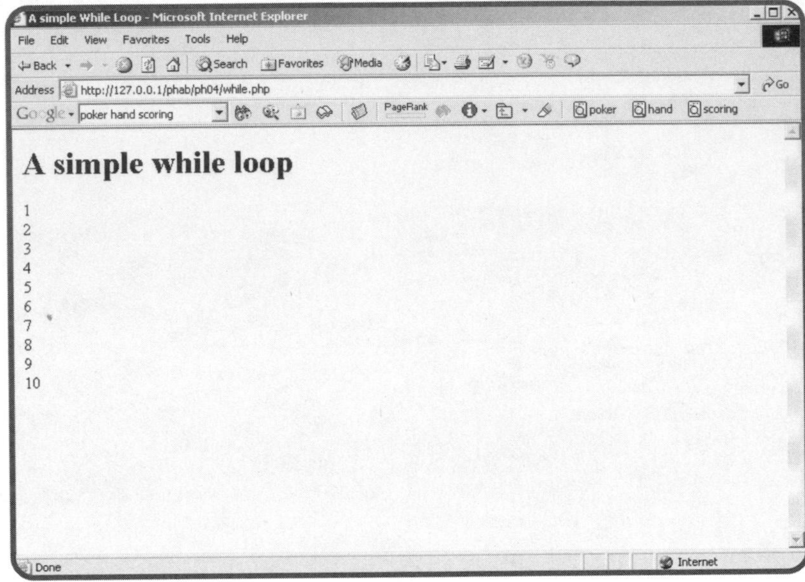

FIGURE 4.6

Although the output of this program looks a lot like the basic `for` loop, it uses a different construct to achieve the same result.

Repeating Code with a while Loop

The code for the `while.php` program is much like the `for` loop demo, but you can see that the loop is a little bit simpler:

```
<html>

<head>
<title>
A simple While Loop
</title>
```

```
</head>

<body>

<h1>A simple while loop</h1>

<?

$i = 1;

while ($i <= 10){
  print "$i <br>\n";
  $i++;
} // end while

?>

</body>
</html>
```

The `while` loop requires only one parameter, which is a condition. The loop will continue as long as the condition is evaluated as true. As soon as the condition is evaluated as false, the loop will exit. This particular program starts by initializing the variable `$i`, then checking to see if it's greater than or equal to ten in the `while` statement. Inside the loop body, the program prints out the current value of `$i` and increments `$i`.

Recognizing Endless Loops

The flexibility of the `while` construct gives it power, but with that power comes some potential for problems. `while` loops are easy to build, but a loop that does not work properly can cause a lot of problems. It's possible that the code in the loop will never execute at all. Even worse, you might have some sort of logical error that causes the loop to continue indefinitely. As an example, look at the following code:

```
<html>

<head>
<title>
A bad While Loop
</title>
</head>

<body>

<h1>A bad while loop</h1>

<?

$i = 1;

while ($i <= 10){
  print "$i <br>\n";
  $j++;
} // end while

?>

</body>
</html>
```

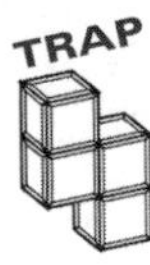

The badWhile.php program is intended to show what happens when you have an endless loop in your code. If you run this program, it's possible it will cause a temporary slowdown of your Web server. Be sure your server is configured to stop a PHP process when the user presses the Stop button on the browser. (This is a default setting on most installations of PHP.)

The badWhile.php program has a subtle but deadly error. Look carefully at the source code and see if you can spot it. The code is just like the first `while` program, except instead of incrementing `$i`, I incremented `$j`. The variable `$j` has nothing to do with `$i`, and `$i` never changes. The loop keeps going on forever, because it cannot end until `$i` is greater than or equal to ten, which will never happen. This program is an example of the classic "endless loop." Every programmer alive has written them accidentally, and you will too.

Usually the culprit of an endless loop is a sloppy variable name, spelling, or capitalization. If you use a variable like `$myCounter` as the sentry variable, but then increment `$MyCounter`, PHP will keep track of two entirely different variables, and your program won't work correctly. This is another reason to be consistent on your variable naming and capitalization conventions.

Building a Well-Behaved Loop

Fortunately, there are some guidelines for building a loop that behaves as you wish. Even better, you've already learned most of the important ideas, because these fundamental concepts are built in to the structure of the `for` loop. When you write a `while` loop, you are responsible for these three things:

- Creating a sentry variable
- Building a condition
- Ensuring the loop can exit

I'll discuss each of these ideas in the following sections.

Create and Initialize a Sentry Variable

If your loop will be based on the value of a variable (there are some other alternatives), make sure you identify that variable, make sure it has appropriate scope, and make sure it has a reasonable starting value. You might also check that value to ensure the loop runs at least one time (at least if that's your intent). Creating a variable is much like the initialization stage of a `for` construct.

Build a Condition to Continue the Loop

Your condition will usually compare a variable and a value. Make sure you have a condition that can be met, and that can be broken. The hard part is not building the loop, but ensuring the program gets out of the loop at the correct time. This condition is much like the condition in the `for` loop.

Ensure the Loop Can Exit

There must be some trigger that changes the sentry variable so the loop can exit. This code must exist inside the code body. Be sure it is possible for the sentry variable to achieve the value necessary to exit the loop by making the condition false.

Working with Basic Arrays

Programming is about the combination of control structures (like loops) and data structures (like variables). You've learned the very powerful looping structures. Now it's time to look at a data structure that works naturally with loops. *Arrays* are special variables made to hold lists of information. PHP makes it quite easy to work with arrays. Look at Figure 4.7. This program, called `basicArray.php`, demonstrates two arrays.

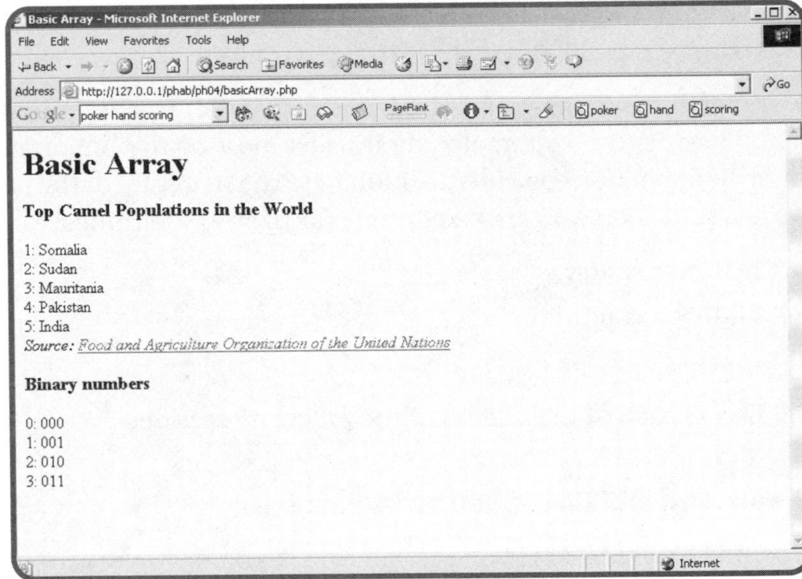

FIGURE 4.7

The information displayed on this page is stored in two array variables.

First, I'll let you look over the entire program, then I'll show you how it does its work.

```
<html>
<head>
<title>
Basic Array
</title>
```

```
</head>

<body>

<h1>Basic Array</h1>

<?

//simply assign values to array
$camelPop[1] = "Somalia";
$camelPop[2] = "Sudan";
$camelPop[3] = "Mauritania";
$camelPop[4] = "Pakistan";
$camelPop[5] = "India";

//output array values
print "<h3>Top Camel Populations in the World</h3>\n";
for ($i = 1; $i <= 5; $i++){
  print "$i: $camelPop[$i]<br>\n";
} // end for loop

print "<i>Source: <a href = http://www.fao.org/ag/aga/glipha/index.jsp> Food and Agriculture
Organization of the United Nations</a></i>\n";

//use array function to load up array
$binary = array("000", "001", "010", "011");

print "<h3>Binary numbers</h3>\n";
for ($i = 0; $i < count($binary); $i++){
  print "$i: $binary[$i]<br>\n";
```

```
} // end for loop

?>

</body>
</html>
```

Generating a Basic Array

Look at the lines that describe `$camelPop`:

```
//simply assign values to array
$camelPop[1] = "Somalia";
$camelPop[2] = "Sudan";
$camelPop[3] = "Mauritania";
$camelPop[4] = "Pakistan";
$camelPop[5] = "India";
```

The `$camelPop` variable is a variable meant to hold the five countries with the largest camel populations in the world. (If this array stuff isn't working for you, at least you've learned something in this chapter!) Since `$camelPop` is going to hold the names of five different countries, it makes sense that this is an array (computer geek lingo for list) rather than an ordinary variable. The only thing different about `$camelPop` and all the other variables you've worked with so far is `$camelPop` can have multiple values. To tell these values apart, use an index in square brackets.

Apparently the boxer George Foreman has several sons also named George. I've often wondered what Mrs. Foreman does when she wants somebody to take out the trash. I suspect she has assigned a number to each George, so there is no ambiguity. This is exactly how arrays work. Each element has the same name, but a different numerical index, so you can tell them apart.

Many languages require you to explicitly create array variables, but PHP is very easygoing in this regard. Simply assign a value to a variable with an index in square braces and you've created an array.

Even though PHP is good-natured about letting you create an array variable on the fly, you might get a warning about this behavior on some Web servers (those that have error reporting set to E_ALL). If that's the case, you can create an empty array with the array() function described in the following sections and then add values to it.

Using a Loop to Examine an Array's Contents

Arrays go naturally with `for` loops. Very often when you have an array variable, you'll want to step through all of its values and do something to each one. In this example, I want to print out the index and the corresponding country's name. Here's the `for` loop that performs this task:

```
//output array values

print "<h3>Top Camel Populations in the World</h3>\n";

for ($i = 1; $i <= 5; $i++){

  print "$i: $camelPop[$i]<br>\n";

} // end for loop
```

Because I know the array indices will vary between 1 and 5 (inclusive), I set up my loop so the value of `$i` will go from 1 to 5. Inside the loop, I simply print out the index (`$i`) and the corresponding country (`$camelPop[$i]`) The first time through the loop, `$i` will be 1, so `$camelPop[$i]` is `$camelPop[1]`, which is "Somalia." Each time through the loop, the value of `$i` will be incremented, so eventually every element of the array will be displayed.

The advantage of combining loops and arrays is convenience. If you want to do something with each element of an array, you only have to write the code one time, then put that code inside a loop. This is especially powerful when you start to design programs that work with large amounts of data. If, for example, I wanted to list the camel population of every country in the UN database rather than simply the top five countries, all I would have to do is make a bigger array and modify the `for` loop.

Using the array() Function to Pre-Load an Array

Often you'll start out knowing exactly which values you want to place in an array. PHP provides a shortcut for loading up an array with a set of values.

```
//use array function to load up array

$binary = array("000", "001", "010", "011");
```

In this example, I created an array of the first four binary digits (starting at zero). You can use the `array` keyword to assign a list of values to an array. Note that when you use this technique, the indices of the elements are automatically created for you.

Most computer languages automatically begin counting things with zero rather than one (the way humans tend to count). This can cause confusion. When PHP builds an array for you, the first index will automatically be zero, not one.

Detecting the Size of an Array

Arrays are meant to add flexibility to your code. You don't actually need to know how many elements are in an array, because PHP provides a function called `count()` that can determine how many elements an array has. In the following code, I used the `count()` function to determine the array size.

```
print "<h3>Binary numbers</h3>\n";

for ($i = 0; $i < count($binary); $i++){

  print "$i: $binary[$i]<br>\n";

} // end for loop
```

Note that my loop sentry goes from zero to one less than the number of elements in the array. If you have four elements in an array and the array begins with zero, the largest index will be three. This is a standard way of looping through an array.

Since it is so common to step through arrays, PHP provides another kind of loop that makes this even easier. You'll get a chance to see that looping structure in Chapter 5, "Better Arrays and String Handling." For now, just make sure you understand how an ordinary `for` loop is used with an array.

Improving "This Old Man" with Arrays and Loops

The `basicArray.php` program shows how to build arrays, but it doesn't illustrate the power of arrays and loops working together. To see how these features can help you, let's revisit an old friend from the last Chapter 3, "Controlling Your Code with Conditions and Functions." The version of the "This Old Man" program featured in Figure 4.8 looks a lot like it did in Chapter 3, but the code is quite a bit more compact.

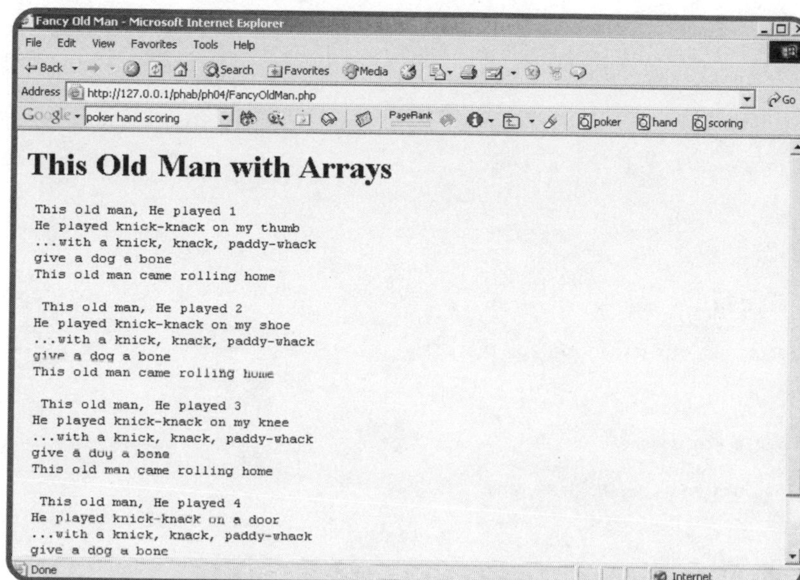

FIGURE 4.8

The Fancy Old Man program uses a more compact structure that is easy to modify.

The improvements in this version of the program are only apparent when you look under the hood.

```
<html>
<head>
<title>
Fancy Old Man
</title>
</head>
<body>
<h1>This Old Man with Arrays</h1>
<pre>
<?
$place = array(
  "",
  "on my thumb",
  "on my shoe",
  "on my knee",
```

```
  "on a door");

//print out song
for ($verse = 1; $verse <= 4; $verse++){

print <<<HERE
 This old man, He played $verse
 He played knick-knack $place[$verse]
 ...with a knick, knack, paddy-whack
 give a dog a bone
 This old man came rolling home



HERE;
  } // end for loop

?>
</pre>
</body>
</html>
```

This improved version takes advantage of the fact that the only things that really change from verse to verse is the verse number, and the place where the old man plays paddy-whack (whatever that means). You can organize the places into an array, and that would greatly simplify writing out the song lyrics.

Building the Place Array

I noticed that each place is a string value associated with some number. I used the `array()` directive to pre-load the `$place` array with appropriate values. There isn't a place corresponding to zero, so I simply left the zero element blank.

```
$place = array(
  "",
  "on my thumb",
  "on my shoe",
```

```
"on my knee",
"on a door");
```

Note that like most places in PHP, carriage returns don't really matter when you're writing the source code. I decided to put each place on a separate line, just because it looked neater that way.

Writing Out the Lyrics

The song itself is incredibly repetitive. Each verse is identical with the others except for the verse number and the corresponding place. For each verse, the value of the `$verse` variable will be the current verse number. The corresponding place is stored in `$place[$verse]`. The code to print out the entire song is a large print statement in a `for` loop.

```
//print out song
for ($verse = 1; $verse <= 4; $verse++){

print <<<HERE
 This old man, He played $verse
 He played knick-knack $place[$verse]
 ...with a knick, knack, paddy whack
 give a dog a bone
 This old man came rolling home


HERE;
 } // end for loop
```

The Fancy Old Man program illustrates very nicely the trade-off associated with using arrays. Creating a program that uses arrays correctly often takes a little more planning than using control structures alone (as the programs in Chapter 3). However, the extra work up front can really pay off because the program can be much easier to modify and extend.

Keeping Persistent Data

Most traditional kinds of programming presume that the user and the program are engaging in a continual dialog. A program begins running, might ask the user some questions, responds to these inputs, and continues interacting with the user until the user somehow indicates an interest in leaving the program. Programs written on a Web server are different. The PHP programs you are writing have an incredibly short life span. When the user makes a request to your PHP program through a Web browser, the server runs the PHP interpreter (the program that converts your PHP code into the underlying machine language your server really understands). The result of the program is a Web page that is sent back to the user's browser. Once your program sends a page to the user, the PHP program shuts down because its work is done. Web servers do not maintain contact with the browser after sending a page. Each request from the user is seen as an entirely new transaction. The poker dice program featured at the beginning of this chapter appears to interact with the user indefinitely. Actually, the same program is being called repeatedly. The program acts differently in different circumstances. Somehow it needs to keep track of what state it's currently in.

IN THE REAL WORLD

The underlying Web protocol (HTTP) that Web servers use does not keep connections open any longer than necessary. This behavior is referred to as being a *stateless protocol*. There are some very good reasons for this behavior. Imagine if your program were kept running as long as anybody anywhere on the Web was looking at it. What if a person fired up your program, then went to bed? Your Web server would have to maintain a connection to that page all night. Also, remember that your program might be called by thousands of people all at the same time. It could be very hard on your server to have all these concurrent connections open. Having stateless behavior improves your Web server's performance, but that performance comes at a cost. Essentially, your programs have complete amnesia every time they run, and you'll somehow need a mechanism for determining what the current state is.

Counting with Form Fields

There are a couple of ways to store information, which you'll learn about later in this book. The easiest approach is to hide the data in the user's page. To illustrate, take a look at Figures 4.9 and 4.10.

Each time you click on the Submit button of the `persistence` program, the counters increment by one. The behavior of the `persistence` program appears to contradict the basic nature of server-side programs because the program seems to remember the previous value of the counter and increment it each time. In fact, if two users

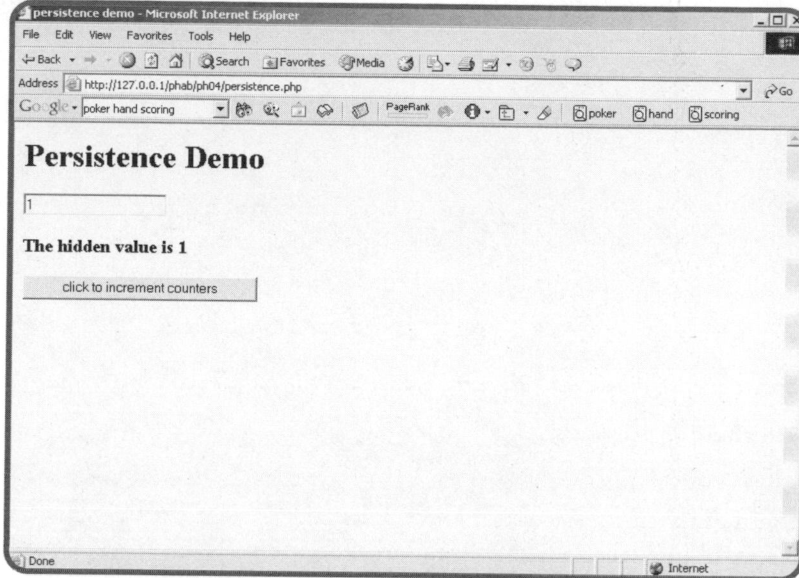

FIGURE 4.9

The program has two counters, which both read one when the program is run the first time.

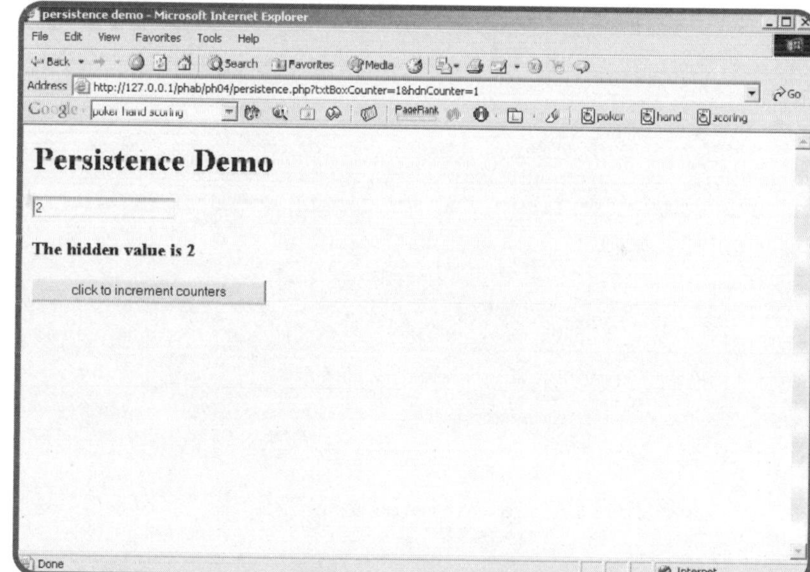

FIGURE 4.10

After the user clicks the Submit button, both values are incremented.

were accessing the `persistence` program at the same time, each would count correctly. Look at the source code to see how it works:

```
<html>

<head>

<title>
```

```
persistence demo
</title>
</head>

<body>

<h1>Persistence Demo</h1>
<form>
<?
//increment the counters
$txtBoxCounter++;
$hdnCounter++;

print <<<HERE

<input type = "text"
       name = "txtBoxCounter"
       value = "$txtBoxCounter">

<input type = "hidden"
       name = "hdnCounter"
       value = "$hdnCounter">
<h3>The hidden value is $hdnCounter</h3>
<input type = "submit"
       value = "click to increment counters">
HERE;

?>

</form>
</body>
</html>
```

Storing Data in the Text Box

The program has two variables, `$txtBoxCounter` and `$hdnCounter`. For now, concentrate on `$txtBoxCounter`. This variable is the variable that is related to the text box. When the program begins, it grabs the value of `$txtBoxCounter` (if it exists) and adds one to it. When the program prints out the text box, it automatically places the `$txtBoxCounter` value in the text box. Since the form has no action attribute defined, the program will automatically call itself when the user clicks on the Submit button. This time, there will be a value in `$txtBoxCounter` (the value 1). When the program runs again, it will increment `$txtBoxCounter` and store the new value (now 2) in the text box. Each time the program runs, it stores the value it will need on the *next* run in the text box.

Using a Hidden Field for Persistence

The text box is convenient for this example because you can see it, but there are serious problems with using a text box in this way in real programs. Text boxes are editable by the user, which means the user could put any kind of information in them, and really mess up your day. Hidden form fields are the unsung heroes of server-side programming. Look at `$hdnCounter` in the source code. This hidden field also has a counter, but since it is hidden, the user never sees it. However, the value of the `$hdnCounter` variable will be sent to the PHP program indicated by the form's `action` attribute. That program can do anything with it, including printing it out in the HTML code body.

Very often when you find yourself wanting to keep track of information between pages, you'll store the information in hidden fields on the user's page.

> **IN THE REAL WORLD**
>
> **The "hidden fields" technique shown here works fine for storing small amounts of information, but it is very inefficient and insecure when you are working with more serious forms of data. As you progress through this book, you'll learn many other ways of making data persist, including the use of cookies, session variables, files, and databases.**

Writing the Poker Dice Program

It's time to take another look at the Poker Dice program that made its debut at the beginning of this chapter. As usual, this program doesn't do anything you haven't already learned. It is a little more complex than the trivial sample programs I've been showing you in this chapter, but it's surprisingly compact considering how much it does. It won't surprise you that arrays and loops are the secret to this program's success.

Setting up the HTML

As always, a basic HTML page serves as the foundation for the PHP program. I chose to add a simple style sheet to this page to make tan characters on a green background.

```
<html>
<head>
<title>poker dice</title>
<style type = "text/css">
body {
  background: green;
  color: tan;
}

</style>
</head>

<body>
<center>
<h1>Poker Dice</h1>

<form>

<?
```

Building the Main Code Body

The poker dice program is long enough to merit functions. I've broken it down into smaller segments to describe it here, but you may also want to look at the code in its entirety from the CD-ROM that accompanies this book.

The main part of the code is used to set up the general flow of the program. Most of the work is done in other functions called from this main area.

```
//check to see if this is first time here
if (empty($cash)){
  $cash = 100;
} // end if

rollDice();

if ($secondRoll == TRUE){
  print "<h2>Second roll</h2>\n";
  $secondRoll = FALSE;
  evaluate();
} else {
  print "<h2>First roll</h2>\n";
  $secondRoll = TRUE;
} // end if

printStuff();
```

The first order of business is to see if this is the first time the user has come to this page. It's important to understand how timing works in this program. The user will feel like he or she is playing the same game for several turns, but actually each time he or she rolls the dice, the entire program runs again. The program will have different behavior based on which form elements (if any) have values. If the user has never been to the page before, the value for the `$cash` variable will be null. The first `if` statement checks this condition. If the `$cash` variable has not yet been created, the user will get a starting value of $100. (I wish real casinos worked like this...)

The program then calls the `rollDice()` function, which will be described momentarily. This function rolls the dice and prints them to the screen.

If you look carefully at the program as it is running, you'll see it runs in two different modes. Each turn consists of two possible rolls. On the first roll, the user is given the ability to save a roll with a checkbox, and no scoring is performed. On the second roll, there are no checkboxes (because the user will need to start with all fresh dice on the next turn) and the program keeps track of the player's score by adding money for various combinations.

The `$secondRoll` variable is used to keep track of whether the user is on the second roll. I chose to give it the value `TRUE` when the user is on the second roll and `FALSE` when on the first roll. If `$secondRoll` is `TRUE`, the program will call the `evaluate()` function, which will tally any losses or winnings. Regardless, I inform the user which roll it is, and change the value of `$secondRoll` so it reflects what should happen the *next* time this program is called (which will happen when the user clicks on the Submit button).

Making the rollDice() Function

The job of the `rollDice()` function is—well—to roll the dice. It's a somewhat long function, so I'll print it all out for you here, then I'll explain it in smaller chunks. Essentially, this function builds an HTML table based on five die rolls. It is able to determine if the user has chosen to keep any previous dice, and only rolls a new die if the user did not choose to keep it. If it is the first roll, the program prints a checkbox, which allows the user to select a die to keep.

```
function rollDice(){
  global $die, $secondRoll, $keepIt;

  print "<table border = 1><td><tr>";

  for ($i = 0; $i < 5; $i++){
    if ($keepIt[$i] == ""){
      $die[$i] = rand(1, 6);
    } else {
      $die[$i] = $keepIt[$i];
    } // end if
    $theFile = "die" . $die[$i] . ".jpg";

    //print out dice images
    print <<<HERE
    <td>
    <img src = "$theFile"
         height = 50
         width = 50><br>

HERE;
```

```
      //print out a checkbox on first roll only

      if ($secondRoll == FALSE){

        print <<<HERE

      <input type = "checkbox"

             name = "keepIt[$i]"

             value = $die[$i]>

      </td>


 HERE;


      } // end if

   } // end for loop


   //print out submit button and end of table

   print <<<HERE

   </tr></td>

   <tr>

     <td colspan = "5">

     <center>

     <input type = "submit"

            value = "roll again">

     </center>

     </td>

   </tr>

   </table>


HERE;


} // end rollDice
```

The checkboxes that appear sometimes are special. The general strategy for them is this: If it's the first turn, I'll print out a checkbox under each die. The checkboxes are all called `keepIt`, and all have an index. When PHP sees these variables with the same name but different indices, it will automatically create an array. Checkboxes in PHP are a little different than some of the other form elements, because they only send a value if they are checked. Any checkbox the user does not check will not be passed to the program. If the checkbox has been checked, the value associated with that checkbox will be passed to the program.

Rolling the Dice if Necessary

The program uses two arrays to keep track of the dice. The `$die` array is used to store the current values of all the dice. The `$keepIt` array will contain no values unless the user has checked the corresponding checkbox (which will only happen on the first roll, because the checkboxes will not be printed on the second roll).

```
if ($keepIt[$i] == ""){
      $die[$i] = rand(1, 6);
    } else {
      $die[$i] = $keepIt[$i];
    } // end if
    $theFile = "die" . $die[$i] . ".jpg";
```

For each die, if the user chose to keep the previous value, that previous value will be stored in the appropriate element of the `$keepIt` array. If so, the `$keepIt` value will be transferred over to the `$die` array. Otherwise, the program will roll a new random value for the die.

Printing Out the Table Contents

Once the function has determined a value for each die (by copying it from `$keepIt` or rolling a new value as appropriate) it is time to print out the image corresponding to each die.

```
//print out dice images
    print <<<HERE
    <td>
    <img src = "$theFile"
         height = 50
         width = 50><br>

HERE;
    //print out a checkbox on first roll only
```

```
    if ($secondRoll == FALSE){
      print <<<HERE
    <input type = "checkbox"
           name = "keepIt[$i]"
           value = $die[$i]>
    </td>

HERE;

    } // end if
```

If it's the first roll, the function also prints out the `keepIt` checkbox corresponding to this die. Note how the name of the checkbox will correspond to the die name. (Remember, the value `$i` will be translated to a number before the HTML page is printed.) The value of the current die is stored as the value of the `keepIt` checkbox.

If you're still baffled, that's okay. It can be hard to see how all this works together. It might help to run the program a couple of times and look carefully at the HTML source that's being generated. To fully understand a PHP program, you can't always look at it simply on the surface as the end user will. You may need to see the HTML elements that are hidden to the user to fully understand what's going on.

Printing Up the End of the Table

After the loop that rolls and prints out the dice, it's a simple matter to print the Submit button and the end of table HTML.

```
//print out submit button and end of table
  print <<<HERE
  </tr></td>
  <tr>
    <td colspan = "5">
    <center>
    <input type = "submit"
           value = "roll again">
    </center>
    </td>
```

```
  </tr>

  </table>


HERE;
```

Note that since no action was specified in the form, PHP will default to the same page that contains the form. This is convenient for programs like this that call themselves repeatedly.

Creating the evaluate() Function

The purpose of the `evaluate()` function is to examine the `$die` array and see if the user has achieved patterns worthy of reward. Again, I'll print out the entire function here, and then show you some highlights below.

```
function evaluate(){
  global $die, $cash;
  //set up payoff
  $payoff = 0;

  //subtract some money for this roll
  $cash -= 2;

  //count the dice
  $numVals = array(6);
  for ($theVal = 1; $theVal <= 6; $theVal++){
    for ($dieNum = 0; $dieNum < 5; $dieNum++){
      if ($die[$dieNum] == $theVal){
        $numVals[$theVal]++;
      } // end if
    } // end dieNum for loop
  } // end theVal for loop

  //print out results
  //  for ($i = 1; $i <= 6; $i++){
  //    print "$i:  $numVals[$i]<br>\n";
```

```
//  } // end for loop

 //count how many pairs, threes, fours, fives
 $numPairs = 0;
 $numThrees = 0;
 $numFours = 0;
 $numFives = 0;

 for ($i = 1; $i <= 6; $i++){
   switch ($numVals[$i]){
     case 2:
       $numPairs++;
       break;
     case 3:
       $numThrees++;
       break;
     case 4:
       $numFours++;
       break;
     case 5:
       $numFives++;
       break;
   } // end switch
 } // end for loop

 //check for two pairs
 if ($numPairs == 2){
   print "You have two pairs!<br>\n";
   $payoff = 1;
 } // end if

 //check for three of a kind and full house
 if ($numThrees == 1){
```

```
  if ($numPairs == 1){
    //three of a kind and a pair is a full house
    print "You have a full house!<br>\n";
    $payoff = 5;
  } else {
    print "You have three of a kind!<br>\n";
    $payoff = 2;
  } // end 'pair' if
} // end 'three' if

//check for four of a kind
if ($numFours == 1){
  print "You have four of a kind!<br>\n";
  $payoff = 5;
} // end if

//check for five of a kind
if ($numFives == 1){
  print "You got five of a kind!<br>\n";
  $payoff = 10;
} // end if

//check for flushes
if (($numVals[1] == 1)
  && ($numVals[2] == 1)
  && ($numVals[3] == 1)
  && ($numVals[4] == 1)
  && ($numVals[5] == 1)){
  print "You have a flush!<br>\n";
  $payoff = 10;
} // end if

if (($numVals[2] == 1)
```

```
    && ($numVals[3] == 1)
    && ($numVals[4] == 1)
    && ($numVals[5] == 1)
    && ($numVals[6] == 1)){
    print "You have a flush!<br>\n";
    $payoff = 10;

  } // end if
  print "You bet 2<br>\n";
  print "Payoff is $payoff<br>\n";
  $cash += $payoff;

} // end evaluate
```

The general strategy of the `evaluate()` function is to subtract two dollars for the player's bet each time. (Change this to make the game easier or harder.) Then I created a new array called `$numVals`, which tracks how many times each possible value appears. Analyzing the `$numVals` array is an easier way to track the various scoring combinations than looking directly at the `$die` array. The rest of the function checks each of the possible scoring combinations and calculates an appropriate payoff.

Counting Up the Dice Values

When you think about the various scoring combinations in this game, it's important to know how many of each value the user rolled. The user will get points for pairs, three, four, and five of a kind, and flushes (five values in a row). I made a new array called `$numVals` which has six elements. `$numVals[1]` will contain the number of ones the user rolled. `$numVals[2]` shows how many twos, and so on.

```
//count the dice
  for ($theVal = 1; $theVal <= 6; $theVal++){
    for ($dieNum = 0; $dieNum < 5; $dieNum++){
      if ($die[$dieNum] == $theVal){
        $numVals[$theVal]++;
      } // end if
    } // end dieNum for loop
```

```
} // end theVal for loop


//print out results
//  for ($i = 1; $i <= 6; $i++){
//    print "$i:  $numVals[$i]<br>\n";
//  } // end for loop
```

To build the `$numVals` array, I stepped through each possible value (1 through 6) with a `for` loop. I then used another `for` loop to look at each die and determine if it showed the appropriate value. (In other words, I checked for ones the first time through the outer loop, then twos, then threes, and so on.) If I found the current value, I incremented `$numVals[$theVal]` appropriately.

Notice the lines at the end of this segment that are commented out. There was no need to move on with the scorekeeping code if the `$numVals` array was not working as expected, so I put in a quick loop that would tell me how many of each value the program found. This was a quick way to make sure my program was working properly before I added new functionality to it. It's smart to periodically check your work and make sure that things are working as you expected. When things were working correctly, I decided to place comments in front of each line to temporarily turn it off. By doing this, I removed the code, but it is still there if something goes wrong and I need to look at the `$numVals` array again.

Counting Up Pairs, Twos, Threes, Fours, and Fives

The `$numVals` array has most of the information I need, but it's not quite in the right format yet. The user will earn cash for pairs, and for three, four, and five of a kind. To check for these conditions, I'll use some other variables and another loop to look at `$numVals`.

```
//count how many pairs, threes, fours, fives
$numPairs = 0;
$numThrees = 0;
$numFours = 0;
$numFives = 0;


for ($i = 1; $i <= 6; $i++){
  switch ($numVals[$i]){
```

```
      case 2:
        $numPairs++;
        break;
      case 3:
        $numThrees++;
        break;
      case 4:
        $numFours++;
        break;
      case 5:
        $numFives++;
        break;
    } // end switch
  } // end for loop
```

First, I created variables to track pairs, and threes, fours, and fives of a kind. I initialized all these variables to zero. I then stepped through the `$numVals` array to see how many of each value occurred. If, for example, the user rolled 1, 1, 5, 5, 5, `$numVals[1]` will equal 2 and `$numVals[5]` will equal 3. After the `switch` statement executes, `$numPairs` will equal 1 and `$numThrees` will equal 1. All the other `$num` variables will still contain zero. Creating these variables will make it very easy to determine which scoring situations (if any) have occurred.

Looking for Two Pairs

All the work setting up the scoring variables pays off, because it's now very easy to determine when a scoring condition has occurred. I chose to award the user one dollar for two pairs (and nothing for one pair.) If the value of `$numPairs` is 2, the user has gotten two pairs, and the `$payoff` variable is given the value 1.

```
  //check for two pairs
  if ($numPairs == 2){
    print "You have two pairs!<br>\n";
    $payoff = 1;
  } // end if
```

Of course, you're welcome to change the payoffs as you wish. As it stands, this game is incredibly generous, but that makes it fun for the user.

Looking for Three of a Kind and Full House

I decided to combine the checks for three of a kind and full house (which is three of a kind and a pair). The code first checks for three of a kind by looking at `$numThrees`. If the user has three of a kind, it then checks for a pair. If both these conditions are true, it's a full house, and the user is rewarded appropriately. If there isn't a pair, there is still a (meager) reward for the three of a kind.

```
//check for three of a kind and full house
if ($numThrees == 1){
  if ($numPairs == 1){
    //three of a kind and a pair is a full house
    print "You have a full house!<br>\n";
    $payoff = 5;
  } else {
    print "You have three of a kind!<br>\n";
    $payoff = 2;
  } // end 'pair' if
} // end 'three' if
```

Checking for Four and Five of a Kind

Checking for four and five of a kind is trivial. All that is necessary is to look at the appropriate variables.

```
//check for four of a kind
if ($numFours == 1){
  print "You have four of a kind!<br>\n";
  $payoff = 5;
} // end if

//check for five of a kind
if ($numFives == 1){
  print "You got five of a kind!<br>\n";
  $payoff = 10;
} // end if
```

Checking for Straights

Straights are a little trickier, because there are two possible straights. The player could have the values 1-5 or 2-6. To check these situations, I used two compound conditions.

```
//check for straights
if (($numVals[1] == 1)
  && ($numVals[2] == 1)
  && ($numVals[3] == 1)
  && ($numVals[4] == 1)
  && ($numVals[5] == 1)){
  print "You have a straight!<br>\n";
  $payoff = 10;
} // end if

if (($numVals[2] == 1)
  && ($numVals[3] == 1)
  && ($numVals[4] == 1)
  && ($numVals[5] == 1)
  && ($numVals[6] == 1)){
  print "You have a straight!<br>\n";
  $payoff = 10;
```

Notice how each `if` statement has a condition made of several sub-conditions joined by the `&&` operator. The `&&` operator is called a *boolean and* operator. You can read it as "and." The condition will be evaluated to `true` only if all the sub conditions are true.

The two conditions are very similar to each other. They simply check the two possible flush situations.

Printing Out the Results

The last function in the program prints out variable information to the user. The `$cash` value describes the user's current wealth. Two hidden elements are used to store information the program will need on the next run. The `secondRoll` element contains a true or false value indicating whether the *next* run should be considered the second roll. The `cash` element describes how much cash should be attributed to the player on the next turn.

```
function printStuff(){
  global $cash, $secondRoll;

  print "Cash: $cash\n";

  //store variables in hidden fields
  print <<<HERE
  <input type = "hidden"
         name = "secondRoll"
         value = "$secondRoll">

  <input type = "hidden"
         name = "cash"
         value = "$cash">

HERE;
} // end printStuff
```

Summary

You are beginning to round out your basic training as a programmer. You have added rudimentary looping behavior to your bag of tricks. Your programs can repeat based on conditions you establish. You know how to build `for` loops that work forwards, backwards, and by skipping values. You also know how to create `while` loops. You know the guidelines for creating a well-behaved loop. You know how to form arrays manually and with the `array()` directive. You can step through all elements of an array using a loop. You learned how your program can keep track of persistent variables by storing them in form fields in your output pages. You've put all these skills together to build an interesting game. In Chapter 5, you'll extend your ability to work with arrays and loops by building more powerful arrays and using specialized looping structures.

CHALLENGES

1. Modify the poker dice game in some way. Add a custom background, change the die images, or modify the payoffs to balance the game to your liking.
2. Write the classic "I'm thinking of a number" game. Have the computer randomly generate a number, then let the user guess its value. Tell the user if he or she is too high, too low, or correct. When the user guesses correctly, tell how many turns it has been. No arrays are necessary for this game, but it will be necessary to store values in hidden form elements.
3. Write the guessing game in reverse. This time the user generates a random number between 1 and 100 and the computer guesses the number. Let the user choose from too high, too low, or correct. Your algorithm should always be able to guess the number in seven turns or less.
4. Write a program that deals out a random poker hand. Use playing card images from http://waste.org/~oxymoron/cards/ or another source. Your program does not need to score the hand. It simply needs to deal out a hand of five random cards. Use an array to handle the deck.

Better Arrays and String Handling

So far, you have learned quite a bit about how to work with information in your PHP programs. In this chapter, you will learn some important new skills to improve the ways you work with data. You will learn about some more sophisticated ways to work with arrays, and how to manage text information with more flair. Specifically, you will learn how to:

- Manage arrays with the `foreach` loop.
- Create and use associative arrays.
- Extract useful information from some of PHP's built-in arrays.
- Build basic two-dimensional arrays.
- Build two-dimensional associative arrays.
- Break a string into smaller segments.
- Search for one string inside another.

Introducing the Word Search Creator

By the end of this chapter, you will be able to create a fun program that generates word search puzzles. The user will enter a series of words into a list box, as shown in Figure 5.1.

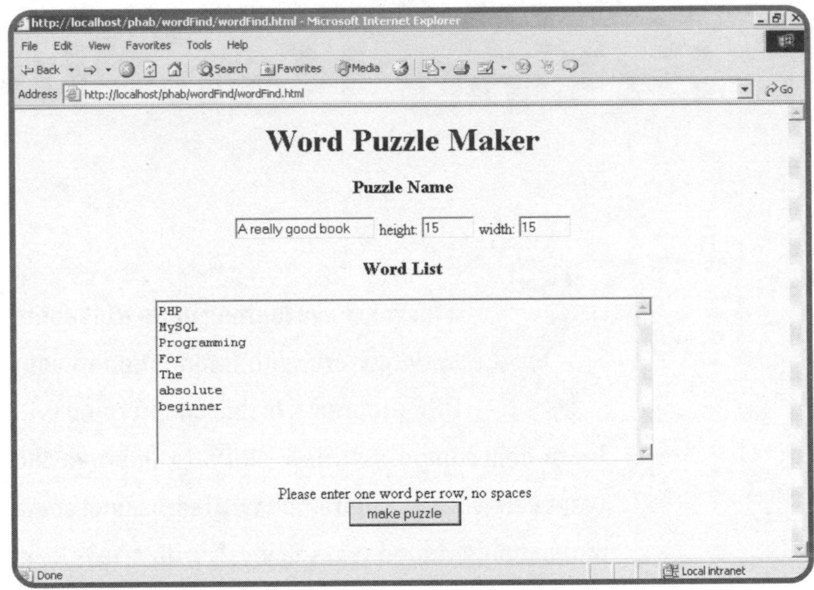

FIGURE 5.1

The user enters a list of words, and a size for the finished puzzle.

The program then tries to generate a word search based on the user's word list. (It isn't always possible, but the program can usually generate a legal puzzle.) One possible solution for the word list shown in Figure 5. 1 is demonstrated in Figure 5.2.

If desired, the program can also generate an answer key based on the puzzle. This capability is shown in Figure 5.3.

The secret to the word find game (and indeed most computer programs) is the way the data is handled. Once I had determined a good scheme for working with the data in the program, the actual programming wasn't too tough.

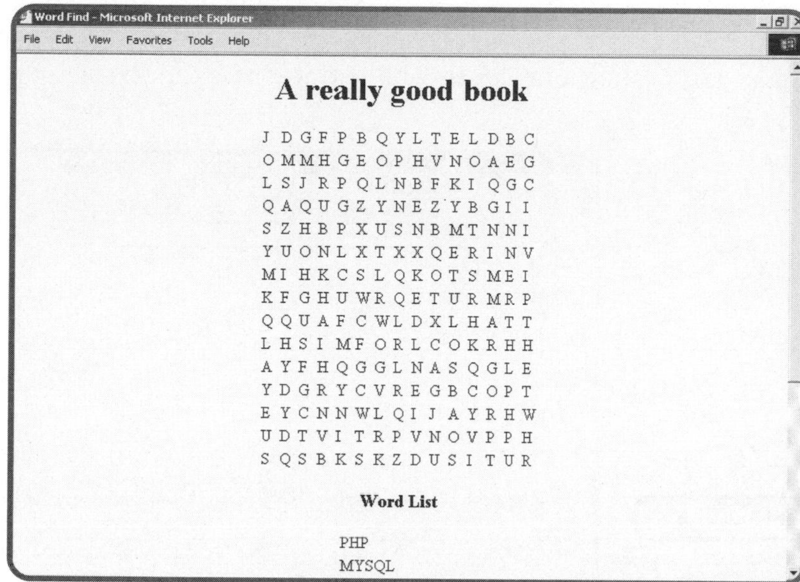

FIGURE 5.2

This puzzle contains all the words in the list.

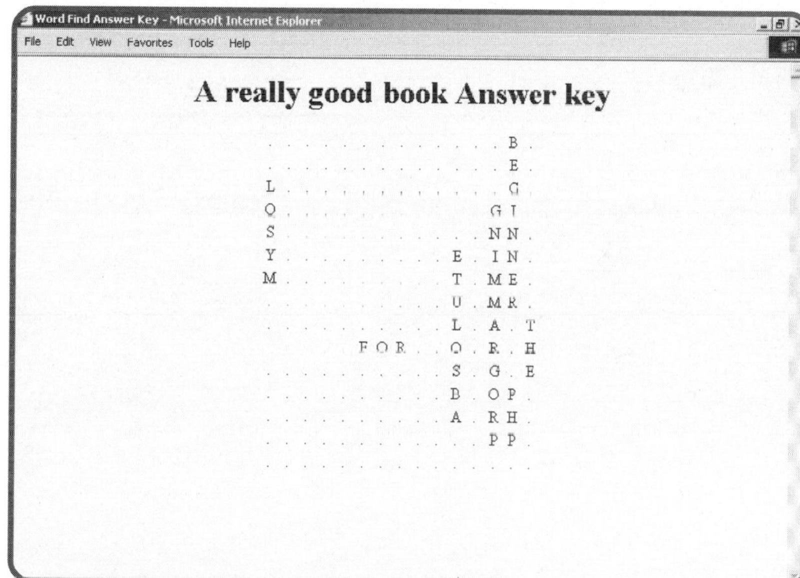

FIGURE 5.3

Here's the answer key for the puzzle.

Using the foreach loop to Work with an Array

As I mentioned in Chapter 4, "Loops and Arrays: The Poker Dice Game," `for` loops and arrays are natural companions. In fact, PHP supplies a special kind of loop that makes it even easier to step through each element of an array.

Introducing the foreach.php Program

The program shown in Figure 5.4 illustrates how the `foreach` loop works.

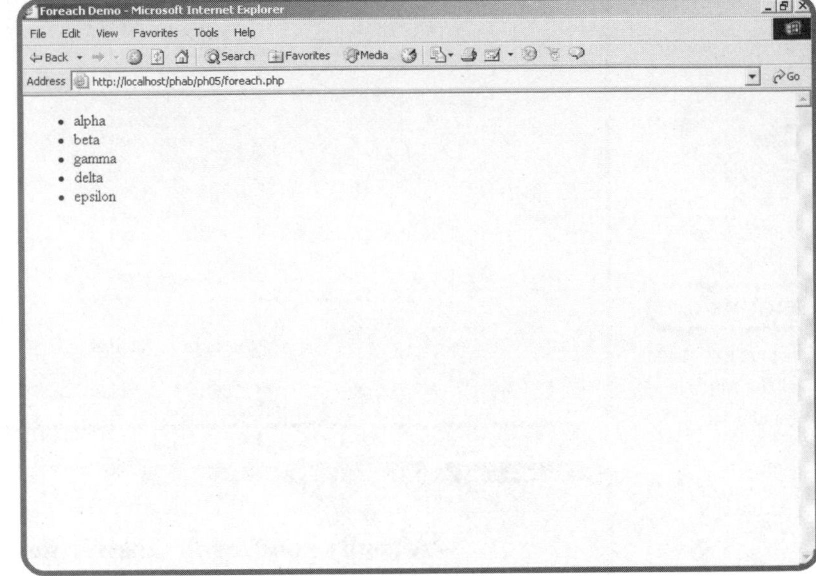

FIGURE 5.4

Although it looks just like normal HTML, this page was created with an array and a `foreach` loop.

The HTML page is unremarkable, but it was generated by surprisingly simple code.

```
<html>
<head>
<title>Foreach Demo</title>
</head>
<body>
<h1>Foreach Demo</h1>
<?

$list = array("alpha", "beta", "gamma", "delta", "epsilon");

print "<ul>\n";
foreach ($list as $value){
  print "  <li>$value</li>\n";
} // end foreach
```

```
print "</ul>\n";

?>
</body>
</html>
```

All the values that will be in the list are created in the `$list` variable using the `array` function.

The `foreach` loop works a lot like a `for` loop, except it is a bit simpler. The first parameter of the `foreach` construct is an array (in this case, `$list`). The keyword `as` then indicates the name of a variable that will hold each value in turn. In this case, the `foreach` loop will step through the `$list` array as many times as necessary. Each time through the loop, the function will populate the `$value` variable with the current member of the `$list` array. In essence, this `foreach` loop:

```
foreach ($list as $value){
  print "  <li>$value</li>\n";
} // end foreach
```

works just like the following traditional `for` loop:

```
for ($i = 0; $i < length($list); $i++);
  $value = $list[$i];
  print "  <li>$value</li>\n";
} // end for loop
```

The main difference between a `foreach` loop and a `for` loop is the presence of the index variable (`$i` in this example). If you're using a `foreach` loop and you need to know the index of the current element, you can use the `key()` function.

The `foreach` loop can be an extremely handy shortcut for stepping through each value of an array. Since this is a common task, knowing how to use the `foreach` loop is an important skill. As you learn some other kinds of arrays, you'll see how to modify the `foreach` loop to handle these other array styles.

Creating an Associative Array

PHP is known for its extremely flexible arrays. You can easily generate a number of interesting and useful array types in addition to the ordinary arrays you've already made. One of the handiest types of arrays is called an "associative array."

While it sounds complicated, an associative array is much like a normal array. While regular arrays rely on numeric indices, an associative array has a string index. Figure 5.5 shows a page created with two associative arrays.

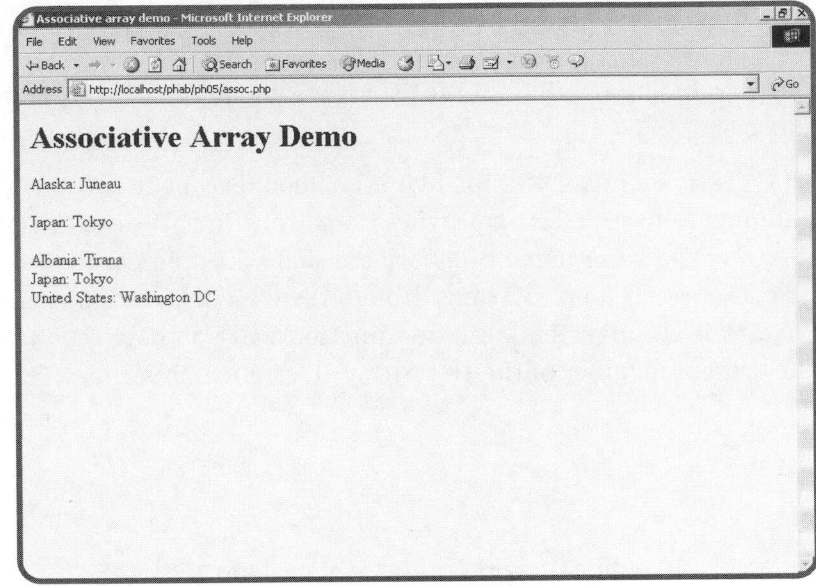

FIGURE 5.5

This page uses associative arrays to relate countries and states to their capital cities.

Examining the assoc.php Program

Imagine that you want to store a list of capital cities. You could certainly store the cities in an array. However, if your main interest is in the relationship between a state and its capital, it could be difficult to maintain the relationship using arrays. In this particular instance, it would be nice if you could use the name of the state as the array index rather than a number.

Building an Associative Array

Here is the code from `assoc.php` that generates the array of state capitals:

```
$stateCap["Alaska"] = "Juneau";

$stateCap["Indiana"] = "Indianapolis";

$stateCap["Michigan"] = "Lansing";
```

The associative array is just like a normal array, except the index values are strings. Note that the indices must be inside quotes. Once you have created an associative array, it is used much like a normal array, as well.

In the Real World

If all this "associative array" talk is making you dizzy, don't panic. It's actually just a new name for something you're very familiar with. Think about the way HTML attributes work. Each tag has a number of attributes that you can use in any order. For example, a standard button might look like this:

```
<input type = "button"
       value = "Save the world.">
```

This button has two attributes. Each attribute is made up of a name/value pair. The keywords "type" and "value" are *names* (or indices, or keys, depending on how you want to think of it) and the terms "button" and "Save the world." are the *values* associated with those names. CSS uses a different syntax for exactly the same idea. The CSS element

```
p {background-color:red;
   color:yellow;
   font-size:14pt}
```

indicates a series of modifications to the paragraph tag. While the syntax is different, the same pattern applies. The critical part of a CSS definition is a list of name/value pairs.

There's one more place associative arrays naturally pop up. As information comes into your program from an HTML form, it comes in as an associative array. The name of each element becomes an index, and the value of that form element is translated to the value of the array element. Later in this chapter you'll see how you can take advantage of this.

An associative array is simply a data structure used when the name/value relationship is the easiest way to work with some kind of data.

```
print "Alaska: ";
print $stateCap["Alaska"];
print "<br><br>";
```

Once again, note that the index of the array is a quoted string. The associative form is terrific for data like the state capital information. In essence, it lets you "look up" the capital city if you know the state name.

Building an Associative Array with the array() Function

If you know the values you want to have in your array, you can use the `array()` function to build an associative array. However, building associative arrays requires a slightly different syntax than the garden variety arrays you encountered in the last chapter. I build the `$worldCap` array using the `array()` syntax:

```
$worldCap = array(
  "Albania"=>"Tirana",
  "Japan"=>"Tokyo",
  "United States"=>"Washington DC"
  );
```

When you are building an ordinary array, the `array()` function requires the data, but doesn't require you to specify the indices. It automatically generates the index of each element by grabbing the next available integer. In an associative array, you are responsible for providing both the data and the index. The general format for this assignment uses a special kind of assignment operator. The => operator indicates an element holds some kind of value. I generally read it as "holds," so you can say "Japan holds Tokyo." In other words, "Japan" => "Tokyo" indicates that PHP should generate an array element with the index "Japan" and store the value "Tokyo" in that element. You can access the value of this array just like any other associative array.

```
print "Japan: ";
print $worldCap["Japan"];
print "<br><br>";
```

Using foreach with Associative Arrays

The `foreach` loop is just as useful with associative arrays as it is with the vanilla kind. However, it uses a slightly different syntax. Take a look at this code from the `assoc.php` page:

```
foreach ($worldCap as $country => $capital){
  print "$country: $capital<br>\n";
} // end foreach
```

A `foreach` loop for a regular array uses only one variable because the index can be easily calculated. In an associative array, each element in the array will have a unique index and value. The associative form of the `foreach` loop takes this into account by indicating two variables. The first variable holds the index. The second variable refers to the value associated with that index. Inside the loop, you can refer to the current index and value using whatever variable names you designated in the `foreach` structure. Each time through the loop, you will be given a name/value pair. In this example, the name will be stored in the variable `$country`, because all the indices in this array are names of countries. Each time through the loop, `$country` will have a different value. In each iteration, the value of the `$capital` variable contains the array value corresponding to the current value of `$country`.

Unlike traditional arrays, you cannot rely on associative arrays to return in any particular order when you use a `foreach` loop to access elements of the array. If you need elements to show up in a particular order, you'll need to call them explicitly.

Using Built-In Associative Arrays

Associative arrays are extremely handy because they reflect a kind of information storage that is very frequently used. In fact, you've been using associative arrays in disguise ever since Chapter 2 of this book. Whenever your PHP program receives data from a form, that data is actually stored in a number of associative arrays for you. A variable was automatically created for you by PHP for each form element. However, you can't always rely on that particular bit of magic. Increasingly, server administrators have been turning this "automatic variable creation" off for security reasons. In fact, the default setup for PHP is now to have this behavior (with the odd name `render_globals`) turned off. It's handy to know how PHP gets data from the form as a good example of associative arrays. It's also useful because you may find yourself needing to know how to get form data without the variables being created explicitly for you.

Introducing the formReader.php Program

The `formReader.php` program is actually one of the first PHP programs I ever wrote, and it's one I use frequently. It's very handy, because it can take the input from any HTML form and report back the names and values of each of the form elements on the page. To illustrate, Figure 5.6 shows a typical Web page with a form.

When the user clicks the Submit Query button, `formReader` responds with some basic diagnostics, as you can see from Figure 5.7.

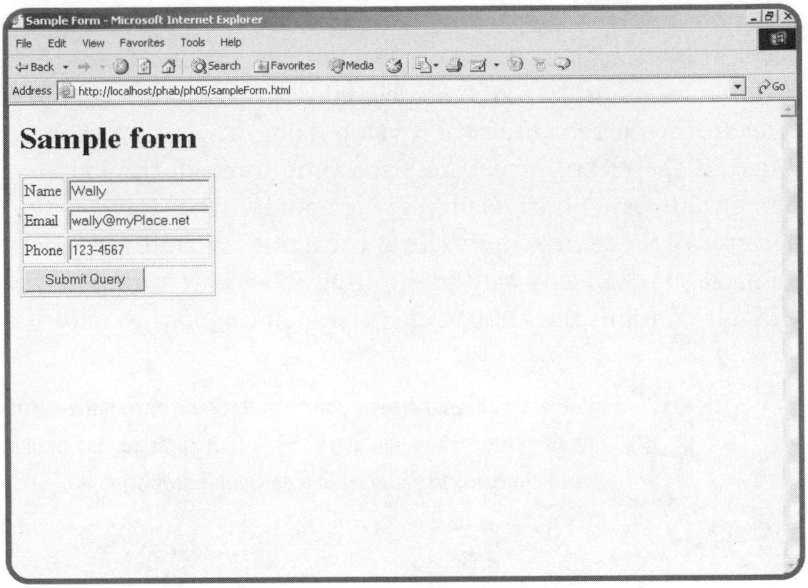

FIGURE 5.6

This form has three basic fields. It will call the formReader.php program.

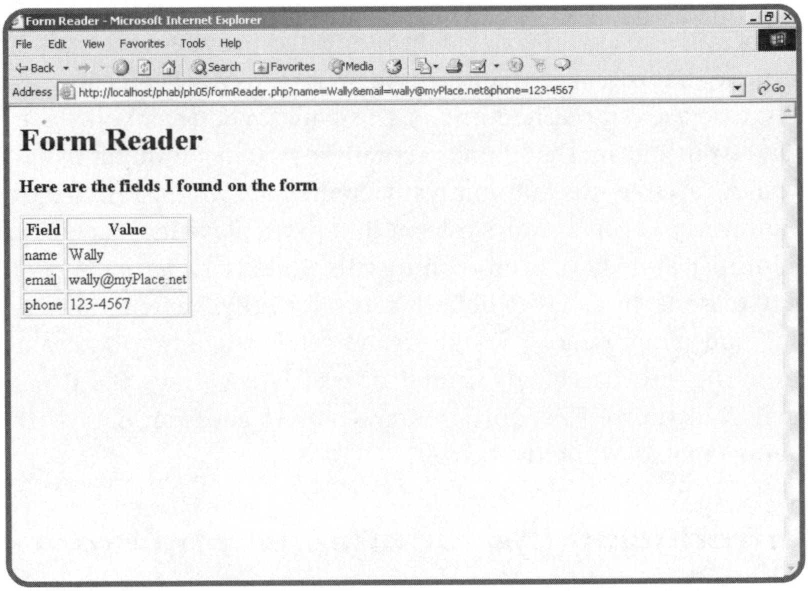

FIGURE 5.7

The `formReader` program determines each field and its value.

Reading the $_REQUEST Array

The `formReader` program does its work by taking advantage of an associative array built into PHP. Until now, you've simply relied on PHP to create a variable for you based on the input elements of whatever form calls your program. This automatic variable creation is called `register_globals`. While this is an extremely convenient feature, it can be dangerous, so some administrators turn it off. Even when `register_globals` is active, it can be useful to know other ways of accessing the information that comes from the form.

All the fields sent to your program are automatically stored in a special associative array called `$_REQUEST`. Each field name on the original form becomes a key, and the value of that field becomes the value associated with that key. If you have a form with a field called `userName`, you can get the value of the field by calling `$_REQUEST["userName"]`.

The `$_REQUEST` array is also useful because you can use a `foreach` loop to quickly determine the names and values of all form elements known to the program. The source code of the `formReader.php` program illustrates how this is done.

```
<!doctype html public "-//W3C//DTD HTML 4.0 //EN">
<html>
<head>
      <title>Form Reader</title>
</head>
<body>
<h1>Form Reader</h1>
<h3>Here are the fields I found on the form</h3>
<?
print <<<HERE
<table border = 1>
<tr>
  <th>Field</th>
  <th>Value</th>
</tr>
HERE;

foreach ($_REQUEST as $field => $value){
  print <<<HERE
  <tr>
    <td>$field</td>
    <td>$value</td>
```

```
  </tr>
HERE;
} // end foreach
print "</table>\n";

?>

</body>
</html>
```

Note how I stepped through the `$_REQUEST` array. Each time through the `foreach` loop, the current field name is stored in the `$field` variable, and the value of that field is stored in `$value`.

I use this script when I'm debugging my programs. If I'm not getting the form elements I expected from a form, I'll put a loop like this in at the top of my program to make sure I know exactly what's being sent to the program. Often this type of procedure can help you find misspellings or other bugs.

IN THE REAL WORLD

PHP provides some other variables related to `$_REQUEST`. The `$HTTP_POST_VARS` array holds all the names and values sent through a POST request, and `$HTTP_GET_VARS` array holds names and values sent through a GET request. You can use this feature to make your code more secure. If you create variables only from the `$HTTP_POST_VARS` array, for example, all input sent via the `GET` method will be ignored. This will make it harder for users to forge data by putting field names in the browser's address bar. Of course, a clever user can still write a form that contains bogus fields, so you always have to be a little suspicious whenever you get any data from the user.

Creating a Multi-Dimensional Array

Arrays are very useful structures for storing various kinds of data into the computer's memory. Normal arrays are much like lists. Associative arrays are like name/value pairs. A third special type of array acts much like a table of data. For instance, imagine you were trying to write a program to help users determine the distance between major cities. You might start on paper with a table like Table 5.1:

TABLE 5.1 DISTANCES BETWEEN MAJOR CITIES

	Indianapolis	New York	Tokyo	London
Indianapolis	0	648	6476	4000
New York	648	0	6760	3470
Tokyo	6476	6760	0	5956
London	4000	3470	5956	0

It's reasonably common to work with this sort of tabular data in a computer program. PHP (and most languages) provides a special type of array to assist in working with this kind of information. The `basicMultiArray` program featured in Figures 5.8 and 5.9 illustrates how a program can encapsulate a table.

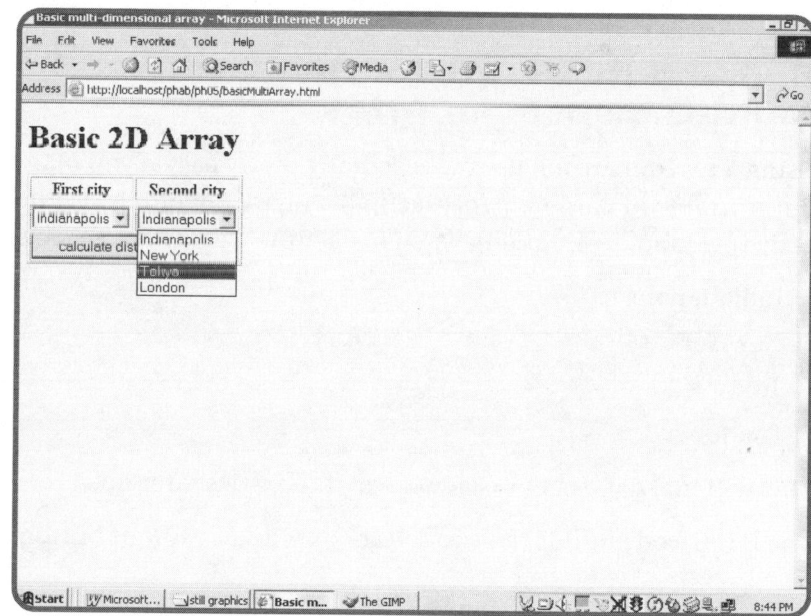

FIGURE 5.8

The user can choose origin and destination cities from select groups.

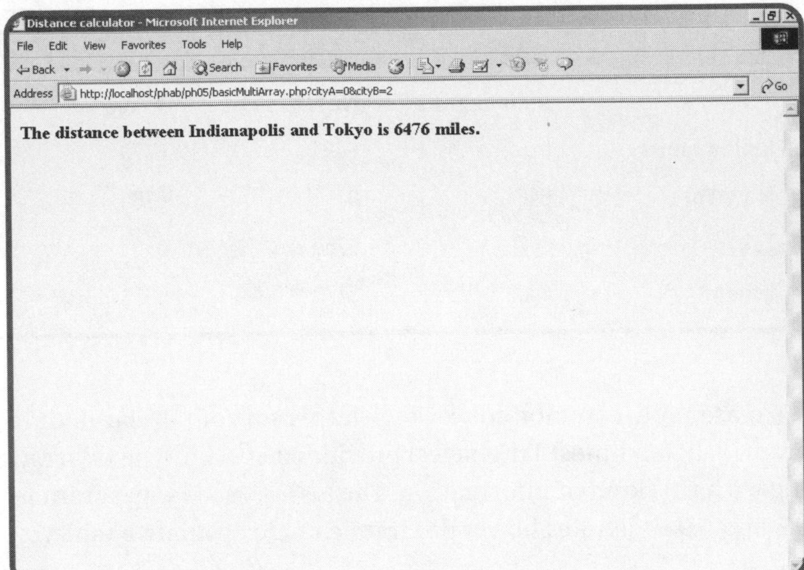

FIGURE 5.9

The program will look up the distance between the cities and return an appropriate value.

Building the HTML for the Basic Multi-Dimensional Array

Using a two-dimensional array is actually pretty easy if you plan well. I first wrote out my table of data on paper (actually, I have a white board in my office for exactly this kind of situation). I assigned a numeric value to each city, so

Indianapolis = 0

New York = 1

Tokyo = 2

London = 3

This will make it easier to keep track of the cities later on.

The HTML code builds the two select boxes and a Submit button in a form.

```
<!doctype html public "-//W3C//DTD HTML 4.0 //EN">
<html>
<head>
        <title>Basic multi-dimensional array</title>
</head>
<body>
```

```
<h1>Basic 2D Array</h1>

<form action = basicMultiArray.php>
<table border = 1>
<tr>
  <th>First city</th>
  <th>Second city</th>
<tr>

<!-- note each option value is numeric -->

<tr>
  <td>
    <select name = "cityA">
      <option value = 0>Indianapolis</option>
      <option value = 1>New York</option>
      <option value = 2>Tokyo</option>
      <option value = 3>London</option>
     </select>
   </td>

  <td>
    <select name = "cityB">
      <option value = 0>Indianapolis</option>
      <option value = 1>New York</option>
      <option value = 2>Tokyo</option>
      <option value = 3>London</option>
    </select>
  </td>
</tr>

<tr>
```

```
  <td colspan = 2>
    <input type = "submit"
           value = "calculate distance">
  </td>
</tr>
</table>
</body>
</html>
```

Recall that when the user submits this form, it will send two variables. The `cityA` variable will contain the *value* property associated with whatever city the user selected, and `cityB` will likewise contain the value of the currently selected destination city. I carefully set up the value properties so they would coordinate with each city's numeric index. If the user chooses New York as the origin city, the value of `$cityA` will be 1, because I decided that New York would be represented by the value 1. The reason I'm giving numeric values is because the information will all be stored in arrays, and normal arrays take numeric indices. (In the next section I'll show you how to do the same thing with associative arrays.)

Responding to the Distance Query

The PHP code that determines the distance between cities is actually quite simple once the arrays are in place.

```
<!doctype html public "-//W3C//DTD HTML 4.0 //EN">
<html>
<head>
       <title>Distance calculator</title>
</head>
<body>
<?
$city = array (
  "Indianapolis",
  "New York",
  "Tokyo",
  "London"
```

```
  );

$distance = array (
  array (0, 648, 6476, 4000),
  array (648, 0, 6760, 3470),
  array (6476, 6760, 0, 5956),
  array (4000, 3470, 5956, 0)
  );

$result = $distance[$cityA][$cityB];
print "<h3>The distance between ";
print "$city[$cityA] and $city[$cityB]";
print " is $result miles.</h3>";

?>
</body>
</html>
```

Storing City Names in the $city Array

I have two arrays in this program. The `$city` array is a completely normal array of string values. It contains a list of city names. I carefully set up the array so the numeric values I assigned to the city would correspond to the index in this array. Remember that array indices usually start with zero, so Indianapolis is zero, New York is one, and so on.

The user won't care that Indianapolis is city 0, so I used the `$city` array to assign names to the various cities. If the user chose city zero (Indianapolis) for the `$cityA` field, I can refer to the name of that city as `$city[$cityA]` because `$cityA` will contain the value `0` and `$city[0]` is "Indianapolis."

Storing Distances in the $distance Array

The distances don't fit in a list, because it requires two values to determine a distance. You must know which city you are coming from and which city you are going to in order to calculate a distance. These two values correspond to rows and columns in the original table. Look again at the code that generates the `$distance` array.

```
$distance = array (
  array (0, 648, 6476, 4000),
  array (648, 0, 6760, 3470),
  array (6476, 6760, 0, 5956),
  array (4000, 3470, 5956, 0)
  );
```

The `$distance` array is actually an array full of other arrays! Each of the inner arrays corresponds to distance from a certain destination city. For example, since Indianapolis is city 0, the first (zeroth?) inner array refers to the distance between Indy and the other cities. If it helps, you can think of each inner array as a row of a table, and the table as an array of rows. It might sound complicated to build a two-dimensional array, but it actually is more natural than you may think. If you compare the original data in Table 5.1 with the code that creates the two-dimensional array, you'll see that all the numbers are in the right place.

There's no need to stop at two dimensions. It's possible to build arrays with three, four, or any other number of dimensions. However, it becomes difficult to visualize how the data works with these complex arrays. Generally, one-and two dimensions are as complex as you'll want your ordinary arrays to get. For more complex data types, you'll probably want to look towards file manipulation tools and relational data structures, which you'll learn throughout the rest of this book.

Getting Data from the $distance Array

Once data is stored in a two-dimensional array, it is reasonably easy to retrieve. To look up information in a table, you need to know the row and column. A two-dimensional array requires two indices, one for the row, and one for the column. To find the distance from Tokyo (City number 2) to New York (City number 1), you can simply refer to $distance[2][1]. The code for the demo program gets the index values from the form:

```
$result = $distance[$cityA][$cityB];
```

This value is stored in the variable `$result` and then sent to the user.

Making a Two-Dimensional Associative Array

You can also create two-dimensional associative arrays. It takes a little more work to set up this array, but it can be worth it because the name-value relationship eliminates the need to keep track of numeric identifiers for each element. Another version of the `multiArray` program illustrates how to use associative arrays to generate the same city distance program.

Since this program looks exactly like the `basicMultiArray` program to the user, I am not showing the screen shots. All of the interesting features of this program are in the source code.

Building the HTML for the Associative Array

The HTML page for the associative version of this program is much like the indexed version, except for one major difference. See if you can spot the difference in the source code.

```
<!doctype html public "-//W3C//DTD HTML 4.0 //EN">
<html>
<head>
<title>2D Array</title>
</head>
<body>
<h1>2D Array</h1>

<form action = multiArray.php>
<table border = 1>
<tr>
  <th>First city</th>
  <th>Second city</th>
<tr>

<!-- note each option value is a string -->

<tr>
```

```
<td>
  <select name = "cityA">
    <option value = "Indianapolis">Indianapolis</option>
    <option value = "New York">New York</option>
    <option value = "Tokyo">Tokyo</option>
    <option value = "London">London</option>
  </select>
</td>

<td>
  <select name = "cityB">
    <option value = "Indianapolis">Indianapolis</option>
    <option value = "New York">New York</option>
    <option value = "Tokyo">Tokyo</option>
    <option value = "London">London</option>
  </select>
</td>
</tr>

<tr>
  <td colspan = 2>
    <input type = "submit"
           value = "calculate distance">
  </td>
</tr>
</table>

</body>
</html>
```

The only difference between this HTML page and the last one is the `value` properties of the `select` objects. In this case, the distance array will be an associative array, so it will not have numeric indices. Since the indices can be text-based, I send the actual city name as the value for `$cityA` and `$cityB`.

Responding to the Query

The code for the associative response is interesting, because it spends a lot of effort to build the fancy associative array. Once the array is created, it's very easy to work with.

```
<!doctype html public "-//W3C//DTD HTML 4.0 //EN">

<html>

<head>

<title>Distance Calculator</title>

</head>

<body>

<h1>Distance Calculator</h1>


<?

//create arrays

$indy = array (

  "Indianapolis" => 0,

  "New York" => 648,

  "Tokyo" => 6476,

  "London" => 4000

  );

$ny = array (

  "Indianapolis" =>648,

  "New York" => 0,

  "Tokyo" => 6760,

  "London" => 3470

  );

$tokyo = array (

  "Indianapolis" => 6476,

  "New York" => 6760,

  "Tokyo" -> 0,

  "London" => 5956

  );

$london = array (

  "Indianapolis" => 4000,
```

```
  "New York" => 3470,
  "Tokyo" => 5956,
  "London" => 0
  );

//set up master array
$distance = array (
  "Indianapolis" => $indy,
  "New York" => $ny,
  "Tokyo" => $tokyo,
  "London" => $london
  );

$result = $distance[$cityA][$cityB];
print "<h3>The distance between $cityA and $cityB is $result miles.</h3>";

?>

</body>
</html>
```

Building the Two-Dimensional Associative Array

The basic approach to building a two-dimensional array is the same whether it's a normal array or uses associative indexing. Essentially, you create each row as an array, and then build an array of the existing arrays. In the traditional array, the indices were automatically created. The development of an associative array is a little more complex, because you need to specify the key for each value. As an example, look at the code used to generate the `$indy` array:

```
$indy = array (
  "Indianapolis" => 0,
  "New York" => 648,
  "Tokyo" => 6476,
  "London" => 4000
  );
```

Inside the array, I used city names as indices. The value for each index refers to the distance from the current city (Indianapolis) to the particular destination. The distance from Indianapolis to Indianapolis is zero, and the distance from Indy to New York is 648, and so on.

I created an associative array for each city, and then put those associative arrays together in a kind of mega-associative array:

```
//set up master array
$distance = array (
  "Indianapolis" => $indy,
  "New York" => $ny,
  "Tokyo" => $tokyo,
  "London" => $london
  );
```

This new array is also an associative array, but each of its indices refers to an array of distances.

Getting Data from the Two-Dimensional Associative Array

Once the two-dimensional array is constructed, it's extremely easy to use. The city names themselves are used as indices, so there's no need for a separate array to hold city names. The data can be output in two lines of code:

```
$result = $distance[$cityA][$cityB];
print "<h3>The distance between $cityA and $cityB is $result miles.</h3>";
```

If you wish, you can combine associative and normal arrays. It would be possible to have a list of associative arrays and put them together in a normal array, or vice-versa. PHPs array-handling capabilities allow for a phenomenal level of control over your data structures.

Manipulating String Values

The Word Search program featured at the beginning of this chapter uses arrays to do some of its magic, but arrays alone are not sufficient to handle the tasks needed for this program. The word search program takes advantage of a number of special string manipulation functions to work extensively with text values. PHP has a huge number of string functions that give you an incredible ability to fold, spindle, and mutilate string values.

Demonstrating String Manipulation with the Pig Latin Translator

As a context for describing string manipulation functions, consider the program featured in Figures 5.10 and 5.11. This program allows the user to enter a phrase into a text box and converts the phrase into a bogus form of Latin.

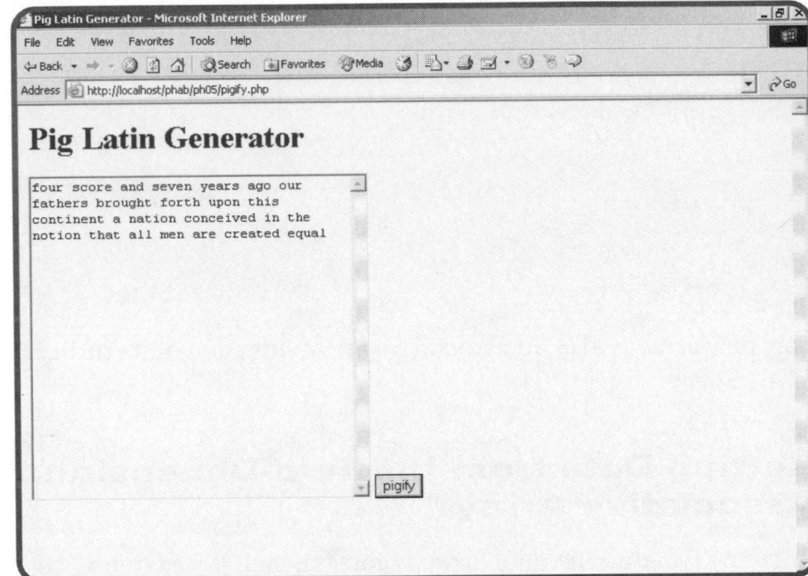

FIGURE 5.10

The `pigify` program lets the user type some text into a text area.

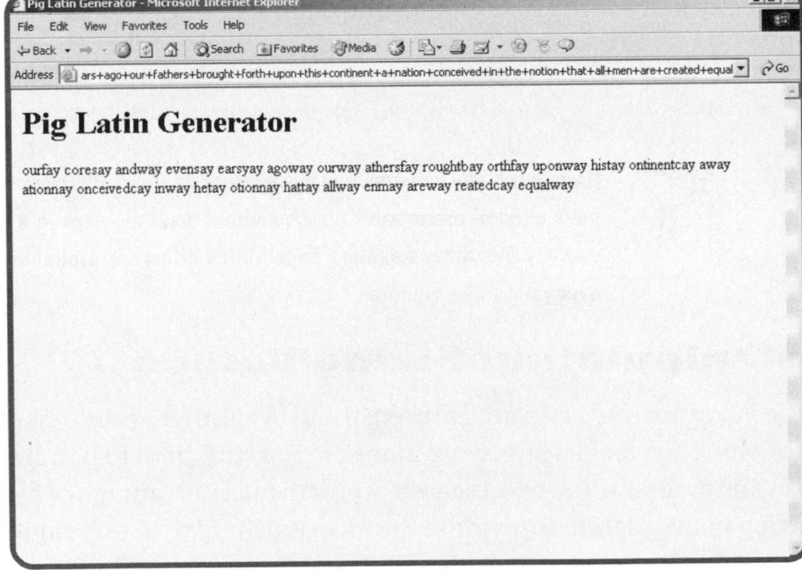

FIGURE 5.11

The program translates immortal prose into incredible silliness.

If you're not familiar with pig Latin, it's a silly kid's game. Essentially, you take the first letter of each word, move it to the end of the word, and add "ay." If the word begins with a vowel, simply end the word with "way."

The `pigify` program will use a number of string functions to manipulate the text.

```
<!doctype html public "-//W3C//DTD HTML 4.0 //EN">
<html>
<head>
       <title>Pig Latin Generator</title>
</head>
<body>
<h1>Pig Latin Generator</h1>
<?
if ($inputString == NULL){
  print <<<HERE
  <form>
  <textarea name = "inputString"
            rows = 20
            cols = 40></textarea>
   <input type = "submit"
          value = "pigify">
   </form>

HERE;
} else {
  //there is a value, so we'll deal with it

  //break phrase into array
  $words = split(" ", $inputString);
  foreach ($words as $theWord){
    $theWord = rtrim($theWord);
    $firstLetter = substr($theWord, 0, 1);
    $restOfWord = substr($theWord, 1, strlen($theWord));
```

```
      //print "$firstLetter) $restOfWord <br> \n";
      if (strstr("aeiouAEIOU", $firstLetter)){
        //it's a vowel
        $newWord = $theWord . "way";
      } else {
        //it's a consonant
        $newWord = $restOfWord . $firstLetter . "ay";
      } // end if
      $newPhrase = $newPhrase . $newWord . " ";
    } // end foreach
    print $newPhrase;

} // end if

?>



</body>
</html>
```

Building the Form

This program uses a PHP page to create an input form and to respond directly to the input. It begins by looking for the existence of the `$inputString` variable. This variable will not exist the first time the user gets to the page. In this situation, the program will build the appropriate HTML page and await user input. After the user hits the Submit button, the program will run again, but this time there will be a value in the `$inputString` variable. The rest of the program uses string manipulation functions to create a pig Latin version of the input string.

Using the Split Function to Break a String into an Array

One of the first tasks is to break the entire string that comes from the user into individual words. PHP provides a couple of interesting functions for this purpose. The `split()` function takes a string and breaks it into an array based on some sort of delimiter. The `split()` function takes two arguments. The first argument is a delimiter and the second is a string to break up. I want each word to be a different element in the array, so I use space (" ") as a delimiter. The following line takes the `$inputString` variable and breaks it into an array called `$words`. Each word will be a new element of the array.

```
$words = split(" ", $inputString);
```

Once the `$word` array is constructed, I stepped through it with a `foreach` loop. I stored each word temporarily in `$theWord` inside the array.

Trimming a String with rtrim()

Sometimes when you split a string into an array, each element of the array will still have the split character at the end. In the pig Latin game, there will be a space at the end of each word, which can cause some problems later. PHP provides a function called `rtrim()` which automatically removes spaces, tabs, newlines, and other white space from the end of a string. I used the `rtrim()` function to clean off any trailing spaces from the `split()` operation, and returned the results back to `$theWord`.

```
$theWord = rtrim($theWord);
```

In addition to `rtrim()`, PHP has `ltrim()`, which trims excess white space from the beginning of a string, and `trim()`, which cleans up both ends of a string. Also, there's a variation of the trim commands that allows you to specify exactly which characters are removed.

Finding a Substring with substr()

The behavior of the algorithm depends on the first character of each word. I'll also need to know all the rest of the word without the first character. The `substr()` function is useful for getting part of a string. It requires three parameters. The first argument is the string you want to get a piece from. The second parameter is which character you want to begin with (starting with zero as usual), and the third parameter is how many characters you want to extract.

I got the first letter of the word with this line:

```
$firstLetter = substr($theWord, 0, 1);
```

It gets one letter from `$theWord` starting at the beginning of the word (position 0). I then stored that value in the `$firstLetter` variable.

It's not much more complicated to get the rest of the word:

```
$restOfWord = substr($theWord, 1, strlen($theWord) -1);
```

Once again, I need to extract values from `$theWord`. This time, I'll begin at character 1 (which humans would refer to as the second character). I don't know directly how many characters to get, but I can calculate it. I should grab one less character than the total number of characters in the word. The `strlen()` function is perfect for this operation, because it returns the number of characters in any string. I can calculate the number of letters I need with `strlen($theWord) - 1`. This new decapitated word is stored in the `$restOfWord` variable.

Using strstr() to Search for One String Inside Another

The next task is to determine if the first character of the word is a vowel. There are a number of approaches to this problem, but perhaps the easiest is to use a searching function. I created a string with all the vowels ("aeiouAEIOU") and then I searched for the existence of the `$firstLetter` variable in the vowel string. The `strstr()` function is perfect for this task. It takes two parameters. The first parameter is the string you are looking for (given the adorable name "haystack" in the online documentation). The second parameter is the string you are searching in (called the "needle"). To search for the value of the `$firstLetter` variable in the string constant `"aeiouAEIOU"`, I used the following line:

```
if (strstr("aeiouAEIOU", $firstLetter)){
```

The `strstr()` function returns the value `FALSE` if the needle was not found in the haystack. If the needle was found, it returns the position of the needle in the haystack parameter. In this case, all I'm really concerned about is whether `$firstLetter` is found in the list of variables. If so, it's a vowel, which will change the way I modify the word.

Using the Concatenation Operator

Most of the time in PHP you can use string interpolation to combine string values. However, sometimes you still need to use a formal operation to combine strings. The process of combining two strings is called *concatenation*. (I love it when simple ideas have complicated names.) The concatenation operator in PHP is the period (.). In pig Latin, if a word begins with a vowel, it should simply end with the string "way." I used string concatenation to make this work.

```
$newWord = $theWord . "way";
```

When the word begins with a consonant, the formula for creating the new word is slightly more complicated, but is still performed with string concatenation.

```
$newWord = $restOfWord . $firstLetter . "ay";
```

Recent testing has shown that the concatenation method of building strings is dramatically faster than interpolation. If speed is an issue, you might want to use string concatenation rather than string interpolation.

Finishing Up the Pig Latin Program

Once I created the new word, I added it and a trailing space to the `$newPhrase` variable. When the `foreach` loop has finished executing, `$newPhrase` will contain the pig Latin translation of the original phrase.

Translating Between Characters and ASCII Values

Although it isn't necessary in the pig Latin program, the word search program will require the ability to randomly generate a character. I'll do this by randomly generating an ASCII value (ASCII is the code used to store characters as binary numbers in the computer's memory) and translating that number to the appropriate character. The `ord()` function is useful in this situation. The upper case letters are represented in ASCII by numbers between 65 and 90. To get a random upper-case letter, I can use the following code:

```
$theNumber = random(65, 90);

$theLetter = ord($theNumber);
```

Returning to the Word Search Creator

By now you've learned all the skills you need to create the word find builder program that debuted at the beginning of this chapter. The program is stored in three files. First, the user enters a word list and puzzle information into an HTML page. This page will call the main `wordFind.php` program, which analyzes the word list, creates the puzzle, and prints it out. Finally, the user will have the opportunity to print an answer key, which is created by a simple PHP program.

Getting the Puzzle Data from the User

The `wordFind.html` page is the user's entry point into the word find system. This page is a standard HTML form with a number of basic elements in it.

```
<html>
<head>
      <title>Word Puzzle Maker</title>
</head>
<body>
<center>
<h1>Word Puzzle Maker</h1>

<form action = "wordFind.php"
      method = "post">
<h3>Puzzle Name</h3>
<input type = "text"
       name = "name"
       value = "My Word Find">
height: <input type = "text"
               name = "height"
               value = "10"
               size = "5">
width: <input type = "text"
               name = "width"
               value = "10"
               size = "5">
<br><br>

<h3>Word List</h3>
<textarea rows=10 cols=60 name = "wordList"></textarea>
<br><br>
Please enter one word per row, no spaces
<br>
<input type="submit" value="make puzzle">
</form>
</center>
</body>
</html>
```

The action property of the form points to the wordFind.php program, which is the primary program in the system. Notice that I used the post method to send data to the program. This is because I expect to be sending large strings to the program, and the get method allows only small amounts of data to be sent to the server.

The form features basic text boxes for the puzzle name, height, and width. This data will be used to determine how the puzzle is built. The wordList text area is expected to house a list of words, which will be used to create the puzzle.

Setting up the Response Page

The bulk of the work in the wordFind system happens in the wordFind.php page. This program has a small amount of HTML to set the stage, but the vast bulk of this file is made up of PHP code.

```
<html>
<head>
<title>
Word Find
</title>
</head>

<body>

<?
// word Find
// by Andy Harris, 2003
// for PHP/MySQL programming for the Absolute Beginner
// Generates a word search puzzle based on a word list
// entered by user. User can also specify the size of
// the puzzle and print out an answer key if desired
```

Notice the comments at the beginning of the code. Since the code for this program is a little bit more involved than most of the programs you have seen before in this book, I have decided to comment it more carefully. It's a really good idea to add comments to your programs so you can more easily determine what they do. You'll be amazed how little you understand your own code after you've been away from it a couple of days. Good comments can make it much easier to maintain your code, and make it easier for others to fix and improve your programs later. My comments here basically lay out the plan for this program.

Working with the Empty Data Set

For testing purposes, I wrote the word find PHP page before I worried about the HTML. For that reason, I simply added in default values for a word list and for the other main variables that determine the board's layout (height, width, and name). In a production version of the program, I don't expect the PHP code will ever be called without an HTML page, but I left the default values in place so you could see how they work.

```
if ($wordList == NULL){
  //make default puzzle
  $word = array(
    "ANDY",
    "HEATHER",
    "LIZ",
    "MATT",
    "JACOB"
    );
  $boardData = array(
    width => 10,
    height => 10,
    name => "Generic Puzzle"
  );
```

This code builds two arrays, which define the entire program. The `$word` array holds the list of words to hide in the puzzle, and the `$boardData` array is an associative array holding critical information about how the board is to be created.

Of course, these are not the values I expect to use, because most of the time this program will be called from an HTML form which will generate the values. The next section of code fills up these variables if the program is called from the appropriate form.

Building the Main Logic for the Program

The main logic for the program begins by retrieving the word list and puzzle parameters from the user's form. Then it tries to convert the list into an array. This type of text analysis is sometimes called *parsing*.

The program then repeatedly tries to build the board until it succeeds. Once the program has successfully created the board, it creates an answer key, then adds in the random letters with the `addFoils()` function. Finally, the program prints out the completed puzzle.

```
} else {
  //get puzzle data from HTML form
  $boardData = array(
    width => $width,
    height => $height,
    name => $name
  );

  //try to get a word list from user input
  if (parseList() == TRUE){
    $legalBoard = FALSE;

    //keep trying to build a board until you get a legal result
    while ($legalBoard == FALSE){
      clearBoard();
      $legalBoard = fillBoard();
    } // end while

    //make the answer key
    $key = $board;
    $keyPuzzle = makeBoard($key);

    //make the final puzzle
    addFoils();
```

```
    $puzzle = makeBoard($board);

    //print out the result page
    printPuzzle();

  } // end parsed list if
} // end word list exists if
```

As you look over this code, you should be able to tell the general flow of the program even if you don't understand exactly how things will happen. The main section of a well-defined program should give you a bird's eye view of the action. Most of the details are delegated to functions. Most of the remaining chapter is devoted to explaining how these functions work. Try to make sure you've got the basic gist of the program's flow; then you'll see how all of it is done.

Parsing the Word List

One important early task involves analyzing the word list that comes from the user. The word list comes as one long string separated by newline (\n) characters. The `parseList()` function converts this string into an array of words. It has some other important functions too, including converting each word to upper case, checking for words that will not fit in the designated puzzle size, and removing unneeded carriage returns.

```
function parseList(){
  //gets word list, creates array of words from it
  //or return false if impossible

  global $word, $wordList, $boardData;

  $itWorked = TRUE;

  //convert word list entirely to upper case
  $wordList = strtoupper($wordList);

  //split word list into array
```

```
  $word = split("\n", $wordList);


  foreach ($word as $currentWord){
    //take out trailing newline characters
    $currentWord = rtrim($currentWord);


    //stop if any words are too long to fit in puzzle
    if ((strLen($currentWord) > $boardData["width"]) &&
        (strLen($currentWord) > $boardData["height"])){
      print "$currentWord is too long for puzzle";
      $itWorked = FALSE;
    } // end if


  } // end foreach
  return $itWorked;
} // end parseList
```

The first thing I did was use the `strtoupper()` function to convert the entire word list into upper case letters. Word search puzzles always seem to use capital letters, so I decided to convert everything to that format.

The long string of characters with newlines is not a useful format for our purposes, so I converted the long string into an array called `$word`. The `split()` function works perfectly for this task. Note that I split on the string `"\n"`. This is the newline character, so it should convert each line of the text area into an element of the new `$word` array.

The next task was to analyze each word in the array with a `foreach` loop. When I tested this part of the program, it became clear that sometimes the trailing newline character was still there, so I used the `rtrim()` function to trim off any unnecessary trailing white space.

If the user enters a word that is larger than the height or width of the puzzle board, it will be impossible to create the puzzle, so I check for this situation by comparing the length of each word to the height and width of the board. Note that if the word is too long, I simply set the value of the `$itWorked` variable to `FALSE`. Earlier in this function, I initialized the value of `$itWorked` to `TRUE`. By the time the function is finished, `$itWorked` will still contain the value `TRUE` if all the words were small enough to fit in the puzzle. If any of the words were too large to fit, the value of `$itWorked` will be false, and the program will not proceed.

Clearing the Board

The word search uses a crude but effective technique to generate legal game boards. It creates random boards repeatedly until it finds one that is legal. While this may seem like a wasteful approach, it is much easier to program than many more sophisticated attempts, and produces remarkably good results for simple problems such as the word search puzzle.

IN THE REAL WORLD

Although this program does use a "brute force" approach to find a good solution, you'll see a number of ways the code is optimized to make a good solution more likely. One example of this you've seen already is the way the program stops if one of the words is too long to fit in the puzzle. This prevents a long processing time while the program tries to fit a word in the puzzle when it cannot be done. As you go through the code, you'll see a number of other places where I do some work to steer the algorithm towards good solutions and away from pitfalls. Because of these efforts, you'll find that the program is actually pretty good at finding word search puzzles unless there are too many words or the game board is too small.

The game board will often be re-created several times during one program execution. I needed a function that could initialize the game board or clean it out easily. The game board is stored in a two-dimensional array called `$board`. When the board is "empty," each cell will contain the period (.) character. I chose this convention because it would still give me something visible in each cell, and would give a character that represents an empty cell. The `clearBoard()` function sets or resets the `$board` array so that it contains a period in every cell.

```
function clearBoard(){
  //initialize board with a . in each cell
  global $board, $boardData;

  for ($row = 0; $row < $boardData["height"]; $row++){
    for ($col = 0; $col < $boardData["width"]; $col++){
      $board[$row][$col] = ".";
    } // end col for loop
```

```
  } // end row for loop
} // end clearBoard
```

This code is the classic nested `for` loop so common to two-dimensional arrays. Note that I used `for` loops rather than `foreach` loops because I was interested in the indices of the loops. The outer `for` loop steps through the rows. Inside each row loop, another loop steps through each column. I assigned the value "." to the `$board` array at the current `$row` and `$col` locations. Eventually, every cell in the array will contain the value "."

I determined the size of the `for` loops by referring to the `$boardData` associative array. Although there are a number of ways I could have done this, I chose the associative array for several reasons. The most important is clarity. It's easy for me to see by this structure that I'm working with the height and width related to board data information. Another advantage of using an associative array in this context is convenience. Since the height, width, and board name are all stored in the `$boardData` array, I could make a global reference to the `$boardData` variable and all its values would come along. It's like having three variables for the price of one.

Filling the Board

Of course, the purpose of clearing the board is to fill it in with the words from the word list. This happens in two stages. The `fillBoard()` function controls the entire process of filling up the whole board, but the details of adding each word to the board are relegated to the `addWord()` function (which you'll see next.)

The board is only complete if each word is added correctly. Each word is added only if each of its letters is added without problems. The program repeatedly calls `fillBoard()` as often as necessary to get a correct solution. Each time `fillBoard()` runs, it may call `addWord()` as many times as necessary until each word is added. The `addWord()` function in turn keeps track of whether it is able to successfully add each character to the board.

The general plan of the fillBoard() function is to generate a random direction for each word, then tell the addWord() function to place the specified word in the specified direction on the board. The looping structure for the fillBoard() function is a little unique, because the loop could exit in two different ways. If any of the words cannot be placed in the requested manner, the puzzle generation will stop immediately, and the function will return the value `FALSE`. However, if the entire word list is successfully placed on the game board, the function should also stop looping, but should report the value TRUE. There are a number of ways to achieve this effect, but I prefer often to use a special Boolean variable for this purpose. Boolean variables are variables meant to contain only the values true and false. Of course, PHP is pretty easy-going about variable types, but your can make a variable act like a Boolean simply by assigning it only the values TRUE or FALSE. In the fillBoard() function, look at how the $keepGoing variable is used. It is initialized to TRUE, and the function's main loop keeps running as long as this is the case. However, the two conditions that can cause the loop to exit (the addWord() function failed to place a word correctly, or the entire word list has been exhausted) both cause the $keepGoing variable to become FALSE. When this happens, the loop will stop, and the function will shortly exit.

```
function fillBoard(){
  //fill board with list by calling addWord() for each word
  //or return false if failed

  global $word;
  $direction = array("N", "S", "E", "W");
  $itWorked = TRUE;
  $counter = 0;
  $keepGoing = TRUE;
  while($keepGoing){
    $dir = rand(0, 3);
    $result = addWord($word[$counter], $direction[$dir]);
    if ($result == FALSE){
      //print "failed to place $word[$counter]";
      $keepGoing = FALSE;
      $itWorked = FALSE;
    } // end if
    $counter++;
    if ($counter >= count($word)){
      $keepGoing = FALSE;
    } // end if
  } // end while
```

```
  return $itWorked;

} // end fillBoard
```

The function begins by defining an array for directions. At this point, I decided only to support placing words in the four cardinal directions, although it would be easy enough to add diagonals. (Hey, that sounds like a *dandy* end-of-chapter exercise!) The `$direction` array holds the initials of the four directions I have decided to support at this time. The `$itWorked` variable is a Boolean which reports whether the board has been successfully filled. It is initialized to `TRUE`. If the `addWord()` function fails to place a word, the value of `$itWorked` will be changed to `FALSE`.

The `$counter` variable will be used to count which word I'm currently trying to place. I increment the value of `$counter` each time through the loop. When `$counter` is larger than the size of the `$word` array, the function has successfully added every word, and can exit triumphantly.

To choose a direction, I simply created a random value between 0 and 3, and referred to the associated value of the `$direction` array.

The last line of the function returns the value of `$itWorked`. The `fillBoard()` function is called by the main program repeatedly until it succeeds. This success or failure is reported to the main program by returning the value of `$itWorked`.

Adding a Word

The `fillBoard()` function handles the global process of adding the word list to the game board, but the process of adding each word to the board is performed by the `addWord()` function. This function expects two parameters, the word to add, and a direction.

The function cleans up the word, and renders slightly different service based on which direction the word will be placed. It places each letter of the word in an appropriate cell while preventing it from being placed outside the boundary of the game board. It also checks to make sure that the cell does not currently house some other letter from another word (unless that letter happens to be the one the function is already trying to place). The function may look long and complex at first, but when you look at it more closely, you'll find that it's extremely repetitive.

```
function addWord($theWord, $dir){

  //attempt to add a word to the board or return false if failed
```

```
global $board, $boardData;

//remove trailing characters if necessary
$theWord = rtrim($theWord);

$itWorked = TRUE;

switch ($dir){
  case "E":
    //col from 0 to board width - word width
    //row from 0 to board height
    $newCol = rand(0, $boardData["width"] - 1 - strlen($theWord));
    $newRow = rand(0, $boardData["height"]-1);

    for ($i = 0; $i < strlen($theWord); $i++){
      //new character same row, initial column + $i
      $boardLetter = $board[$newRow][$newCol + $i];
      $wordLetter = substr($theWord, $i, 1);

      //check for legal values in current space on board
      if (($boardLetter == $wordLetter) ||
          ($boardLetter == ".")){
        $board[$newRow][$newCol + $i] = $wordLetter;
      } else {
        $itWorked = FALSE;
      } // end if
    } // end for loop
    break;

  case "W":
    //col from word width to board width
    //row from 0 to board height
    $newCol = rand(strlen($theWord), $boardData["width"] -1);
```

```
      $newRow = rand(0, $boardData["height"]-1);
      //print "west:\tRow: $newRow\tCol: $newCol<br>\n";

      for ($i = 0; $i < strlen($theWord); $i++){
        //check for a legal move
        $boardLetter = $board[$newRow][$newCol - $i];
        $wordLetter = substr($theWord, $i, 1);
        if (($boardLetter == wordLetter) ||
            ($boardLetter == ".")){
          $board[$newRow][$newCol - $i] = $wordLetter;
        } else {
          $itWorked = FALSE;
        } // end if
      } // end for loop
      break;

    case "S":
      //col from 0 to board width
      //row from 0 to board height - word length
      $newCol = rand(0, $boardData["width"] -1);
      $newRow = rand(0, $boardData["height"]-1 - strlen($theWord));
      //print "south:\tRow: $newRow\tCol: $newCol<br>\n";

      for ($i = 0; $i < strlen($theWord); $i++){
        //check for a legal move
        $boardLetter = $board[$newRow + $i][$newCol];
        $wordLetter = substr($theWord, $i, 1);
        if (($boardLetter == $wordLetter) ||
            ($boardLetter == ".")){
          $board[$newRow + $i][$newCol] = $wordLetter;
        } else {
         $itWorked = FALSE;
        } // end if
```

```
      } // end for loop
      break;

    case "N":
      //col from 0 to board width
      //row from word length to board height
      $newCol = rand(0, $boardData["width"] -1);
      $newRow = rand(strlen($theWord), $boardData["height"]-1);

      for ($i = 0; $i < strlen($theWord); $i++){
        //check for a legal move
        $boardLetter = $board[$newRow - $i][$newCol];
        $wordLetter = substr($theWord, $i, 1);
        if (($boardLetter == $wordLetter) ||
            ($boardLetter == ".")){
          $board[$newRow - $i][$newCol] = $wordLetter;
        } else {
         $itWorked = FALSE;
        } // end if
      } // end for loop
      break;

  } // end switch
  return $itWorked;
} // end addWord
```

The main focus of the `addWord()` function is a `switch` structure based on the word direction. The code inside each switch branch is similar in its general approach.

Closely Examining the East Code

It's customary in Western languages to write from left to right, so the code for "E," which indicates "write towards the East" is probably the most natural to understand. I'll explain how that code works, then I'll show you how the other directions differ. Here's the code fragment that attempts to write a word in the Easterly direction:

```
case "E":

      //col from 0 to board width - word width

      //row from 0 to board height

      $newCol = rand(0,

                $boardData["width"] - 1 - strlen($theWord));

      $newRow = rand(0, $boardData["height"]-1);


      for ($i = 0; $i < strlen($theWord); $i++){

        //new character same row, initial column + $i

        $boardLetter = $board[$newRow][$newCol + $i];

        $wordLetter = substr($theWord, $i, 1);


        //check for legal values in current space on board

        if (($boardLetter == $wordLetter) ||

            ($boardLetter == ".")){

          $board[$newRow][$newCol + $i] = $wordLetter;

        } else {

          $itWorked = FALSE;

        } // end if

      } // end for loop

      break;
```

Determining Starting Values for the Characters

Essentially, the code steps through the word one letter at a time, placing each letter in the next cell to the right. I could have chosen any random cell and checked to see when the code got outside the range of the board, but this would have involved some complicated and clunky code. A more elegant solution is to carefully determine what the range of appropriate starting cells are, and only choose cells within that range. For example, if I'm placing the word "elephant" (with 8 letters) from left to right in a puzzle with a width of ten, the only legal columns would be columns zero and one (remember, computers usually start counting at zero). If I'm placing "elephant" in the same puzzle but from right to left, the last two columns (8 and 9) are the only legal options. Once I recognized this fact, I had to figure out how to encode this idea so it could work with any size words in any size puzzle.

IN THE REAL WORLD

By far the most critical part of this code is the comments at the beginning. Even though I'm a reasonably experienced programmer, it's easy enough to get confused when you start solving problems of any reasonable complexity. Just to remind myself, I placed these comments to explain to myself exactly what the parameters of this chunk of code are.

I referred back to these comments many times while I was writing and debugging the code. If I hadn't given myself clear guidance on what I was trying to do, I would have gotten so lost I probably wouldn't have been able to write the program.

To figure out where to place each word, I need a random value for the row and column, but that random value must be within an appropriate range based on the word length and board width. By trial and error and some sketches on a white board, I determined that `$boardData["width"] - 1` is the largest column in the game board, and `strlen($theWord)` is the length of the current word in characters. If I subtract the word length from the board width, I'll get the largest legal starting value for a left-to-right placement. That's how I got the slightly scary formula

```
$boardData["width"] - 1 - strlen($theWord)
```

The smallest legal starting value for this kind of placement is zero, because column zero will always work when you're going right-to-left and when the word is the same size or smaller than the puzzle (which has already been established).

In an Eastward placement, the row number doesn't matter, because any row in the puzzle will be legal, as all letters will be placed on the same row.

Once I know the largest and smallest legal starting places for the word, I can randomly generate that starting point knowing that the entire word can be placed there legally as long as it doesn't overlap any other words.

I used a `for` loop to pull one character at a time from the word using the `substr()` function. Each character is placed at the same row as the starting character, but at a column offset by the position in the word. Repeating the "elephant" example, if the starting position chosen is column 1, the character "E" will be placed in column 1, because "E" is at the 0th position in the word "elephant," and 1 + 0 = 1. When the counter (`$i`) gets to the letter "L," it will have the value 1, so it will be placed in column 2, and so on.

If the formula for choosing the starting place and the plan for placing subsequent letters in place work correctly, it will be impossible to add a letter outside the puzzle board. However, another bad thing could happen if a character from a previously placed word is in a cell that the current word wants. The code checks the current cell on the game board to see its current status. If the cell contains the value ".", it is empty, and the new character can be freely placed there. If the cell contains the value that the current word wants to place in the cell, the program can likewise continue without interruption. However, if the cell contains any other character, the loop will need to exit, and the program will need reset the board and try again. This is done by setting the value of `$itWorked` to `FALSE`.

Printing in the Other Directions

Once you understand how to print words when the direction is East, you'll see that the other directions are similar. However, for each direction, I needed to figure out what the appropriate starting values were, and what cell to place each letter in. The table below summarizes these value

TABLE 5.2 SUMMARY OF PLACEMENT DATA

	E	W	S	N
min Col	0	word width	0	0
max Col	board width – 1 - word width	board width –1	board width – 1	board width – 1
min Row	0	0	0	word width
max Row	board height -1	board height – 1	board height – 1 – word width	board height – 1
letter col	start + i	start - i	start	start
letter row	start	start	start + i	start – i

A little explanation of Table 5.2 is in order. Within the table, I identified the minimum and maximum column for each direction, as well as the minimum and maximum row. This was actually easiest to figure out by writing some examples out on graph paper. The placement of each letter is based on the starting row and column, with i standing for the position of the current letter within the word. So, in direction W, I'd put the letter at position 2 of my word into the randomly chosen starting row, but at the starting column minus two. This will cause the letters to be printed from right to left. Work out the other examples on graph paper so you can see how they worked out.

IN THE REAL WORLD

This is exactly where computer programming becomes mystical for most people. Up to now, you've probably been following so far, but this business of placing the characters has a lot of math in it, and you didn't get to see me struggle with it. It might look to you as if I just knew what the right formulas were. I didn't. I had to think about it carefully *without* the computer turned on. I got out a whiteboard (my favorite programming tool) and some graph paper, and tried to figure out what I meant mathematically when I said "write the characters from bottom to top." This is hard, but you can do it. The main thing beginners forget to do is turn off the computer. Get out some paper and figure out what it is you're trying to tell the computer to do. Then you can start writing code. You'll still get it wrong (at least I did). But, if you've written down your strategy, you can compare what you expected to happen with what did happen, and you're likely to be able to solve even this kind of somewhat mathematical problem.

Making a Puzzle Board

By the time the `fillBoard()` function has finished calling `addWord()` to add all the words, the answer key is actually complete. Each word is in place, and any cell that does not contain one of the words still has a period. The main program will copy the current `$board` variable over to the `$key` array. The answer key is now ready to be formatted into a form the user can use. However, rather than writing one function to print out the answer key and another function to print out the finished puzzle, I wrote one function that takes the array as a parameter and creates a long string of HTML code placing that puzzle in a table.

```
function makeBoard($theBoard){
  //given a board array, return an HTML table based on the array
  global $boardData;
  $puzzle = "";
  $puzzle .= "<table border = 0>\n";
  for ($row = 0; $row < $boardData["height"]; $row++){
    $puzzle .= "<tr>\n";
    for ($col = 0; $col < $boardData["width"]; $col++){
      $puzzle .= "  <td width = 15>{$theBoard[$row][$col]}</td>\n";
    } // end col for loop
    $puzzle .= "</tr>\n";
  } // end row for loop
```

```
  $puzzle .= "</table>\n";

  return $puzzle;

} // end printBoard;
```

Most of the function deals with creating an HTML table, which will be stored in the variable `$puzzle`. Each row of the puzzle corresponds begins by building an HTML `<tr>` tag, and creates a `<td></td>` pair for each element in the table.

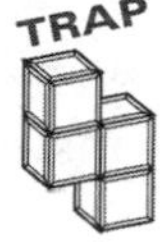

Sometimes PHP has trouble correctly interpolating two-dimensional arrays. If you find that an array is not being correctly interpolated, you can try two things. First, you can simply surround the array reference in braces as I did in the code in `makeBoard()` **Also, you can forego interpolation and use concatenation instead. For example, you could have built each cell with the following code:**

```
$puzzle .= "<td> width = 15>" . $theBoard[$row][$col] . "</td>\n";
```

Adding the Foil Letters

The puzzle itself can be easily derived from the answer key. Once the words in the word list are in place, all it takes to generate a puzzle is to replace the periods in the puzzle with some other random letters. I call these other characters "foil letters" because it is their job to foil the user. This is actually quite easy compared to the process of adding the words.

```
function addFoils(){

  //add random dummy characters to board

  global $board, $boardData;

  for ($row = 0; $row < $boardData["height"]; $row++){

    for ($col = 0; $col < $boardData["width"]; $col++){

      if ($board[$row][$col] == "."){

        $newLetter = rand(65, 90);

        $board[$row][$col] = chr($newLetter);

      } // end if

    } // end col for loop

  } // end row for loop

} // end addFoils
```

The function uses the standard pair of nested loops to cycle through each cell in the array. For each cell that contains a period, it generates a random number between

65 and 90. These numbers correspond to the ASCII numeric codes for the capital letters. I then used the `chr()` function to retrieve the letter that corresponds to that number, and stored the new random letter in the array.

Printing Out the Puzzle

The last step in the main program is to print results to the user. So far, all the work has been done behind the scenes. Now it is necessary to produce an HTML page with the results. The `printPuzzle()` function performs this duty. The actual puzzle and answer key tables have already been formatted as HTML by the `printBoard()` function. The puzzle HTML is stored in the `$puzzle` variable, and the answer key is stored in `$keyPuzzle`.

```
function printPuzzle(){
  //print out page to user with puzzle on it

  global $puzzle, $word, $keyPuzzle, $boardData;
  //print puzzle itself

  print <<<HERE
  <center>
  <h1>{$boardData["name"]}</h1>
  $puzzle
  <h3>Word List</h3>
  <table border = 0>

HERE;

  //print word list
  foreach ($word as $theWord){
    print "<tr><td>$theWord</td></tr>\n";
  } // end foreach
  print "</table>\n";
  $puzzleName = $boardData["name"];

  //print form for requesting answer key.
```

```
    //send answer key to that form (sneaky!)
    print <<<HERE
    <br><br><br><br><br><br><br><br>
    <form action = "wordFindKey.php"
          method = "post">
    <input type = "hidden"
           name = "key"
           value = "$keyPuzzle">
    <input type = "hidden"
           name = "puzzleName"
           value = "$puzzleName">

    <input type = "submit"
           value = "show answer key">
    </form>
    </center>

HERE;

} // end printPuzzle
```

This function mainly deals with printing out standard HTML from variables that have been created during the program's run. The name of the puzzle is stored in `$boardData["name"]`. The puzzle itself is simply the value of the `$puzzle` variable. I printed the word list by the simple expedient of a `foreach` loop creating a list from the `$word` array.

The trickiest part of the code is working with the answer key. It would be easy enough to print the answer key directly on the same HTML page. In fact, this is exactly what I did as I was testing the program. However, the puzzle won't be much fun if the answer is right there, so I allowed the user to press a button to get the answer key. The key is related only to the currently generated puzzle. If the same word list were sent to the `wordfind` program again, it would likely produce a different puzzle with a different answer. The secret is to store the current answer key in a hidden form element and pass this element to another program. I created a form with two hidden fields. I stored the name of the puzzle in a field called `puzzleName` and the entire HTML of the answer key in a field called `key`. When the user presses the Submit key, it will call a program called `wordFindKey`.

In the Real World

Passing the answer key to another program was a kind of dirty trick. It worked for a couple of reasons. First, since the `key` field is hidden and the form sends data through the `post` method, the user is unlikely to know that the answer to the puzzle is literally under his nose. Since I expect this program mainly to be used by teachers who would print out the puzzle anyway, this is fine. Even without the secrecy concerns, it would be necessary to pass the key data by `post` because it is longer than the 256 characters allowed by the `get` method.

Sending the HTML-formatted answer key to the next program made the second program quite simple, but there is another advantage to this approach: It is very difficult to send entire arrays through form variables, but by creating the HTML table, all the data in the array was reduced to one string value, which can be easily passed to another program through a form.

Printing Out the Answer Key

The `wordFindKey` program is actually very simplistic, because all the work of generating the answer key was done by the word find program. All this program has to do is retrieve the puzzle name and answer key from form variables and print them out. Since the key has even been formatted as a table, there is no need for any kind of heavy lifting by the `wordFindKey` program.

```
<!doctype html public "-//W3C//DTD HTML 4.0 //EN">
<html>
<head>
<title>Word Find Answer Key</title>
</head>
<body>

<?
//answer key for word find
//called from wordFind.php

print <<<HERE
<center>
<h1>$puzzleName Answer key</h1>
$key
```

```
</center>


HERE;
?>
</body>
</html>
```

Summary

In this chapter you've started to see how important it is to put together data in meaningful ways. You've looked at a number of more powerful kinds of arrays and tools to manipulate them. You've learned how to use the `foreach` loop to look at each element of an array in turn. You can use string indices to generate associative arrays. You know how to make two-dimensional arrays using both numeric and string indices. You've learned how to do several kinds of string manipulation tricks including searching for one string inside another, extracting substrings, and splitting a string into an array. You put all these skills together in an interesting and non-trivial application. You should be proud of your efforts so far.

CHALLENGES

1. **Add the ability to use diagonals in your puzzles. (Hint: All you'll need to do is combine the formulas I've already established. You don't need any new ones.)**
2. **Create a game of BattleShip for two players on the same computer. The game will print out a grid. (Pre-set the location of the fleets to make it easier.) Let the user choose a location on the grid with a checkbox. Report the result of his firing back, and then give the screen to the second user.**
3. **Write a version of Conway's Life. This program simulates cellular life on a grid with three simple rules.**
   a. **Each cell with exactly three neighbors will become or remain alive.**
   b. **Each cell currently alive with exactly two neighbors remains alive.**
   c. **All other cells will die off.**
4. **Randomly generate the first cell and let the user press a button to generate the next generation.**

Working with Files

As your experience in programming grows, the relative importance of data becomes increasingly apparent. You began your understanding of data with simple variables, but learned how simple and more complex arrays can make your programs more flexible and more powerful. However, data stored in the computer's memory is transient, especially in the server environment. It is often necessary to store information in a form that is more permanent than the constructs you have learned so far. PHP provides a number of powerful functions for working with text files. With these skills, you will be able to create extremely useful programs. Specifically, you will learn how to:

- Open files for read, write, and append access.
- Use file handles to manipulate text files.
- Write data to a text file.
- Read data from a text file.
- Open an entire file into an array.
- Modify text data on the fly.
- Get information about all the files in a particular directory.
- Get a subset of files based on filenames.

Previewing the Quiz Machine

The main program for this chapter is a fun and powerful tool that can be used in many different ways. It is not simply one program, but a system of programs that work together to let you create, administer, and grade multiple choice quizzes automatically.

IN THE REAL WORLD

It would be reasonably easy to build an HTML page that presents a quiz and a PHP program to grade only that quiz. However, if you will want several quizzes, it might be worth the investment in time and energy to build a system that can automate the creation and administration of quizzes. The real power of programming comes into play not just when you solve one particular immediate problem, but when you can generate a general solution that can be applied to an entire range of related problems. The quiz machine is an example of exactly such a system. It takes a little more effort to build such a system in the beginning, but the effort really pays off when you have a system you can re-use many times.

Entering the Quiz Machine System

Figure 6.1 shows the main page of the system. The user will need a password to take a test, and a different administrator password to edit a test. In this case, I've entered the administrative password (it's "*absolute*" – like in "absolute beginner's guide") into the appropriate password box, and I'm going to edit the Monty Python quiz.

Editing a Quiz

If the user has the correct password, the screen shown in Figure 6.2 appears, displaying the requested quiz in a special format on the screen.

The quiz administrator can edit the quiz in a number of ways. Each quiz has a name, instructor e-mail address, and a password. Each question is stored in a single line with the question, four possible answers, and the correct answer separated by colon (:) characters.

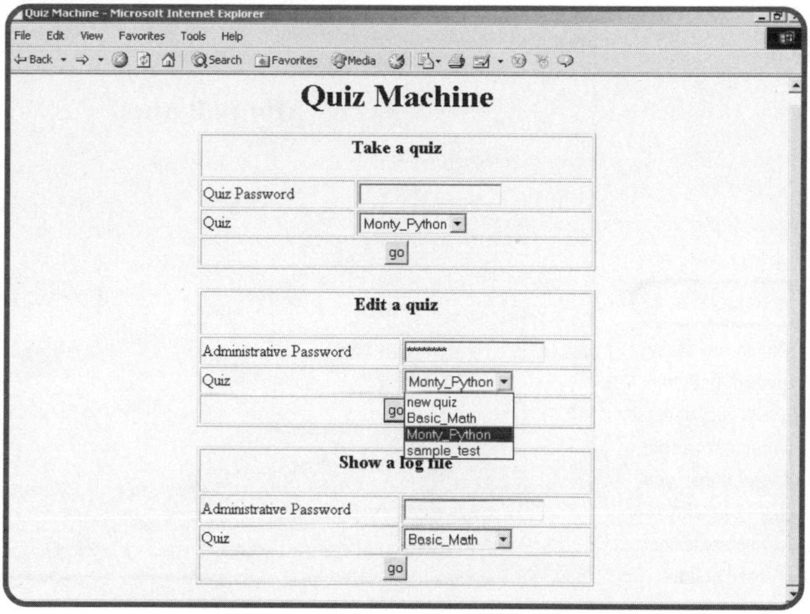

FIGURE 6.1

The user is an administrator, preparing to edit a quiz.

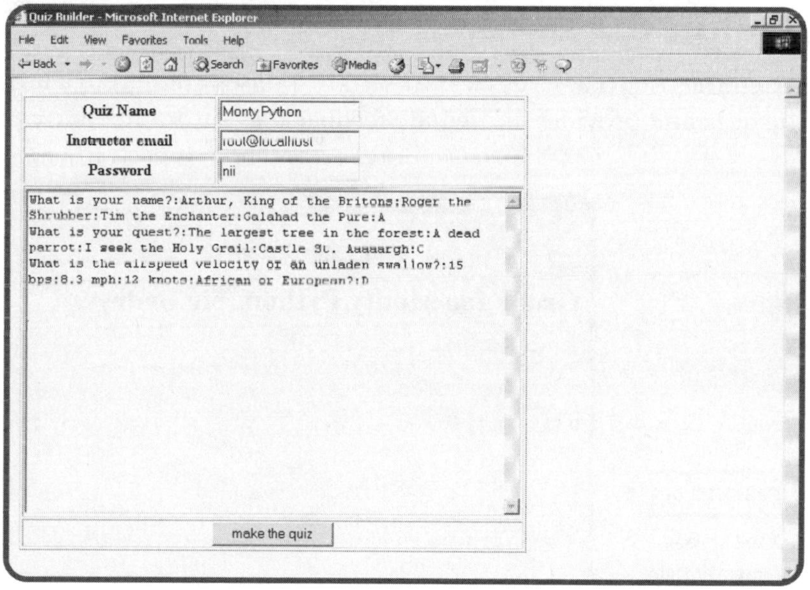

FIGURE 6.2

The user has chosen to edit the Monty Python quiz.

Taking a Quiz

Users with knowledge of the appropriate password can take any of the quizzes known to the system. If a user chooses to take the Monty Python quiz, the screen shown in Figure 6.3 appears.

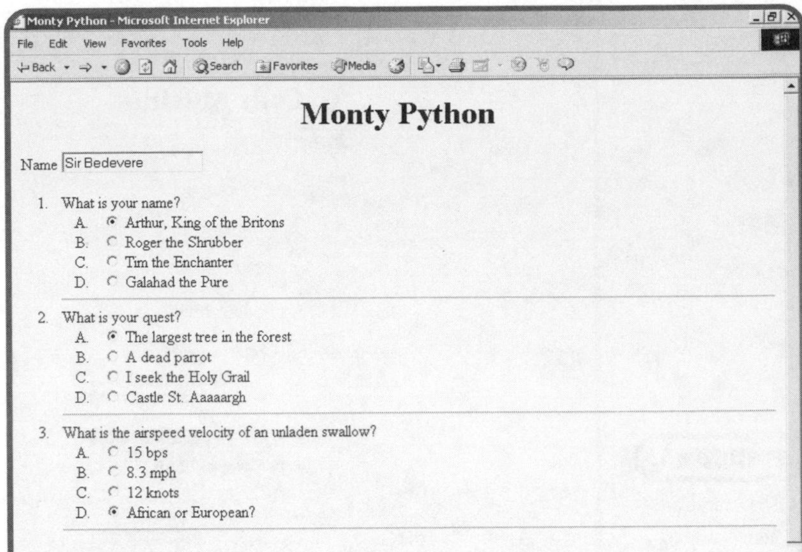

FIGURE 6.3

The user is taking the Monty Python quiz. If you want to become a serious programmer, you should probably rent this movie. It's part of the culture.

Seeing the Results

When the user takes a quiz, the user's responses are sent to a program that grades the quiz and provides immediate feedback, as shown in Figure 6.4

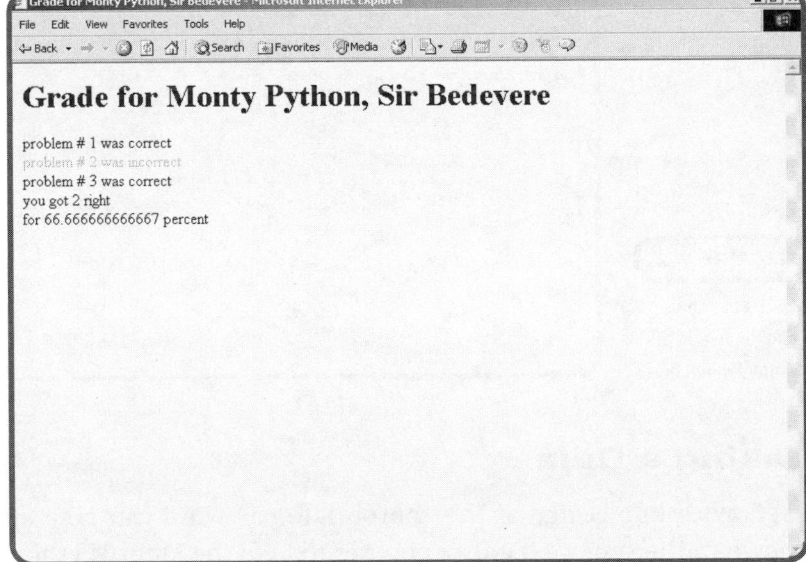

FIGURE 6.4

The grading program provides immediate feedback to the user and stores the information in a file so the administrator can see it later.

Viewing the Quiz Log

The system keeps a log file for each quiz so the administrator can tell the scores of each person who took the quiz. Figure 6.5 shows how people have done on the Monty Python quiz.

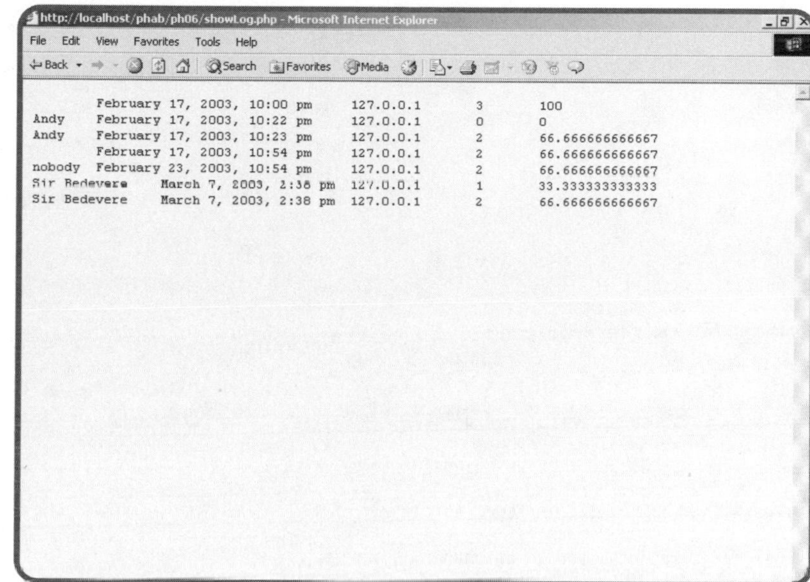

FIGURE 6.5

The log retrieval program presents an activity log for each quiz.

Although the resulting log looks very simplistic, it is generated in a format that can easily be imported into most gradebook programs and spreadsheets. This is very handy if the quiz will be used in a classroom setting.

Saving a File to the File System

Your PHP programs can access the server's file system to store and retrieve information. Your programs can create new files, add data to files, and read information from the files. You'll start by writing a program that creates a file and adds data to it.

Introducing the saveSonnet.php Program

The `saveSonnet.php` program shown in the following code listing opens a file on the server and writes one of Shakespeare's sonnets to that file on the server.

Normally I show you a screen shot of every program, but since this particular program doesn't actually display anything on the screen, that won't be useful to you. The next couple of programs will read this file and display it on the screen, and I'll show you what they look like when the time comes.

```
<head>
<title>SaveSonnet</title>
</head>
<body>
<?

$sonnet76 = <<<HERE
Sonnet # 76, William Shakespeare

Why is my verse so barren of new pride,
So far from variation or quick change?
Why with the time do I not glance aside
To new-found methods, and to compounds strange?
Why write I still all one, ever the same,
And keep invention in a noted weed,
That every word doth almost tell my name,
Showing their birth, and where they did proceed?
O! know sweet love I always write of you,
And you and love are still my argument;
So all my best is dressing old words new,
Spending again what is already spent:
For as the sun is daily new and old,
So is my love still telling what is told.

HERE;

$fp = fopen("sonnet76.txt", "w");
fputs($fp, $sonnet76);
```

```
fclose($fp);

?>
</body>
</html>
```

Most of the code stores the content's of Shakespeare's 76th sonnet to a variable called `$sonnet76`. The remaining three lines save the data in the variable to a text file.

Opening a File with fopen()

The `fopen()` command is used to open a file. Note that you can only create files on the Web server. You cannot directly create a file on the client machine, because you do not have access to that machine's file system. (If you did, any server-side program would be able to create viruses with extreme ease.) However, as a server-side programmer, you already have the ability to create files on the server. The programs you are writing are themselves files. Your programs can write files as if they are you.

Actually the ownership of files created by your PHP programs can be a little more complicated, depending on your operating system, server, and PHP configurations. Generally, any file created by your program will be owned by a special user called PHP or by the account you were in when you wrote the program. This makes a big difference in an OS like UNIX where file ownership is a major part of the security mechanism. The best way to discover how this works is to write a program that creates a file and then look at that file's properties.

The first parameter of the `fopen()` function is the filename. This filename can include directory information, or it can be a relative reference.

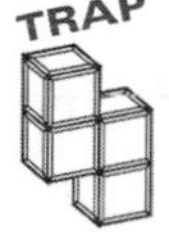

You should always test your programs, especially if they use a relative reference for a filename. It's possible that your current directory is not the default directory. Also, the filename is based on the actual file system of the server, rather than the URL of the file.

You can create a file anywhere on the server that you have access to. Your files can be in the parts of your directory system open to the Web server (usually subdirectories of `public_html` or `htdocs`). Sometimes, though, you might not want your files to be directly accessible to users by typing a URL. You can control access to these files by placing them outside the public html space and by setting the permissions so they can be read by you (and programs you create) but not by anyone else.

Creating a File Handle

When you create a file with the `fopen()` command, the function returns an integer called a *file handle* (sometimes also called a *file pointer*). This special number will be used to refer to the file in subsequent commands. You won't usually be concerned about the actual value of this handle, but you will need to store it in a variable (I usually use `$fp`) so that your other file access commands know which file to work with.

Examining File Access Modifiers

The final parameter in the `fopen()` command is an access modifier. PHP supports a number of access modifiers that determine how your program will interact with the file. Files are usually opened for reading, writing, or appending. You can also use a file for simultaneous input and output, but such files are often not needed in PHP, because the relational database techniques you'll learn in the next couple of chapters provide the same capability with more flexibility and a lot less work. However, the other forms of file access (read, write, and output) are extremely useful, because they provide easy access to the file information. (See Table 6.1 for a list of file access modifiers with descriptions.)

TABLE 6.1 FILE ACCESS MODIFIERS

Modifier	Type	Description
"r"	read-only	program can read from the file
"w"	write	writes to the file, overwriting it if it already exists
"a"	append	writes to the end of the file
"r+" "w+"	read and write	

The file access modifiers determine what you can do with the file. Read mode opens a file for input, so your program can read information in from the file. You cannot write data to a file that is opened in read mode. You'll see an example of the read mode in action in the next section, "Loading a File from the Drive System." Write mode allows you to open a file for output access. If the file does not exist, PHP automatically creates it for you.

Be very careful about opening a file in write mode. If a file already exists and you open it for write access, PHP will create a new file, overwriting the old file and destroying its contents.

Append mode allows you to write to a file without destroying the current contents. When you write to a file in append mode, all new data is added to the end of the file.

> **IN THE REAL WORLD**
>
> **The "r+" and "w+" modifiers are used for another form of file access, called "random access," which allows simultaneous reading and writing to the same file. While this is a very useful tool, I won't spend a lot of time on it in this introductory book. The sequential access methods you'll learn in this chapter are fine for simple file storage problems, and the relational database functions that you'll learn in the remainder of this book aren't any more difficult than the random access model, and provide far more power.**

Writing to a File

The `saveSonnet` program opens up the `sonnet76.txt` file for write access. If there was already a file in the current directory, it is destroyed. The file pointer for the text file is stored in the `$fp` variable. Once this is done, I can use the `fputs()` function to actually write data to the file.

You might be noticing a trend here. Most of the file access functions begin with the letter `f` (`fopen()`, `fclose()`, `fputs()`, `fgets()`, `feof()`.) This is a convention inherited from the C language. It can sometimes help you remember that a particular function works with files. Of course, every statement in PHP that begins with `f` isn't necessarily a file function (`foreach` is a good example), but most of the function names in PHP that begin with `f` are file-handling commands.

The `fputs()` function requires two parameters. The first is a file pointer. This tells PHP where to write the data. The second parameter is the text to write out to the file.

Closing a File

The `fclose()` function tells the system that your program is done working with the file, and should close it up.

Drive systems are much slower than computer memory, and they take a long time to spool up to speed. For that reason, when a program encounters an `fputs()` command, it doesn't always immediately save the data to a file on the disk. Instead, it adds the data to a special buffer and only writes the data when a sufficient amount is on the buffer or the program encounters an `fclose()` command. This is why it's important to close your files. If the program ends without encountering an `fclose()` statement, PHP is supposed to automatically close the file for you, but what's supposed to happen and what actually happens are often two very different things.

Loading a File from the Drive System

It is important that you can also retrieve information from the file system. If you open a file with the "r" access modifier, you will be able to read information from the file.

Introducing the loadSonnet.php Program

The `loadSonnet.php` program, shown in Figure 6.6 loads up the sonnet saved by `saveSonnet.php` and displays it as befits the work of the Bard.

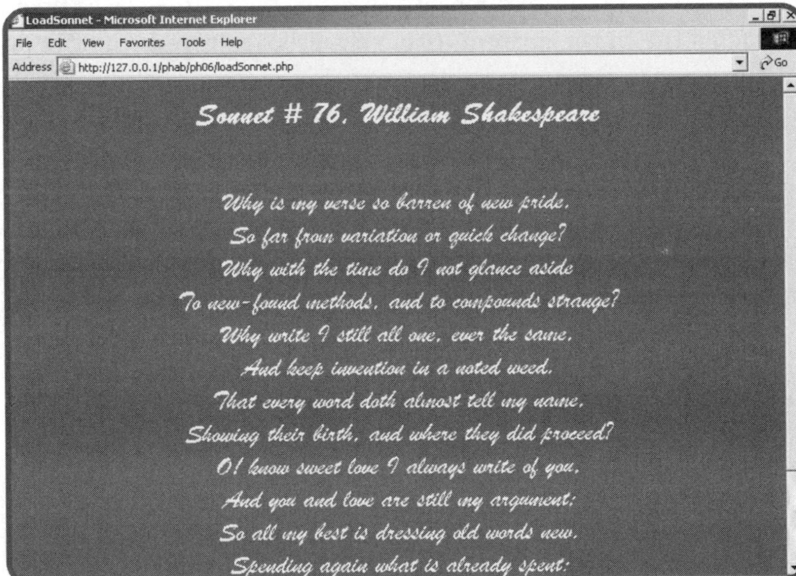

FIGURE 6.6

The file has been loaded from the drive system and prettied up a bit with some CSS tricks.

The code for the `loadSonnet` program follows:

```
<html>
<head>
```

```
<title>LoadSonnet</title>
<style type = "text/css">
body{
  background-color:darkred;
  color:white;
  font-family:'Brush Script MT', script;
  font-size:20pt
}
</style>

</head>
<body>
<?
$fp = fopen("sonnet76.txt", "r");

//first line is title
$line = fgets($fp);
print "<center><h1>$line</h1></center>\n";

print "<center>\n";
//print rest of sonnet
while (!feof($fp)){
  $line = fgets($fp);
  print "$line <br>\n";
} // end while

print "</center>\n";

fclose($fp);

?>

</body>
</html>
```

Using CSS to Beautify the Output

The best way to improve the appearance of text is with CSS styles. By setting up a simple stylesheet, I was able to very quickly improve the appearance of the sonnet without changing the actual text of the sonnet at all. Notice especially how I indicated multiple fonts in case my preferred font was not installed on the user's system.

Using the "r" Access Modifier

In order to read from a file, you must get a file pointer by opening that file for "r" access. If the file does not exist, you will get the result `FALSE` rather than a file pointer.

You can actually open files anywhere on the Internet for read access. If you supply a URL as a filename, you will be able to read the URL as if it were a local file. However, you cannot open URL files for output.

I opened "sonnet76.txt" with the `fopen()` command using the "r" access modifier, and again copied the resulting integer to the `$fp` file pointer variable.

Checking for the End of the File with feof()

When you are reading data from a file, your program doesn't generally know how long the file will be. The `fgets()` command that you will frequently use to get data from a file reads one line of the file at a time. Since you can't be sure how many lines are in a file until you read it, PHP provides a special function called `feof()`, which stands for file end of file (apparently named by the department of redundancy department). This function returns the value `FALSE` if there are any more lines of data left in the file, and `TRUE` when the program is at the end of the data file. Most of the time when you read data from the file, you'll use a `while` loop that continues as long as `feof()` is not true. The easiest way to set up this loop is with a statement like this:

```
while (!feof($fp)){
```

The `feof()` function requires a file pointer as its sole parameter.

Reading Data from the File with fgets()

The `fgets()` function gets one line of data from the file, returns that value as a string, and moves a special pointer to the next line of the file. Usually this function is called inside a loop that continues until `feof()` is true.

Reading a File into an Array

It is often useful to work with a file as an array of data in memory. Frequently you might find yourself doing some operation on each line of an array. PHP provides a couple of features that simplify this type of operation. The `cartoonifier.php` program demonstrates one way of manipulating an entire file without using a file pointer.

Introducing the cartoonifier.php Program

The `cartoonifier.php` program illustrated in Figure 6.7 is a truly serious and weighty use of advanced server technology.

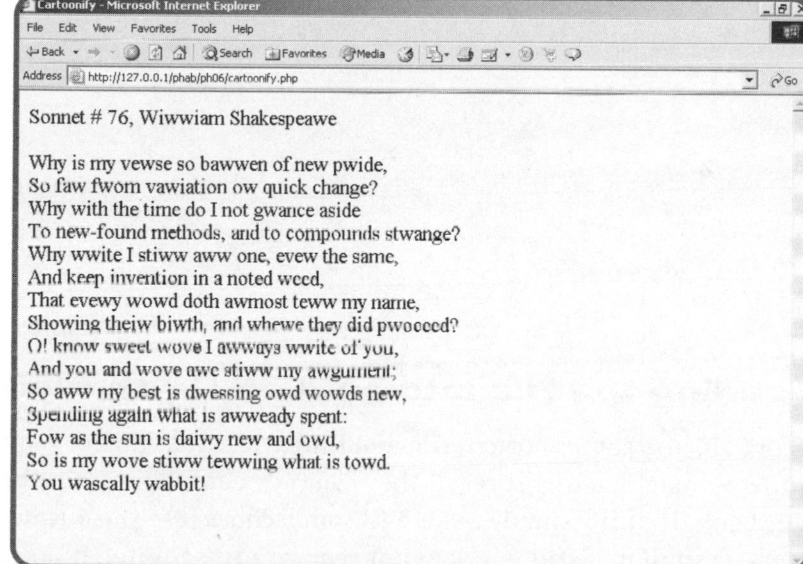

FIGURE 6.7

The cartoonifier program shows what would happen if Shakespeare were a cartoon character.

This program loads the entire sonnet into an array, steps through each line of the poem, and converts it to a unique cartoon dialect by performing a search and replace operation.

```
<html>
<head>
<title>Cartoonify</title>
</head>
<body>
<?
```

```
$fileName = "sonnet76.txt";

$sonnet = file($fileName);
$output = "";

foreach ($sonnet as $currentLine){
  $currentLine = str_replace("r", "w", $currentLine);
  $currentLine = str_replace("l", "w", $currentLine);
  $output .= rtrim($currentLine) . "<br>\n";
} // end foreach
  $output .= "You wascally wabbit!<br>\n";

print $output;

?>
</body>
</html>
```

Loading the File into an Array with file()

There are also some shortcut file handling tricks that do not require you to create a file pointer. You might recall the `readFile()` command from the first chapter of this book. That file simply reads a file and echoes it to the output. The `file()` command is similar, because it does not require a file pointer. It opens a file for input and returns an array, with each line of the file occupying one element of the array. This can be an extremely easy way to work with files, because you can then use a `foreach` loop to step through each line of the file and perform modifications on it.

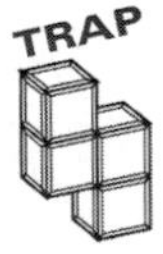

Reading an file into an array is attractive because it's easy and because once the file is in memory, you can work with it very quickly. The problem comes when you are working with very large files. The computer's memory is finite, and large files can quickly cause you problems. For larger data files, you'll probably want to use a one-line at a time approach using the `fgets()` function inside a loop.

Using str_replace() to Modify File Contents

Inside the `foreach` loop, it's a simple matter to convert all occurrences of "r" and "l" to the letter "w" with the `str_replace()` function. The resulting string is then added to the `$output` variable which will ultimately be printed to the screen.

IN THE REAL WORLD

This particular application is silly and pointless, but the ability to replace all occurrences of one string with another in a text file is very useful in a variety of circumstances. For example, you could replace every occurrence of the left brace (<) character in an HTML document with the `<` sequence. This would result in a source code listing that could be directly viewed on the browser. Also, you might use such technology for form letters, where you take information in a text template and replace it with values pulled from the user or from another file.

Working with Directory Information

When you are working with file systems, you often also need to work with the directory structure that contains the files. PHP contains several commands that assist in the manipulation of directories.

Introducing the imageIndex.php Program

The `imageIndex.php` program featured in Figure 6.8 is a simple utility that generates an index of all jpg and gif image files in a particular directory.

When the user clicks on any thumbnail image, a full version of the image will be displayed. The techniques used to display the image files can be used to get selected sets of files from any directory.

```
<html>
<head>
<title>imageIndex</title>
</head>
<body>

<?
// image index
```

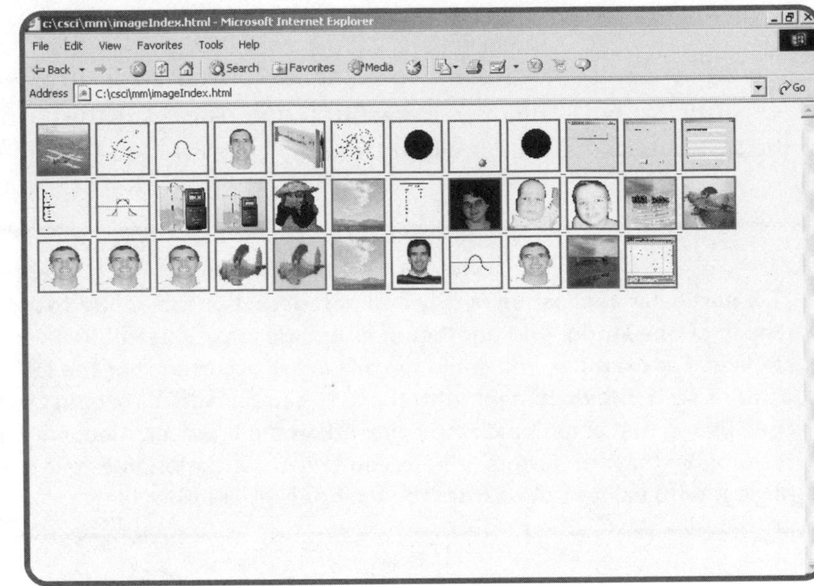

FIGURE 6.8

This HTML file was automatically created by `imageIndex.php`.

```
// generates an index file containing all images in a particular directory


//point to whatever directory you wish to index.
//index will be written to this directory as imageIndex.html
$dirName = "C:\csci\mm";
$dp = opendir($dirName);
chdir($dirName);

//add all files in directory to $theFiles array
while ($currentFile !== false){
  $currentFile = readDir($dp);
  $theFiles[] = $currentFile;
} // end while

//extract gif and jpg images
$imageFiles = preg_grep("/jpg$|gif$/", $theFiles);

$output = "";
foreach ($imageFiles as $currentFile){
```

```
  $output .= <<<HERE
<a href = $currentFile>
  <img src = "$currentFile"
       height = 50
       width = 50>
</a>

HERE;

} // end foreach

//save the index to the local file system
$fp = fopen("imageIndex.html", "w");
fputs ($fp, $output);
fclose($fp);
//readFile("imageIndex.html");
print "<a href = $dirName/imageIndex.html>image index</a>\n";

 ?>

</body>
</html>
```

Creating a Directory Handle with openDir()

Of course directory operations focus on a particular directory. It's often smart to store a directory name in a variable so it can be easily changed, as directory conventions change when you migrate your programs to different systems. In the `imageIndex` program, I stored the target directory in a variable called `$dirName`. The directory can be stored as a relative reference (in which case it will be located in reference to the current program's directory) or absolute (in the current file system).

Getting a List of Files with readdir()

The `readdir()` function is used to read a file from a valid directory pointer. Each time you call the `readdir()` function, it returns the name of the next file it finds, until there are no files left. If the function cannot find another file, it will return the value `FALSE`. I find it very useful to store all the files of a directory into an array, so I'll usually use a loop like this:

```
while ($currentFile !== false){
  $currentFile = readDir($dp);
  $theFiles[] = $currentFile;
} // end while
```

This loop keeps going until the `$currentFile` variable is false, which will happen when there are no files left in the directory. Each time through the loop, it uses the `readdir()` function to load a new value into `$currentFile`, then adds the value of `$currentFile` to the `$theFiles` array. Note that when I assign a value to an array without specifying the index, the item is simply placed at the next available index value. This is an easy way to load up an array in PHP.

The special !== operator is a little bit different than the comparison operators you have seen before. It is used here to prevent a very specific type of error. It's possible that the user might have a file actually called "false" in the directory. If that's the case, the more normal condition `$currentFile != false` would give a strange result, because PHP could confuse a file named "false" with the actual literal value `false`. The !== operator specifies a comparison between actual objects rather than values, and it will work correctly in this particular odd circumstance.

Selecting Particular Files with preg_grep()

Once all the files from a particular directory are stored in an array, you'll often want to select a subset of those files to work with. In this particular case, I'm interested in graphic files, which end with the characters "gif" or "jpg." The oddly-named `preg_grep()` function is perfect for this type of situation. It borrows some clever ideas from UNIX shells and the perl programming language. Grep is the name of a UNIX command that allows you to filter files according to a pattern. The "preg" part indicates that this form of grep uses perl-style regular expressions. Regardless of the funny name, the function is very handy. If you look back at the code in `imageIndex.php`, you'll see the line

```
$imageFiles = preg_grep("/jpg$|gif$/", $theFiles);
```

This code selects all the files that end with "jpg" or "gif" and copies them to another array called `$imageFiles`.

Using Basic Regular Expressions

While it would be possible to use string manipulation functions to determine which files to copy to the new array, there are many situations where you might want the ability to work with string data in a more detailed way. In this particular situation, I wanted all the files with "gif" *or* "jpg" in them. There isn't an easy way to compare for two possible values with normal string manipulations. Also, I didn't want *any* filename containing these two values, but only those filenames that *end* with "gif" or "jpg." Regular expressions are a special convention often used to handle exactly this kind of situation, and much more. To illustrate, I'll explain how the `"/jpg$|gif$/"` expression works. Regular expressions are usually marked by slashes at the beginning and the end. The first and last characters of the expression are these slashes. The pipe (|) character indicates *or*, so I'm looking for "jpg" or "gif." The dollar sign ($) indicates the end of a string in the context of regular expressions, so "jpg$" will only match on the value "jpg" if it's at the end of a string. So, the expression `"/jpg$|gif$/"` will match on any string that ends with "jpg" or "gif."

Regular expressions are extremely powerful if a bit cryptic. PHP supports a number of special functions that use regular expressions in addition to `preg_grep`. Look in the online help under "Regular Expression Functions – Perl compatible" for a list of these functions as well as more details on how regular expressions work in PHP. If you find regular expressions baffling, you can usually find a string manipulation function or two that will do the same general job. (See Table 6.2 for a list of basic regular expressions.)

Storing the Output

Once the `$imageFiles` array is completed, the program uses the data to build an HTML index of all images, and stores that data to a file. Since it's been a few pages since you've seen that code, I'll reproduce a piece of it here.

```
foreach ($imageFiles as $currentFile){
  $output .= <<<HERE
<a href = $currentFile>
  <img src = "$currentFile"
       height = 50
       width = 50>
```

Table 6.2 Summary of Basic Regular Expression Operators

operator	description	sample pattern	matches	doesn't match
.	any character but newline	.	e	\n
^	beginning of string	^a	apple	banana
$	end of string	a$	banana	apple
[*characters*]	any characters in braces	[abcABC]	a	d
[*char range*]	describe range of characters	[a-zA-z]	r	9
\d	any digit	\d\d\d-\d\d\d\d	123-4567	the-thing
\b	word boundary	\bthe\b	the	theater
+	one or more occurrences of preceding character	\d+	1234	text
*	zero or more occurrences of preceding character	[a-zA-z]\d*		
{*digit*}	repeat preceding character that many times	\d{3}-\d{4}	123-4567	999-99-9999
|	or operator	apple|banana	apple, banana	peach
(*pattern segment*)	store results in pattern memory returned with numeric code	(^.).*/1	gig, blab (any word that starts and ends w/ same letter)	any other word

```
</a>

HERE;

} // end foreach

//save the index to the local file system
$fp = fopen("imageIndex.html", "w");
fputs ($fp, $output);
fclose($fp);

print "<a href = $dirName/imageIndex.html>image index</a>\n";
```

I used a `foreach` loop to step through each element of the `$imageFiles` array. I added the HTML to generate a thumbnail version of each image to a variable called `$output`. Finally, I opened a file called `imageIndex.html` in the current directory for writing, put the value of `$output` to the file, and closed the file handle. Finally, I added a link to the file.

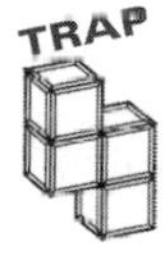

You might be tempted to use a `readFile()` command to immediately view the contents of the file. (I was.) This may not work correctly, because the Web browser is assuming the `imageList.php` directory is the current directory. Inside the program, I changed to another directory within the local file system, but the Web browser has no way of knowing that. When I did a `readFile()`, the HTML was full of broken links, because all of the relative links in the HTML page were pointing towards files in another directory. When I add a link to the page instead, the Web browser itself can find all the images, because it's being sent to the correct directory.

Working with Formatted Text

Text files are easy to work with, but they are extremely unstructured. Sometimes you might want to impose a little bit of formatting on a text file in order to work with data in the file. You'll learn some more formal data management skills in the next couple of chapters, but with a few simple tricks you can do quite a lot with plain text files.

Introducing the mailMerge.php Program

To illustrate how text files can be used for basic data storage, I created a simple mail merge program. The results of this program are shown in Figure 6.9.

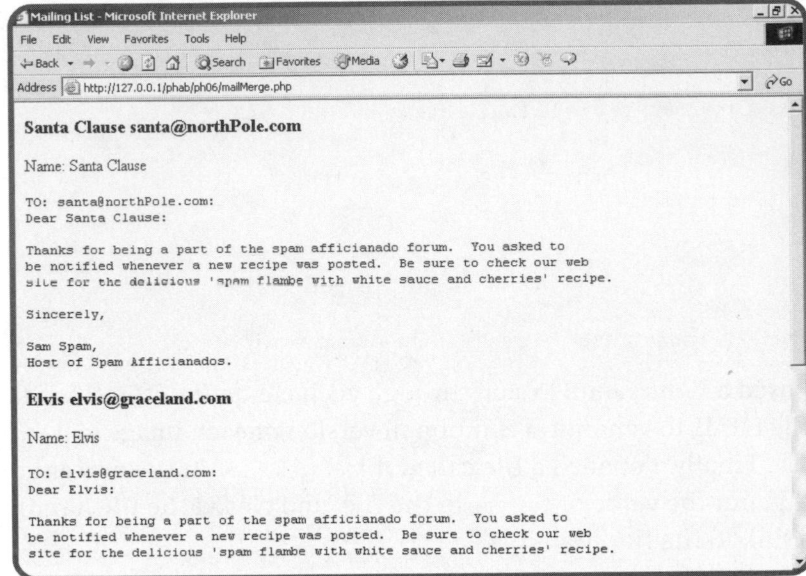

FIGURE 6.9

The program created several form letters from a list of names and e-mail addresses.

You can see that the same letter was used repeatedly, but each time it used a different name and e-mail address. The name and e-mail information was pulled from a file.

Determining a Data Format

The data file (shown in Figure 6.10) for this program is simply a file created in Notepad. Each line consists of a name and an e-mail address, separated by a tab character.

This particular format (one line per record, each field separated by tabs) is called a tab-delimited file, and it is extremely popular, because you can easily create it in a text editor, spreadsheet, or any other kind of program you wish. It's also quite easy to use another character as a separator. Spreadsheet programs often save in a comma-delimited format (CSV for comma-separated values) but string data does not work well in this format because it might already have commas embedded in it.

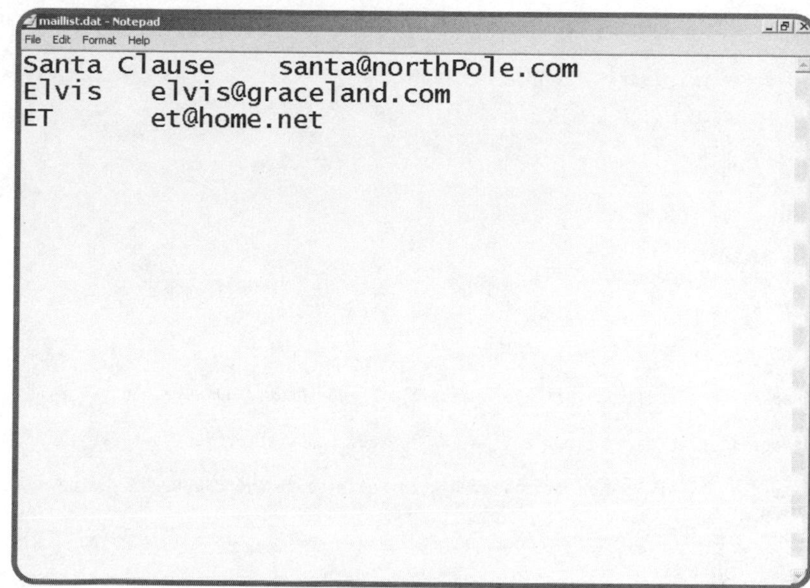

FIGURE 6.10

The data file for this program was created in Notepad.

Examining the mailMerge.php Code

The basic strategy for the mailMerge program is very simple. Take a look at the code for the program, and you might be surprised at how easy it is.

```
<html>
<head>
<title>Mailing List</title>
</head>
<body>
<form>

<?
//Simple Mail merge
//presumes tab-delimited file called maillist.dat

$theData = file("maillist.dat");

foreach($theData as $line){
  $line = rtrim($line);
```

```
  print "<h3>$line</h3>";
  list($name, $email) = split("\t", $line);
  print "Name: $name";

  $message = <<<HERE
TO: $email:
Dear $name:

Thanks for being a part of the spam afficionado forum. You asked to
be notified whenever a new recipe was posted. Be sure to check our web
site for the delicious 'spam flambe with white sauce and cherries' recipe.

Sincerely,

Sam Spam,
Host of Spam Afficionados.

HERE;

  print "<pre>$message</pre>";

} // end foreach

?>
</body>
</html>
```

Loading the Data with the file() Command

The first step is to load the data into the form. Instead of using the file pointer technique from earlier in the chapter, I used a special shortcut that can be extremely handy. The `file()` command takes a filename and automatically loads that file into an array. Each line of the file becomes an element of the array. This is especially useful when your text file contains data, because each line in my data file represents one individual's data.

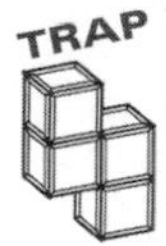

The `file()` command is so easy you might be tempted to use it all the time, but it loads the entire file into memory, so you should only use it for relatively small files. When you use the `fgets()` technique, you only need to have one line from the file in memory at a time, so the `fgets()` method can be effectively used on any size file without affecting performance. Using `file()` on a very large file can be extremely slow.

Splitting a Line into an Array to Scalar Values

You might recall the `split()` function from Chapter 5, "Better Arrays and String Handling." This function is used to separate elements of a string based on some delimiter. I used the `split()` function inside a `foreach` loop to break each line into its constituent values. However, I really didn't want an array in this situation. Instead, I wanted the first value on the line to be read into the `$name` variable, and the second value should be stored in `$email`. The `list()` function allows you to take an array and distribute its contents into scalar (non-array) variables. In this particular situation, I never stored the results of the `split()` function in an array at all, but immediately `list`ed the contents into the appropriate scalar variables. Once the data is in the variables, it can be easily interpolated into a mail-merge message.

In the Real World

The next obvious step for this program would be to automatically send each message as an e-mail. PHP provides a function called `mail()` which makes it quite easy to add this functionality. However, the way the function works is very dependent on how the server is set up, and it won't work with equal reliability on every server.

Also, there are good reasons to send e-mail through a program, and reasons that aren't so good. It's completely legitimate to send e-mails to people when they request it, or to have a program send you e-mails when certain things happen. For example, my own more secure version of the tester program sends me an e-mail to alert when certain conditions that might indicate cheating occur. A program that sends unsolicited e-mail to people is rude, and will cause bad feelings about your site.

Creating the Quiz Machine Program

The quiz tool from the beginning of this chapter is actually an entire system of programs designed to work together, in this case, five different programs Each quiz is stored in two separate files, which are automatically generated by the programs. Figure 6.11 is a flow diagram that illustrates how the various programs fit together.

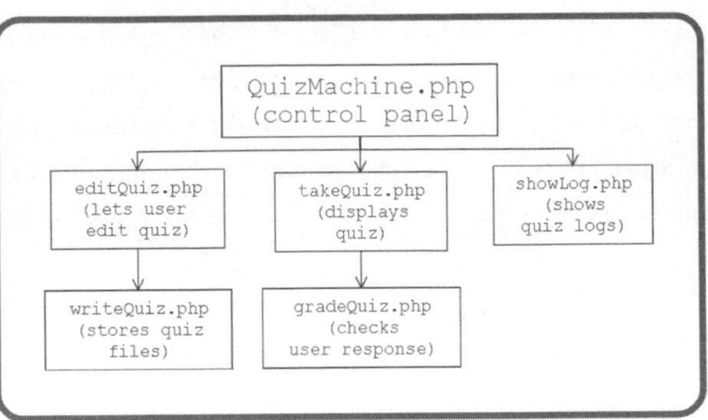

FIGURE 6.11

This diagram illustrates a user's movement through the quiz machine system.

The `QuizMachine.php` program is the entry point into the system for both the test administrator and the person who will be taking the quiz. It essentially consists of three forms that allow access to the other parts of the program. To ensure a minimal level of security, all other programs in the system require some sort of password access. The `QuizMachine` program primarily serves as a gateway to the other parts of the system. If the user has administrative access (determined by a password), he or she can select an exam and call the `editQuiz.php` page. This page loads up the actual master file of the quiz (if it already exists) or sets up a prototype quiz, and places the quiz data in a Web page as a simple editor. The `editQuiz` program calls the `writeQuiz.php` program, which takes the results of the `editQuiz` form, and writes it to a master test file as well as an HTML page.

If the user wants to take a quiz, the system moves to the `takeQuiz.php` page, which checks the user's password and presents the quiz if authorized. When the user indicates he or she is finished, the `gradeQuiz.php` program grades the quiz and stores the result in a text file.

Finally, the administrator can examine the log files resulting from any of the quizzes by indicating a quiz from the `QuizMachine` page. The `showLog.php` program will display the appropriate log file.

Building the QuizMachine.php Control Page

The heart of the quiz system is the `quizMachine.php` page. This is the only page that the user will enter directly. All the other parts of the system will be called from this page or from one of the pages it calls. The purpose of this page is to act as a control panel. It consists of three parts, corresponding to the three primary jobs that can be done with this system: Writing or editing quizzes, taking quizzes, and analyzing the results of quizzes. In each of these cases, the user will have a particular quiz in mind, so the control panel automatically provides a list of appropriate files in each segment. Also, each of these tasks requires a password, to provide at least some level of security.

The main part of the `QuizMachine.php` program simply sets up the opening HTML and calls a series of functions, which will actually do all the real work.

```
<html>
<head>
<title>Quiz Machine</title>
</head>
<body>
<center>
<h1>Quiz Machine</h1>

<?

getFiles();
showTest();
showEdit();
showLog();
```

The program will call `getFiles()` first. This function will examine a directory and get a list of the files in that directory. This list of filenames will be used in the other functions. The next three functions all generate HTML forms. Each of these forms contains a select list that is dynamically generated from the file list. The button corresponding to each form submits the form to the appropriate PHP page in the system.

You might want to make another version of this main page for the people who will take your test. On that page, you wouldn't even show the administrative options. It's very easy to make such a page. Simply copy the `QuizBuilder.php` program to another file, and comment out the calls to the `showEdit()` and `showLog()` functions.

Getting the File List

Since most of the code in the `QuizBuilder` program works with a list of files, the `getFiles()` function is charged with that important task.

```
function getFiles(){
  //get list of all files for use in other routines

  global $dirPtr, $theFiles;

  chdir(".");
  $dirPtr = openDir(".");
  $currentFile = readDir($dirPtr);
  while ($currentFile !== false){
    $theFiles[] = $currentFile;
    $currentFile = readDir($dirPtr);
  } // end while

} // end getFiles
```

The first thing this function does is to change the file system so it is pointing at the current directory, and set up a pointer variable to that directory.

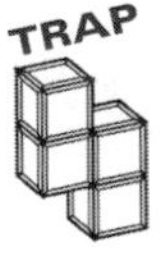

The directory that holds the PHP programs is open for anybody to see. You might want to have your test files not so conspicuous. To simplify this example, I kept all the test files in the same directory as the program itself, but you can keep all the data files in a different directory if you wish. For security reasons, you might choose to store all the data files in a part of your directory that is not available to the Web (away from your `public_html` structure, for instance) so that people can't see the answer key by browsing to it. If you choose to do this, you'll need to change each directory reference throughout the system.

I then created an array called `theFiles`, which holds the name of every file in the directory. The `theFiles` variable is global, so it will be shared with the program and other functions that declare a reference to it.

Showing the "Take a Test" List

Most of your users will not be creating or editing quizzes. Instead, they will be taking them. In order to take a test, the user must choose a test and have the password associated with that test. To simplify choosing a test, the `showTest()` function grabs all the HTML files in the quiz directory and places them in a select list. The password goes in an ordinary password field. The code in `showTest()` creates a form that calls the `takeQuiz.php` program when it is submitted.

```
function showTest(){
  //print a list of tests for user to take

  global $theFiles;
  print <<<HERE
<form action = "takeQuiz.php"
      method = "post">

<table border = 1
       width = 400>
<tr>
  <td colspan = 2><center>
    <h3>Take a quiz</h3>
  </td>
</tr>

<tr>
  <td>Quiz Password</td>
  <td>
    <input type = "password"
           name = "password">
  </td>
</tr>

<tr>
  <td>Quiz</td>
```

```
  <td>
    <select name = "takeFile">

HERE;

  //select only quiz html files
  $testFiles = preg_grep("/html$/", $theFiles);

  foreach ($testFiles as $myFile){
    $fileBase = substr($myFile, 0, strlen($myFile) - 5);
    print "    <option value = $fileBase>$fileBase</option>\n";
  } // end foreach

  print <<<HERE
    </select>
  </td>
</tr>

<tr>
  <td colspan = 2><center>
    <input type = "submit"
           value = "go">
  </center></td>
</tr>
</table>

</form>

HERE;

} // end showTest
```

Although the code is long, almost all of it is pure HTML. The only part that's really PHP code is the part that selects HTML files and places them in the select group.

This code fragment uses the `preg_grep()` to select filenames ending in "HTML" and creates an option tag for that file. Note that I stripped out the `.html` part of the filename, because I won't really need it, and it would complicate some of the code coming up in the `takeQuiz` program.

Showing the Edit List

The `showEdit()` function works a lot like `showTest()`. This function is used to display a list of the master files on the system. Although it will often be exactly the same as the list of tests, it won't always be the same, because there can be master files that haven't yet been made into HTML files.

```
function showEdit(){
  // let user select a master file to edit

  global $theFiles;
  //get only quiz master files
  $testFiles = preg_grep("/mas$/", $theFiles);

  //edit a quiz
  print <<<HERE
<form action = "editQuiz.php"
      method = "post">
<table border = 1
       width = 400>
<tr>
  <td colspan = 2><center>
    <h3>Edit a quiz</h3>
  </center></td>
</tr>

<tr>
  <td>Administrative Password</td>
  <td>
    <input type = "password"
           name = "password"
```

```
          value = "">
  </td>
</tr>

<tr>
  <td>Quiz</td>
  <td>
    <select name = "editFile">
      <option value = "new">new quiz</option>

HERE;
  foreach ($testFiles as $myFile){
    $fileBase = substr($myFile, 0, strlen($myFile) - 4);
    print "  <option value = $myFile>$fileBase</option>\n";
  } // end foreach

  print <<<HERE
    </select>
  </td>
</tr>

<tr>
  <td colspan = 2><center>
    <input type = "submit"
          value = "go">
  </center></td>
</tr>
</table>
</form>

HERE;

} // end showEdit
```

The showEdit() function is just like showQuiz() but the form points to the editQuiz.php program, and the file list is based on those files ending in "mas."

There's one other subtle but important difference. Look at the code for the select element and you'll see I added a "new quiz" option. If the user chooses this option, the editQuiz() function won't try to load a quiz file into memory, but will set up for a new quiz instead.

Showing the Log List

The last segment is meant for the quiz administrator. It allows the user with admin access to view the log of any quiz on the system. This will show who has taken the test, where and when they took it, and the score. When the user clicks on the Submit button associated with this part of the page, the showLog.php program will take over.

```
function showLog(){

  //let user choose from a list of log files
  global $theFiles;

  print <<<HERE

<form action = "showLog.php"
      method = "post">
<table border = 1
       width = 400>
<tr>
  <td colspan = 2><center>
    <h3>Show a log file</h3>
  </td>
</tr>

<tr>
  <td>Administrative Password</td>
  <td>
    <input type = "password"
           name = "password"
```

```
          value = "">
    </td>
  </tr>

  <tr>
    <td>Quiz</td>
    <td>
      <select name = "logFile">

HERE;

  //select only log files
  $logFiles = preg_grep("/log$/", $theFiles);
  foreach ($logFiles as $myFile){
    $fileBase = substr($myFile, 0, strlen($myFile) - 4);
    print "      <option value = $myFile>$fileBase</option>\n";
  } // end foreach

  print <<<HERE
    </select>
  </td>
</tr>

<tr>
  <td colspan = 2><center>
    <input type = "submit"
           value = "go">
  </td>
</tr>
</table>
</form>

HERE;
```

```
} // end showLog

?>

</center>
</body>
</html>
```

I decided that all log files would end with `.log`, so the program can easily get a list of log files to place in the select group.

Editing a Test

For simplicity's sake I decided on a very simple test format. The first three lines of the test file will contain the test's name, the instructor's e-mail address, and a password for the test. The test data itself will follow. Each problem will take up one line (although it can wrap freely— a line is defined by a carriage return character). The problem will have a question followed by four possible answers and the correct answer. Each of these elements will be separated by the colon (:) character.

IN THE REAL WORLD

If you think there are too many rules for how the questions are formatted, I agree. This is a limitation of the sequential file access technique you are using to store the data in this chapter. In later chapters, you'll learn some other ways to work with data that aren't quite so picky. However, this is a relatively easy way to store your data, so I wrote the program to assist the process as much as practical. In general, you'll want to write your program so the user never has to know the underlying data structure.

The `editQuiz.php` program is designed to assist the user in creating and editing quizzes. It's actually a very simple program, because the real work will happen after the user is finished editing and presses the Submit button.

Getting Existing Test Data

The first chore is to determine which quiz the user is requesting. Remember that the value "`new`" indicates that the user wants to build a new test, so that value is treated specially. Any other value will be the foundation of a test filename, so I open the appropriate master file and load its values into the appropriate elements on the form.

```
<html>
<head>
<title>Quiz Builder</title>
</head>
<body>
<?

if ($password != "absolute"){
  print <<<HERE

<font color = "red" size = +3>
Invalid Password!
</font>

HERE;
} else {
  //check to see if user has chosen a form to edit
  if ($editFile == "new"){
    //if it's a new file, put in some dummy values
    $quizName = "sample test";
    $quizEmail = "root@localhost";
    $quizData = "q:a:b:c:d:correct";
    $quizPwd = "php";
  } else {
    //open up the file and get the data from it
    $fp = fopen($editFile, "r");
    $quizName = fgets($fp);
    $quizEmail = fgets($fp);
    $quizPwd = fgets($fp);
    while (!feof($fp)){
      $quizData .= fgets($fp);
    } // end while
    fclose($fp);
 } // end 'new form' if
```

I decided to code the value "absolute" (from the name of this book series) as an administrative password. Each test will have its own password, and the administrative functions (like editing a quiz) have their own password. If the `password` field has any other value besides my chosen password, the program will indicate a problem and refuse to move forward.

This use of an administrative password will keep casual snoops out of your system, but it's nowhere near bullet-proof security. This system is not appropriate for situations where you must be absolutely certain that the tests are secure.

Once you know the user is authorized to edit tests, you need to determine if it's a new test or an existing quiz. If the quiz is new, I simply add some sample data to variables, which will be used for the upcoming form. If the user wants to see an existing test, I open the file for read access, and grab the first three lines, which will correspond to the `$quizName`, `$quizEmail`, and `$quizPwd` fields.

I then use a `foreach` loop to load up the rest of the file into the `$quizData` variable.

You might wonder why the quiz needs a password field if it already took a password to get to this form. The quiz system has multiple levels of security. Anybody can get to the `quizBuilder.php` page. However, in order to move to one of the other pages, the user has to have the right kind of password. Only an administrator should go to the `editPage` and `showLog` programs, so these programs require special administrative password access. Each quiz also has a password associated with it. The password is stored in the quiz master file so that you can associate a different password for each quiz. In this way, the users authorized to take one test won't be taking other tests (and adding confusion to your log files).

Printing Out the Form

Once the variables are loaded with appropriate values, it's a simple matter to print up an HTML form to let the user edit the quiz. The form is almost all pure HTML with the quiz variables interpolated into the appropriate places.

```
print <<<HERE


<form action = "writeQuiz.php"
```

```
     method = "post">

<table border = 1>
<tr>
  <th>Quiz Name</th>
  <td>
    <input type = "text"
           name = "quizName"
           value = "$quizName">
  </td>
</tr>

<tr>
  <th>Instructor email</th>
  <td>
    <input type = "text"
           name = "quizEmail"
           value = "$quizEmail">
  </td>
</tr>

<tr>
  <th>Password</th>
  <td>
    <input type = "text"
           name = "quizPwd"
           value = "$quizPwd">

<tr>
  <td rowspan = 1
      colspan = 2>
    <textarea name = "quizData"
              rows = 20
```

```
            cols = 60>
$quizData</textarea>
  </td>
</tr>

<tr>
  <td colspan = 2><center>
    <input type = "submit"
           value = "make the quiz">
  </center></td>
</tr>

</table>
</form>
HERE;
} // end if

?>
</body>
</html>
```

Writing the Test

Once the administrator has finished editing a quiz file, that quiz file must be stored to the file system, and an HTML page for the quiz needs to be generated. The `writeQuiz.php` program performs these duties.

Setting up the Main Logic

The first job is to create two files. The quiz name can be the foundation of the filename, but many file systems choke at spaces within filenames, so I use the `str_replace()` function to replace all spaces in `$quizName` to underscore characters (_). Then I create a filename for the master file ending in .mas and another filename for the actual quiz ending in .html. To create the HTML file, I open it up for write output. Then I use the `buildHTML()` function (which will be described shortly) to build the HTML code, and I write that code out to the html file and close the file.

The master file is built in pretty much the same way, except it calls the `buildMas()` function in order to create the appropriate text for the file.

```
<html>
<head>
<title>Write Quiz</title>
</head>
<body>
<?
//given a quiz file from editQuiz,
//generates a master file and an HTML file for the quiz

//open the output file
$fileBase = str_replace(" ", "_", $quizName);
$htmlFile = $fileBase . ".html";
$masFile = $fileBase . ".mas";

$htfp = fopen($htmlFile, "w");
$htData = buildHTML();
fputs($htfp, $htData);
fclose($htfp);

$msfp = fopen($masFile, "w");
$msData = buildMas();
fputs($msfp, $msData);
fclose($msfp);

//preview the actual master file
print <<<HERE
<pre>
$msData
</pre>

HERE;
```

To make sure things were going well, I added a check to the end of the page that prints out the actual contents of the master file. The output of this program lets the administrator check to see that the test is working correctly. The administrator can actually take the test and submit it to the grading program from this page. If there is a problem with the test, it's convenient to have the actual contents of the .mas file visible on the page. Of course, the final HTML page will not contain this data, because it holds the answers.

Building the Master File

The master file routine is very straightforward.

```
function buildMas(){
  //builds the master file
  global $quizName, $quizEmail, $quizPwd, $quizData;
  $msData = $quizName . "\n";
  $msData .= $quizEmail . "\n";
  $msData .= $quizPwd . "\n";
  $msData .=  $quizData;
  return $msData;
} // end buildMas
```

The critical part of this file is remembering the file structure rules, so any program that reads this file doesn't get confused. The quiz name should go on the first line, followed by a newline character. The `$quizEmail` and `$quizPwd` variables follow on their own lines, and finally all the `$quizData` (which will usually be several lines) should go to the end of the file. Note that the function doesn't actually store the data to the file, but returns it to the main program. This allows a little more flexibility, so I can write the data to both the file and the page.

Building The HTML File

The function that creates the HTML is a little more involved, but it still isn't too hard. The basic strategy is this: Build an HTML form containing all the questions. For each line of the master file, build a radio group. Place the question and all the possible answers in a set of nested `<ol>` elements. At the end of the page, there should be one Submit button. When the user clicks on the Submit button, the system will call the `gradeQuiz.php` page, which will evaluate the user's responses.

```
function buildHTML(){
  global $quizName, $quizData;
  $htData = <<<HERE
<html>
<head>
<title>$quizName</title>
</head>
<body>

HERE;

  //get the quiz data
  $problems = split("\n", $quizData);
  $htData .= <<<HERE
<center>
<h1>$quizName</h1>
</center>

<form action = "gradeQuiz.php"
      method = "post">

Name
<input type = "text"
       name = "student">

<ol>

HERE;
  $questionNumber = 1;

  foreach ($problems as $currentProblem){
      list($question, $answerA, $answerB, $answerC, $answerD, $correct) =
```

```
        split (":", $currentProblem);
        $htData .= <<<HERE
<li>
  $question
  <ol type = "A">
    <li>
      <input type = "radio"
             name = "quest[$questionNumber]"
             value = "A">
      $answerA
    </li>

    <li>
      <input type = "radio"
             name = "quest[$questionNumber]"
             value = "B">
      $answerB
    </li>

    <li>
      <input type = "radio"
             name = "quest[$questionNumber]"
             value = "C">
      $answerC
    </li>

    <li>
      <input type = "radio"
             name = "quest[$questionNumber]"
             value = "D">
      $answerD
```

```
    </li>

  </ol>

</li>

HERE;
    $questionNumber++;

  } // end foreach
  $htData .= <<<HERE
</ol>

<input type = "hidden"
       name = "quizName"
       value = "$quizName">

<input type = "submit"
       value = "submit quiz">

</form>

HERE;

  print $htData;
  return $htData;
} // end buildHTML

?>
</body>
</html>
```

Most of the critical information this function needs is stored in `$quizData`. Each line of `$quizData` stores one question, so I use a `split()` function to break `$quizData` into an array called `$problems`. I use a `foreach` loop to step through each problem. Each problem contains a list of values, which is separated into a series of scalar variables with the combination of `split()` and `list()`.

Within the `foreach` loop, I also added the HTML code necessary to print out the current question's information. Take a careful look at the code for the radio buttons. Recall that radio buttons that will operate as a group should all have the same name. I did this by calling them all `quest[$questionNumber]`. The `$questionNumber` variable will contain the current question number, and this value will be interpolated before the HTML code is written. Question number 1 will have four different radio buttons called quest[1]. The `gradeQuiz` program will see this as an array called `$quest`.

At the end of the HTML, I added the quiz name as a hidden field, and the Submit button.

Taking a Quiz

The point of all this work is to have a set of quizzes your users can take, so it's good to have a program to present the quizzes. Actually, since the quizzes are saved as HTML pages, you could simply provide a link to a quiz and be done with it, but I wanted a little more security. I wanted the ability to store my quiz files outside the normal `public_html` file space, and I wanted to have basic password protection so people won't take a quiz until I know it's ready. (I won't release the password until I'm ready for people to take the quiz.) Also, I can easily turn a quiz "off" by simply changing the password.

The only real job of the `takeQuiz` page is to check the user's password against the password of the indicated test, and allow access to the quiz if appropriate.

```
<?

//takeQuiz.php

//given a quiz file, prints out that quiz


//get the password from the file

$masterFile = $takeFile . ".mas";

$fp = fopen($masterFile, "r");

//the password is the third line, so get the first two lines, but ignore them

$dummy = fgets($fp);

$dummy = fgets($fp);
```

```
$magicWord = fgets($fp);
$magicWord = rtrim($magicWord);
fclose($fp);


if ($password == $magicWord){
  $htmlFile = $takeFile . ".html";
  //print out the page if the user got the password right
  readFile($htmlFile);
} else {
  print <<<HERE
  <font color = "red"
        size = +3>
Incorrect Password.<br>
You must have a password in order to take this quiz
</font>


HERE;
} // end if
?>
```

The password associated with a test is stored in the test file, so once I know which test the user wants to take, I can open that file and extract the password from it. The password is stored in the third line of the file, and the only way to get to it with a sequential access file like this is to load the first two lines into a dummy variable and then load the password into a variable called `$magicWord`. If the user indicated a password that matches `$magicWord`, I use the `readFile()` function to send the contents of the quiz HTML page to the browser. If not, I send a message indicating the password was not correct.

This would also be a dandy place to set up a little more security. In a production version of this system, I keep a log file of every access, so I'll know if somebody has been trying to get at my system 1,000 times from the same machine within a second (sure sign of some kind of automated attack) or other mischief. I can also check to see that later on when a page has been submitted, it comes from the same computer that requested the file in the first place. If I want, I can also check the times of request and submission in order to reject quizzes that have been out longer than some time limit.

Grading the Quiz

One advantage of this kind of system is the potential for instantaneous feedback for the user. As soon as the user clicks the Submit button, the quiz will be automatically graded by the `gradeQuiz.php` program, which also stores a log of the student's results for the administrator.

Opening the Files

The `gradeQuiz` program, like all the programs in this system, relies on files to do all its important work. In this case, the program will use the master file to get the answer key for the quiz, and will write to a log file.

```
<?
print <<<HERE
<html>
<head>
<title>Grade for $quizName, $student</title>
</head>
<body>

</body>
<h1>Grade for $quizName, $student</h1>
HERE;

//open up the correct master file for reading
$fileBase = str_replace(" ", "_", $quizName);
$masFile = $fileBase . ".mas";
$msfp = fopen($masFile, "r");

$logFile = $fileBase . ".log";

//the first three lines are name, instructor's email, and password
$quizName = fgets($msfp);
$quizEmail = fgets($msfp);
$quizPwd = fgets($msfp);
```

The master file is opened with read access. The first three lines are unimportant, but I must still read them in to get to the quiz data.

Creating an Answer Key

I start by generating an answer key from the master file. I'll step through each question in the file, and extract all the normal variables from it (although all I'm really interested in is the `$correct` variable). I then store the value of `$correct` into an array called `$key`. At the end of this loop, the `$key` array will hold the correct answer for each question in the quiz.

```
//step through the questions building an answer key
$numCorrect = 0;
$questionNumber = 1;
while (!feof($msfp)){
  $currentProblem = fgets($msfp);

  list($question, $answerA, $answerB, $answerC, $answerD, $correct) =
  split (":", $currentProblem);
  $key[$questionNumber] = $correct;
  $questionNumber++;
} // end while
fclose($msfp);
```

Checking the User's Response

The user's responses will come from the HTML form as an array called `$quest`. The correct answers are in an array called `$key`. To grade the test, I can simply step through both arrays at the same time, comparing the user's response with the correct response. Each time these values are the same, the user has gotten an answer correct. When the values are not the same, the user was incorrect (or there was a problem with the test itself–don't discount that as a possibility).

```
//Check each answer from user
for ($questionNumber = 1; $questionNumber <= count($quest); $questionNumber++){
  $guess = $quest[$questionNumber];
  $correct = $key[$questionNumber];
  $correct = rtrim($correct);
```

```
    if ($guess == $correct){
      //user got it right
      $numCorrect++;
      print "problem # $questionNumber was correct<br>\n";
    } else {
      print "<font color = red>problem # $questionNumber was incorrect</font><br>\n";
    } // end if
  } // end for
```

I chose to give a certain amount of feedback telling whether the question was correct or not, but I decided not to display the right answer. You might wish to give the user more or less information, depending on how you're using the quiz program.

Reporting the Results to Screen and Log File

After checking each answer, the program reports the results to the user as a raw score and a percentage. The program also opens up a log file for append access and adds the current data to it. Append access is just like write access, but rather than overwriting an existing file, it adds any new data to the end of it.

```
print "you got $numCorrect right<br>\n";
$percentage = ($numCorrect /count($quest)) * 100;
print "for $percentage percent<br>\n";

$today = date ("F j, Y, g:i a");
//print "Date: $today<br>\n";
$location = getenv("REMOTE_ADDR");
//print "Location: $location<br>\n";

//add results to log file
$lgfp = fopen($logFile, "a");
$logLine = $student . "\t";
$logLine .= $today . "\t";
$logLine .= $location . "\t";
$logLine .= $numCorrect . "\t";
```

```
$logLine .= $percentage . "\n";

fputs($lgfp, $logLine);
fclose($lgfp);

?>

</html>
```

I added a few more elements to the log file that might be useful to a test administrator. Of course, I added the student's name and the current date. You might want to look at the online help for the `date()` function to see all the various ways you can display the current date. I also added a location variable, which uses the `$REMOTE_ADDR` environment variable to indicate which machine the user was on when he or she submitted the exam. This can be useful information, because it can alert you to certain kinds of hacking. (A person taking the same quiz several times on the same machine but with a different name, for example.) The `gradeQuiz` program adds the number correct and the percentage to the log file as well, then closes the file. Notice that the data in the log file is delimited with tab characters. This is done so an analysis program could easily work with the file using the split command. Also, most spreadsheet programs can readily read a tab-delimited file, so the log file can be easily imported into a spreadsheet for further analysis.

You could really improve the logging functionality if you wanted to do some in-depth test analysis. For example, you could easily store each user's response to each question in the quiz. This would give you a database of performance on every question, so you could easily determine which questions are causing difficulty.

Viewing the Log

The `showLog.php` program is actually very similar to the `takeQuiz` program. It checks the password to ensure the user has admin access, then opens up the log using the `file()` function. It prints out the results of the file inside a `<pre></pre>` pair, so the tab characters will be preserved.

```
<?
//showLog.php
//shows a log file
```

```
//requires admin password

if ($password == "absolute"){
  $lines = file($logFile);
  print "<pre>\n";
  foreach ($lines as $theLine){
    print $theLine;
  } // end foreach
  print "</pre>\n";

} else {
  print <<<HERE
<font color = "red"
      size = +2>
You must have the appropriate password to view this log
</font>

HERE;
} // end if

?>
```

You could improve this program by writing the data into an HTML table. However, not all spreadsheets can easily work with HTML table data, so I prefer the tab format. It wouldn't be difficult to add some data analysis to the log viewer, including mean scores, standard deviation, and suggested curve values.

Summary

This chapter has explored the use of sequential files as a data storage and retrieval mechanism. You have learned how to open files in read, write, and append modes. You know how file pointers are used to refer to a file. You have written data to a file and loaded data from a file with appropriate functions. You have learned how to load an entire file into an array. You can examine a directory and determine which files are in the directory. You've learned how to use basic regular expressions in the `preg_greq()` function to display a subset of files in the directory. Finally, you've put all this together in a multi-program system that allows multiple levels of access to an interesting data set. You should be proud of your accomplishments.

CHALLENGES

1. Improve the quiz program in one of the ways I've suggested throughout the chapter. Add the ability to e-mail test results, put in some analysis of test scores, improve the quiz editing page, or try something of your own.
2. A couple of values in this system should be global among each of the PHP programs. The root directory of the files and the administrative password are obvious candidates. Write a program that stores these values in an .ini file and modify the quiz programs to get these values from that file when needed.
3. Create a source code viewer. Given a filename, the program should read in the file and convert each instance of < into <, then save this new file to another name. This will allow you to show your source code to others.
4. Create a simple guest book. Let the user enter information into a form, and when she clicks the Submit button, add her comment to the bottom of the page. You can use one or two files for this.

Using MySQL to Create Databases

When you began programming in PHP, you started with very simple variables. Soon you learned how to do more interesting things with arrays and associative arrays. You added the power of files to gain tremendous new skills. Now you'll learn how relational databases can be used to manage data. In this chapter you'll learn how to build a basic database and how to hook it up to your PHP programs. Specifically, you'll learn:

- How to start the MySQL executable.
- How to build basic databases.
- The essential data definition SQL statements.
- How to return a basic SQL query.
- How to use SQLyog to manage your databases.
- How to incorporate databases into PHP programs.

Introducing the Adventure Generator Program

Databases are a serious tool but they can be fun, too. The adventure generator program shown in Figures 7.1 through 7.4 shows how a database can be used to fuel an adventure game generator. The adventure generator is a system that allows users to create and play simple "multiple choice" adventures. This style of game consists of several nodes. Each node describes some sort of decision. In each case, the user will be able to choose from up to three choices. The user's choice leads to a new decision. If the user makes a sequence of correct choices, he or she will win the game.

This program is interesting as a game, but the really exciting part is how the user can modify this game. A user can use the same system to create and modify adventures. Figure 7.3 shows the data behind the enigma game. Note that you can edit any node of the game by clicking on the appropriate button from this screen.

If the user chooses to edit a segment, the page shown in Figure 7.4 appears.

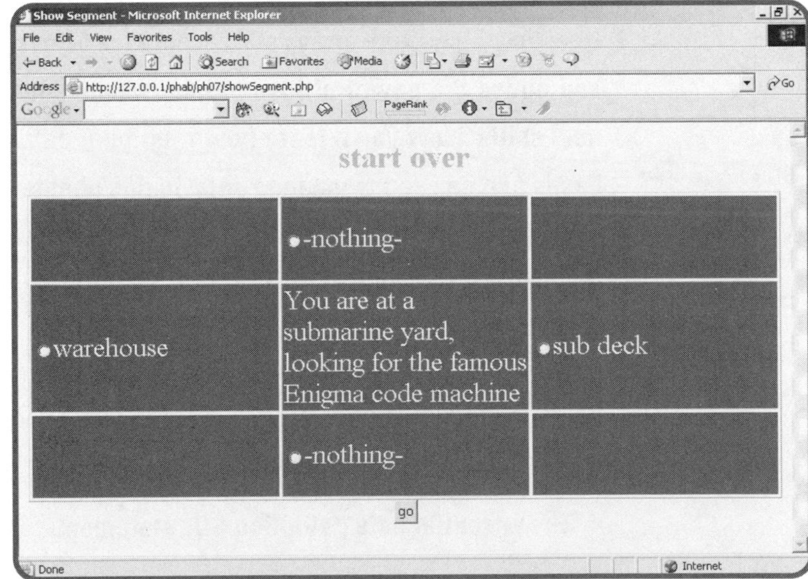

FIGURE 7.1

The user can choose an option. Let's hop onto that sub...

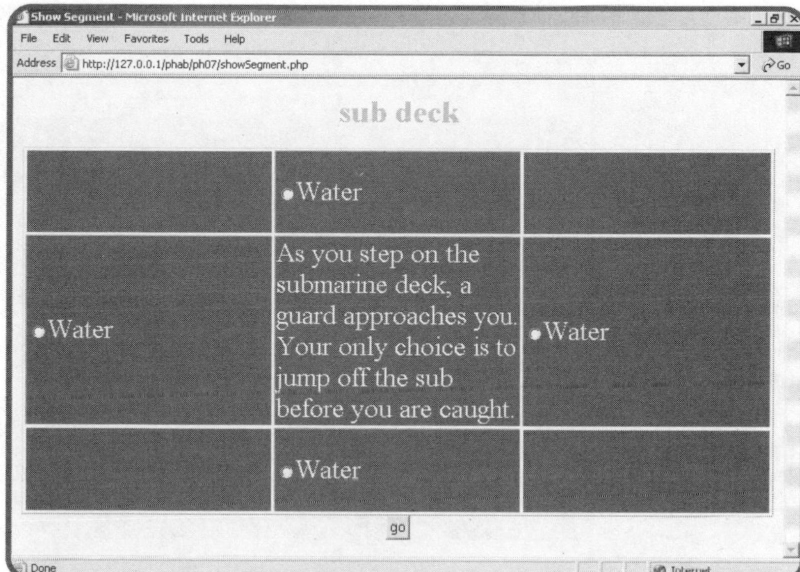

FIGURE 7.2

Maybe the warehouse would have been a better choice after all.

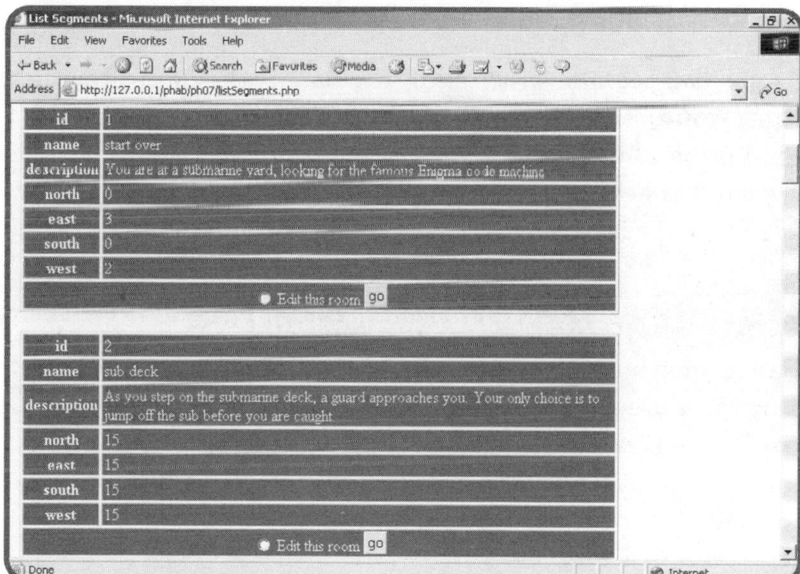

FIGURE 7.3

This page provides information about each segment in the game, including links to directly edit each segment.

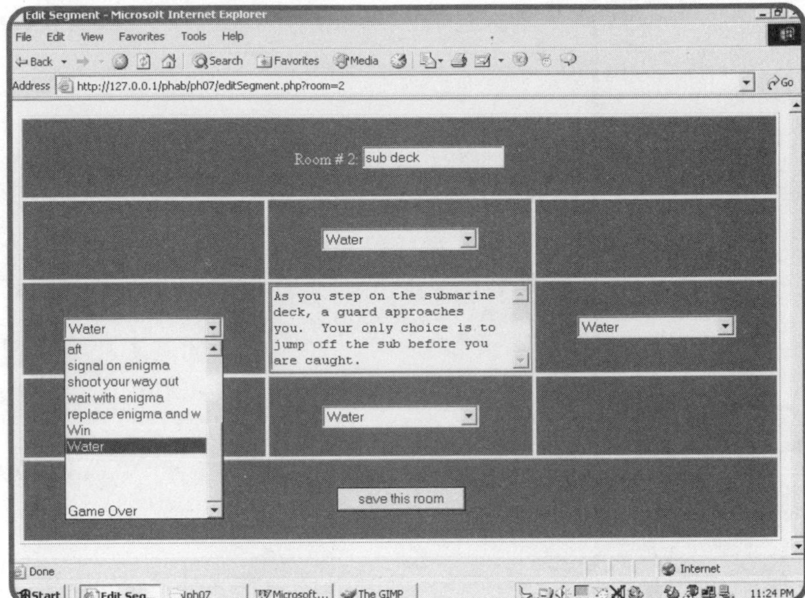

FIGURE 7.4

From this screen it is possible to change everything about a node. All the nodes that have been created so far are available as new locations.

As you can see, the structure of the data is the most important element of this game. You already know some ways to work with data, but this chapter introduces the notion of *relational database management systems* (RDBMS). An RDBMS is a system that helps programmers work with data. The adventure generator program uses a database to store and manipulate all the data.

Using a Database Management System

Data is such an important part of modern programming that entire programming languages are devoted to manipulating databases. The primary standard for database languages is *Structured Query Language* (SQL). SQL is a standardized language for creating databases, storing information into databases and retrieving this information. Special applications and programming environments specialize in interpreting SQL data and acting on it.

Often a programmer will begin by creating a data structure in SQL, then will write a program in some other language (such as PHP) to allow access to that data. The PHP program can then formulate requests or updates to the data, which are passed on to the SQL interpreter. This approach has a couple of advantages. First, once you learn SQL, you can apply it easily to a new programming language. Also, you can easily add multiple interfaces to an existing data set because many programming languages have ways to access an SQL interpreter. Many relational database management systems are available, but the MySQL environment is especially well suited to working with PHP. However, the basic concepts of SQL remain the same no matter what type of database you are working on. Most of the SQL commands described in this chapter work without modification in Microsoft Access, Microsoft SQL Server, and Oracle, as well as a number of other RDBMS packages.

I'll begin this chapter by explaining how to create a simple database in MySQL. There are a number of ways to work with this package, but I'll start by showing you how to write a script that builds a database in a text file. I'll use the SQL language, which is different in syntax and style from PHP. Then I'll show you SQLyog, a wonderful front-end package for working with MySQL databases. In Chapter 8, "Connecting to Database Within PHP," I'll show you how to contact and manipulate your MySQL database from within PHP.

Working with MySQL

There are a number of RDBMS packages available. These programs vary in power, flexibility, and price. However, they all work in essentially the same way. For this book, most examples will use the `MySQL` database. This program is very frequently paired with PHP for a number of reasons. First, MySQL is a very powerful program in its own right. It handles a large subset of the functionality of the most expensive and powerful database packages. It uses a standard form of the well-known SQL data language. MySQL is released under an open source license, and is available for free. It works on many operating systems, and with many languages. It works very quickly and works well even with large data sets. PHP ships with a number of functions designed to support MySQL databases.

Installing MySQL

If you used PHPTriad to install Apache and PHP, you probably also installed MySQL as well. If you are working on a Web server you do not control, you'll need to check with your server administrator to see if MySQL is installed. If your server supports PHP, it's very likely that it also supports MySQL, as these two programs are frequently installed together.

Using the MySQL Executable

MySQL is actually a number of programs. It has a server component that is always running, as well as a number of utility programs. The `MySQL` command line console shown in Figure 7.5 is a basic program run from the command line. It isn't a very pretty program, but it provides powerful access to the database engine.

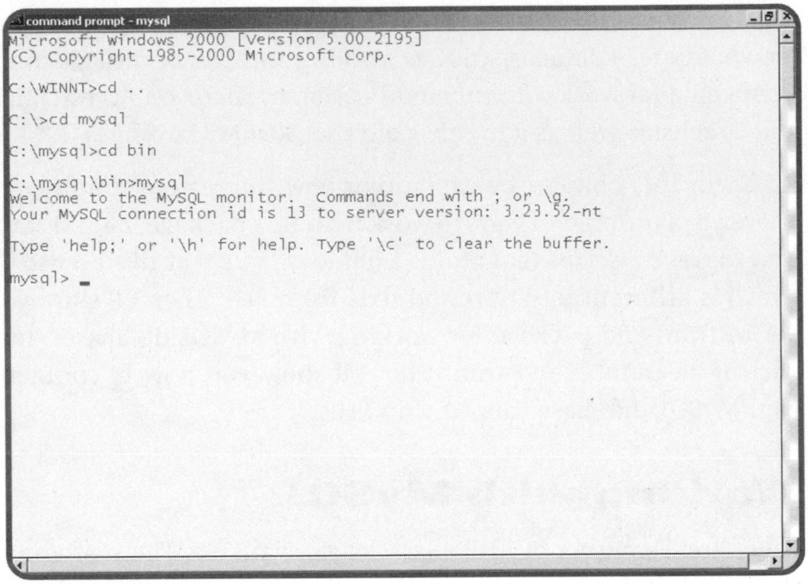

```
Microsoft Windows 2000 [Version 5.00.2195]
(C) Copyright 1985-2000 Microsoft Corp.

C:\WINNT>cd ..

C:\>cd mysql

C:\mysql>cd bin

C:\mysql\bin>mysql
Welcome to the MySQL monitor.  Commands end with ; or \g.
Your MySQL connection id is 13 to server version: 3.23.52-nt

Type 'help;' or '\h' for help. Type '\c' to clear the buffer.

mysql> _
```

FIGURE 7.5

The MySQL program connecting to a database.

There are a number of ways to use MySQL, but the basic procedure involves connecting to a MySQL server, choosing a database, and then using the SQL language to control the database by creating tables, viewing data, and so on.

The MySQL.exe console shipped with MySQL is the most basic way to work with the `MySQL` database. Although it won't win any user interface awards, the program offers low-level access to the database. This interface is important to learn, however, because it is very much like the way your programs will interface with the database system.

Creating a Database

Databases are described by a very specific organization scheme. To illustrate database concepts, I will create and view a simple phone list. The basic structure of the phone list is shown in Table 7.1.

TABLE 7.1 PHONE LIST SUMMARY

id	firstName	lastName	e-mail	phone
0	Andy	Harris	aharris@cs.iupui.edu	123-4567
1	Joe	Slow	jslow@myPlace.net	987-6543

The phone list shows a very typical simple data table. Database people like to give special names to the parts of the database, so I'll use this simple phone list to illustrate. Each row of the table is called a *record*. Records describe discrete entities. The list of records is called a *table*. Each record in a table has the same elements, which are called *fields*, (or sometimes simply *columns*). Every record in the table has the same field definitions, but records can have different values in the fields. The fields in a table are defined in specific ways. Because of the way database tables are stored in files, the computer must always know how much room to allocate for each field, so the size and type of each field is important. This particular database is defined with five fields. The `id` field is an integer. All the other fields contain string data.

Creating a Table

RDBMS programs use a special language called *Structured Query Language*(SQL) to create and manipulate databases. SQL is usually pretty easy to understand, compared to full-blown programming languages. You can usually guess what's going on even without a lot of knowledge. As an example, look at the following SQL code:

```
USE chapter7;

CREATE TABLE phoneList (
  id INT PRIMARY KEY,
  firstName VARCHAR(15),
  lastName VARCHAR (15),
  email VARCHAR(20),
  phone VARCHAR(15)
);

DESCRIBE phonelist;
```

This code is an SQL script. It is like a PHP program in the sense it is a set of instructions for the computer to follow. However, the PHP interpreter doesn't directly interact with the SQL language. Instead, these commands are sent to another program. As a PHP programmer, you'll also be able to write code that sends commands to a database language. Just as your PHP code often writes code in HTML format for the browser to interpret, you'll be writing SQL code for the MySQL interpreter to use.

ADVANTAGES OF SQL

Databases have been an important part of programming since the beginning, but the process of working with data has gone through several evolutions. The advent of a common language that can be used in many applications was a very important step. SQL is a *fourth-generation* language. In general, these languages are designed to solve a particular type of problem. Some fourth generation languages (like SQL) aren't full-blown programming languages, because they don't support data structures like branches and loops. Still, these languages can serve a very useful purpose. SQL is handy because it's widely supported. The SQL commands you will learn in this chapter will apply to most modern database programs with little to no modification. You can take the script you'll learn shortly in MySQL and send the same code to an Oracle or MS SQL Server database (two other very common choices), and all three data programs will build the same database. If you choose to upgrade to a more powerful data package, you can use your existing scripts to manipulate the data. Perhaps the most powerful reason to have a scripting language to control databases relates to programming in traditional languages. You can write a program in any language (like PHP, for example) that generates SQL code. You can then use that code to manipulate the database. This allows you to have complete flexibility, and lets your program act as the interface to your database.

When this code is sent to an SQL-compliant database program (such as MySQL) it will create the database structure shown in Table 7.1.

Using a Database

It is possible that you will have several database projects working in the same relational database system. In my case, each chapter of this book that uses SQL has its own database. Sometimes your system administrator will assign you a database. In any case, you will probably need to invoke that database with the `USE` command.

The syntax of SQL is not exactly like that of PHP. SQL has a different culture, and it makes sense to respect the way SQL code has historically been written. SQL is generally not case-sensitive, but most SQL coders put all SQL commands in all uppercase. Also, when a bunch of SQL commands are placed in a file as this code will be, you usually end each line with a semicolon.

If you don't already have a database to `USE`, you can create one with the `CREATE` command. For example, to create a database called "myStuff," use these commands:

```
CREATE DATABASE mystuff;

USE mystuff;
```

Creating a Table

To create a table, you must indicate the name of the table as well as each field in the table. For each field, you must list what type of data is held in the field, and (at least for text data) how many characters long the field will be. As an example, the following code creates the `phoneList` table:

```
CREATE TABLE phoneList (
  id INT PRIMARY KEY,
  firstName VARCHAR(15),
  lastName VARCHAR (15),
  email VARCHAR(20),
  phone VARCHAR(15)
);
```

You can think of fields as being much like variables, but while PHP is easy-going about what type of data is in a variable, SQL is very picky about the type of data in fields. In order to create an efficient database, MySQL needs to know exactly how many bytes of memory to set aside for every single field in the database. The primary way it does this is to require the database designer to specify the type and size of every field in each table. Table 7.2 lists a few of the primary data types supported by MySQL.

TABLE 7.2 COMMON DATA TYPES IN MYSQL

Data type	Description
INT	Standard integer +/- 2 billion (roughly)
BIGINT	Big integer +/- 9 x 10 ^18th
FLOAT	Floating point decimal number 38 digits
DOUBLE	Double precision floating point 308 digits
CHAR(n)	text with n digits. If actual value is less than n, field will be padded with trailing spaces
VARCHAR(n)	Text with n digits. Trailing spaces will automatically be culled
DATE	Date in YYYY-MM-DD format
TIME	Time in HH:MM:SS format
YEAR	Year in YYYY format

While the data types listed in Table 7.2 are by far the most commonly used, MySQL supports many other data types as well. Look in the online help that ships with MySQL if you need a more specific data type. Other databases will have a very similar list of data types.

You might notice that it is not necessary to specify the length of numeric types (although you can determine a maximum size for numeric types as well as the number of digits you want stored in float and double fields). The storage requirements for numeric variables are based on the type itself.

Working with String Data in MySQL

Text values are usually stored in `VARCHAR` fields. These fields must include the number of characters allocated for the field. Both `CHAR` and `VARCHAR` fields have fixed lengths. The primary difference between them is what happens when the field contains a value shorter than the specified length. If you declare a `CHAR` field to have a length of 10 with

```
firstName VARCHAR(10);
```

and then later store the value `'Andy'` into the field, the field will actually contain `'Andy      '` (that is, Andy followed by six spaces). CHAR fields pad any remaining characters with spaces. The VARCHAR field type removes any padded spaces. Usually you will use the VARCHAR field type to store all your string data.

Determining the Length of a VARCHAR Field

Data design is both a science and an art. Determining the appropriate length for your text fields is one of the oldest problems in data.

If you don't allocate enough room for your text data, you can cause a lot of problems for your users. I once taught a course called CLT SD WEB PRG because the database that held the course names didn't have enough room for the actual name of the course (Client-Side Web Programming). My students renamed it the "Buy a Vowel" course.

However, you can't simply make every text field a thousand characters long, either, because this would be wasteful of system resources. If you have a field that will usually contain only five characters and you allocate one hundred characters, you will still require room on the drive for the extra 95 characters. If your database has thousands of entries, this can be a substantial cost in drive space. In a distributed environment, you'll also have to wait for those unnecessary spaces to come across limited bandwidth. It takes experimentation and practice to determine the appropriate width for your string fields. You'll need to test your application with real users before you can really be sure if you've made the right decision.

Finishing up the CREATE TABLE Statement

Once you understand field data types, the `CREATE TABLE` syntax makes a lot of sense. There are only a few more details to understand. Once you specify `CREATE TABLE`, use a pair of parentheses to indicate the field list. Each field has a name followed by its type (and length, if it's a `CHAR` or `VARCHAR`). The fields are separated by commas. You do not have to put each field on its own line or indent the field definitions, but I prefer to do so, because these practices make the code much easier to read and debug.

Creating a Primary Key

You might be curious about the very first field in the phone list database. Just to refresh your memory, the line that defines that field looks like this:

```
id INT PRIMARY KEY,
```

Most database tables have some sort of field like this that holds a numeric value. This special field is called the *primary key*.

IN THE REAL WORLD

A very simple database like the phone list could theoretically go without a primary key, but such fields are so important to more sophisticated databases that you might as well start putting them into even your first table. It's traditional to put a primary key in every table. In Chapter 9 "Data Normalization," you'll learn more about the relational data model. In that discussion you'll learn how keys are used to build powerful databases, and you'll learn more about creating proper primary keys. In fact, the adventure program you've already seen heavily relies on a key field even though there's only one table in the database.

The code presented so far can be entered directly into the MySQL program. You can see the code and its results in Figure 7.6.

Using the DESCRIBE Command to Check the Structure of a Table

It can be useful to check the structure of a table, especially if somebody else created it or you don't remember exactly what types or sizes of fields are in the table. The `DESCRIBE` command lets you view the structure of a table.

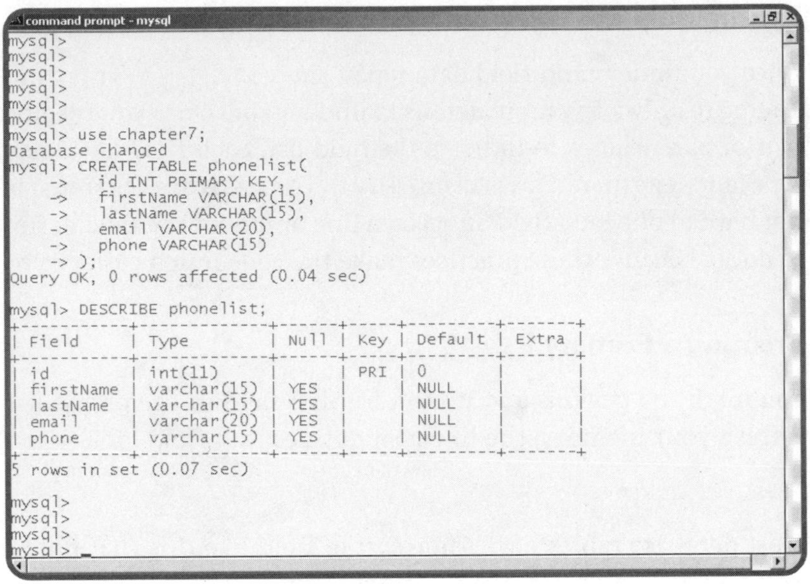

```
mysql>
mysql>
mysql>
mysql>
mysql>
mysql>
mysql> use chapter7;
Database changed
mysql> CREATE TABLE phonelist(
    ->   id INT PRIMARY KEY,
    ->   firstName VARCHAR(15),
    ->   lastName VARCHAR(15),
    ->   email VARCHAR(20),
    ->   phone VARCHAR(15)
    -> );
Query OK, 0 rows affected (0.04 sec)

mysql> DESCRIBE phonelist;
+-----------+-------------+------+-----+---------+-------+
| Field     | Type        | Null | Key | Default | Extra |
+-----------+-------------+------+-----+---------+-------+
| id        | int(11)     |      | PRI | 0       |       |
| firstName | varchar(15) | YES  |     | NULL    |       |
| lastName  | varchar(15) | YES  |     | NULL    |       |
| email     | varchar(20) | YES  |     | NULL    |       |
| phone     | varchar(15) | YES  |     | NULL    |       |
+-----------+-------------+------+-----+---------+-------+
5 rows in set (0.07 sec)

mysql>
mysql>
mysql>
mysql> _
```

FIGURE 7.6

The MySQL command line tool after I created the phonelist table.

Inserting Values

Once you've created a table, you can begin to add data to it. The primary tool for adding records to a table is the `INSERT` command.

```
INSERT INTO phoneList

VALUES (

  0, 'Andy', 'Harris', 'aharris@cs.iupui.edu', '123-4567'

);
```

The `INSERT` statement allows you to add a record into a database. The values must be listed in exactly the same order the fields were defined. Each value is separated by a comma, and all `VARCHAR` and `CHAR` values must be enclosed in single quotes.

If you have a large amount of data to load into a database, you can also use the `LOAD DATA` command. This command accepts a tab-delimited text file with one row per record and fields separated by tabs. It then loads that entire file into the database. This is often the fastest way to load a database with test data. The following line loads data from a file called "addresses.txt" into the `phoneList` table:

```
LOAD DATA LOCAL INFILE "addresses.txt" INTO TABLE phonelist;
```

Figure 7.7 shows the MySQL tool after I have added one record to the table.

In the Real World

As you are building a database, you will need to populate the database with test values. You don't want to use actual data at this point, because your database will not work correctly until you've messed with it for some time. However, your test values should be reflective of the kinds of data your database will actually house. This will help you spot certain problems like field lengths that are too small or fields that are missing.

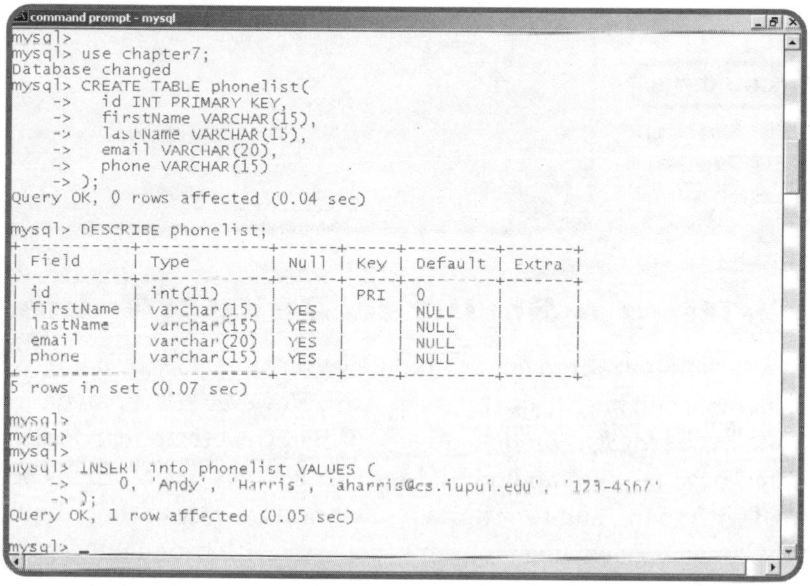

```
mysql>
mysql> use chapter7;
Database changed
mysql> CREATE TABLE phonelist(
    ->   id INT PRIMARY KEY,
    ->   firstName VARCHAR(15),
    ->   lastName VARCHAR(15),
    ->   email VARCHAR(20),
    ->   phone VARCHAR(15)
    -> );
Query OK, 0 rows affected (0.04 sec)

mysql> DESCRIBE phonelist;
+-----------+-------------+------+-----+---------+-------+
| Field     | Type        | Null | Key | Default | Extra |
+-----------+-------------+------+-----+---------+-------+
| id        | int(11)     |      | PRI | 0       |       |
| firstName | varchar(15) | YES  |     | NULL    |       |
| lastName  | varchar(15) | YES  |     | NULL    |       |
| email     | varchar(20) | YES  |     | NULL    |       |
| phone     | varchar(15) | YES  |     | NULL    |       |
+-----------+-------------+------+-----+---------+-------+
5 rows in set (0.07 sec)

mysql>
mysql>
mysql>
mysql> INSERT into phonelist VALUES (
    ->   0, 'Andy', 'Harris', 'aharris@cs.iupui.edu', '123-4567'
    -> );
Query OK, 1 row affected (0.05 sec)

mysql> _
```

FIGURE 7.7

MySQL tells you the operation succeeded, but you don't get a lot more information.

Selecting Results

Of course, you'll want to see the results of all your table-building activities. If you want to see the data in a table, you can use the `SELECT` command. This is perhaps the most powerful command in SQL, but its basic use is quite simple. To see all of the data in the `phonelist` database, use this command:

```
SELECT * FROM phonelist
```

This command grabs all fields of all records of the `phonelist` database and displays them in a table format.

Figure 7.8 shows what happens after I add a `SELECT` statement to get the results of the phone list.

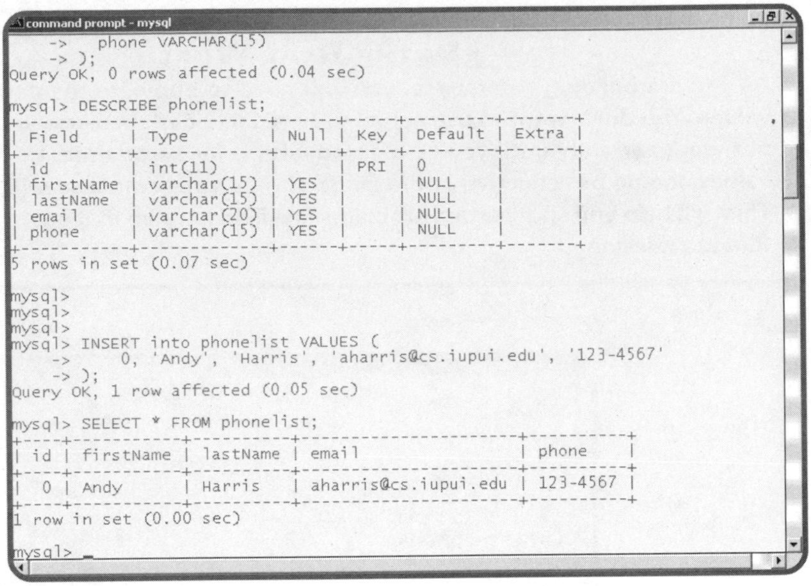

```
command prompt - mysql
    ->    phone VARCHAR(15)
    -> );
Query OK, 0 rows affected (0.04 sec)

mysql> DESCRIBE phonelist;
+-----------+-------------+------+-----+---------+-------+
| Field     | Type        | Null | Key | Default | Extra |
+-----------+-------------+------+-----+---------+-------+
| id        | int(11)     |      | PRI | 0       |       |
| firstName | varchar(15) | YES  |     | NULL    |       |
| lastName  | varchar(15) | YES  |     | NULL    |       |
| email     | varchar(20) | YES  |     | NULL    |       |
| phone     | varchar(15) | YES  |     | NULL    |       |
+-----------+-------------+------+-----+---------+-------+
5 rows in set (0.07 sec)

mysql>
mysql>
mysql>
mysql> INSERT into phonelist VALUES (
    ->     0, 'Andy', 'Harris', 'aharris@cs.iupui.edu', '123-4567'
    -> );
Query OK, 1 row affected (0.05 sec)

mysql> SELECT * FROM phonelist;
+----+-----------+----------+----------------------+----------+
| id | firstName | lastName | email                | phone    |
+----+-----------+----------+----------------------+----------+
|  0 | Andy      | Harris   | aharris@cs.iupui.edu | 123-4567 |
+----+-----------+----------+----------------------+----------+
1 row in set (0.00 sec)

mysql> _
```

FIGURE 7.8

The result of the SELECT statement is a table just like the original plan.

Writing a Script to Build a Table

It is very important to understand how to create tables by hand in SQL, because your programs will have to do this same work. However, it's very tedious to write your SQL code in the MySQL window directly. When you create real data applications, you'll often have to build and rebuild your data tables several times before you are satisfied with them, and this would be awkward directly in the command line interface. Also, as you are writing programs that work with your database, you will likely make mistakes that corrupt the original data. It's good to have a script ready that can easily rebuild the database with test data even if something goes wrong. Most programmers create a script of SQL commands with a text editor (you can use the same editor that you write your PHP code in) and use the `SOURCE` command to load that code in. Below is an SQL script for creating the `phonelist` database.

```
## build phone list

## for mySQL


USE chapter7;

DROP TABLE IF EXISTS phoneList;


CREATE TABLE phoneList (
```

```
  id INT PRIMARY KEY,
  firstName VARCHAR(15),
  lastName VARCHAR (15),
  email VARCHAR(20),
  phone VARCHAR(15)
);

INSERT INTO phoneList
VALUES (
  0, 'Andy', 'Harris', 'aharris@cs.iupui.edu', '123-4567'
);

SELECT * FROM phoneList;
```

This code isn't exactly like the code I used in the interactive session, because there are a few more features that are especially handy when you create SQL code in a script.

Creating Comments in SQL

SQL is actually a language. Although it isn't technically a programming language, it has many of the same features. Like PHP and other languages, SQL supports several types of comment characters. The # sign is often used to signify a comment in SQL. Comments are especially important when you save a group of SQL commands in a file for later reuse. These comments can help you remember what type of database you were trying to build. It's critical to put basic comments in your scripts so you will understand what they should do later.

Dropping a Table

It may seem strange to talk about deleting a table from a database before you've built one, but often (as in this case) a database is created using a script. Before you create a new table, you should check to see if it already exists, and if it does, delete it with the `DROP` command. The

```
DROP TABLE IF EXISTS phoneList;
```

command does exactly that. If the `phoneList` table currently exists, it will be deleted, so there will be no confusion.

Running a Script with SOURCE

You can create an SQL script with any text editor. It is common to save SQL scripts with the `.sql` extension. Inside MySQL, you can use the `SOURCE` command to load and execute an external script. Figure 7.9 shows MySQL after I ran the `buildPhonelist.sql` script.

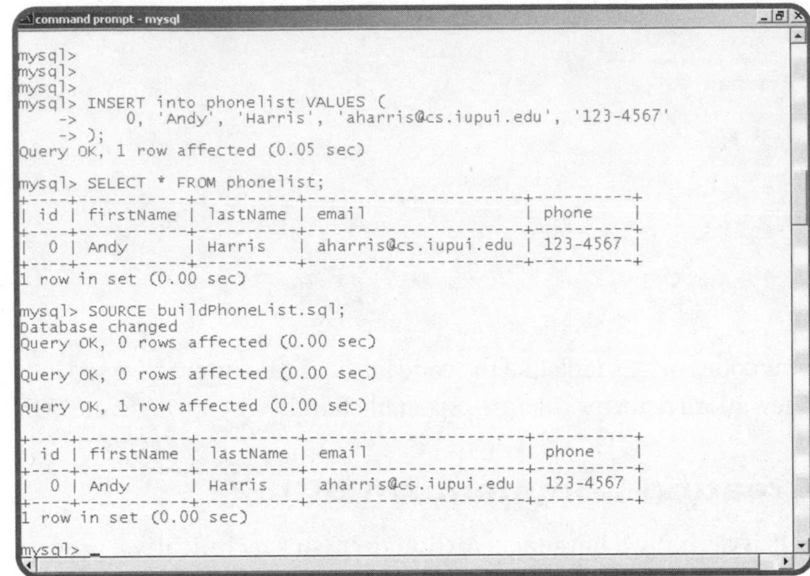

FIGURE 7.9

The SOURCE command allows you to read in SQL instructions from a file.

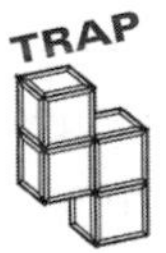

In Windows I often drag a file from a directory view into a command line program like MySQL. Windows will copy the entire filename over, but it will include double quotes, which will cause problems for the MySQL interpreter. If you drag a filename into MySQL, you will need to edit out the quote characters so that MySQL will read the file correctly.

Working with a Database in SQLyog

It's critical to understand the SQL language, but sometimes you may want a more visual way to build and view your databases. If you are running Windows, you can use an excellent front end called SQLyog. This freeware program makes it much easier for you to create, modify, and manipulate databases.

IN THE REAL WORLD

SQLyog is so cool that you'll be tempted to use it all the time. That's fine, but be sure you understand the underlying SQL code, because your PHP programs will have to work with plain text SQL commands. It's fine to use SQLyog while you are building and manipulating your data, but your users won't be using this program. Your application will be the user's interface to your database, so you need to be able to do all commands in plain text from within PHP. I use SQLyog, but I also make sure I always look at the code it produces, so I can write it myself.

SQLyog basically adds the visual editing tools of a program like Microsoft Access to the MySQL environment. It also adds some wonderful tools for adding records, viewing your data structure, and exporting data to a number of useful formats.

Connecting to a Server

MySQL is a client-server application. The MySQL server will usually be running on a Web server where your PHP programs reside. You can connect a MySQL client to any MySQL server. Figure 7.10 shows me connecting to my local MySQL server.

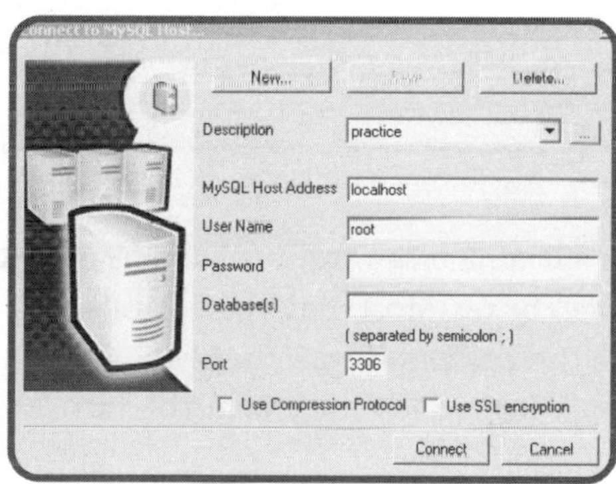

FIGURE 7.10

This screen helps you connect to a data server.

It's important to recognize that you can connect to any data server you have permission to use. This data server doesn't need to be on the same physical machine you are using. This would be useful if you wanted to use SQLyog to view data on a remote Web server you are maintaining, for example. However, many of these remote Web servers do not like this kind of access, so you should still know how to work with the plain MySQL console.

Creating and Modifying a Table

SQLyog provides visual tools to help you create and modify your tables. The phone list is way too mundane for my tastes, so I'll build a new table to illustrate the features of SQLyog. This new table contains a number of randomly generated super heroes. Figure 7.11 shows the dialog used to create a table or alter its structure.

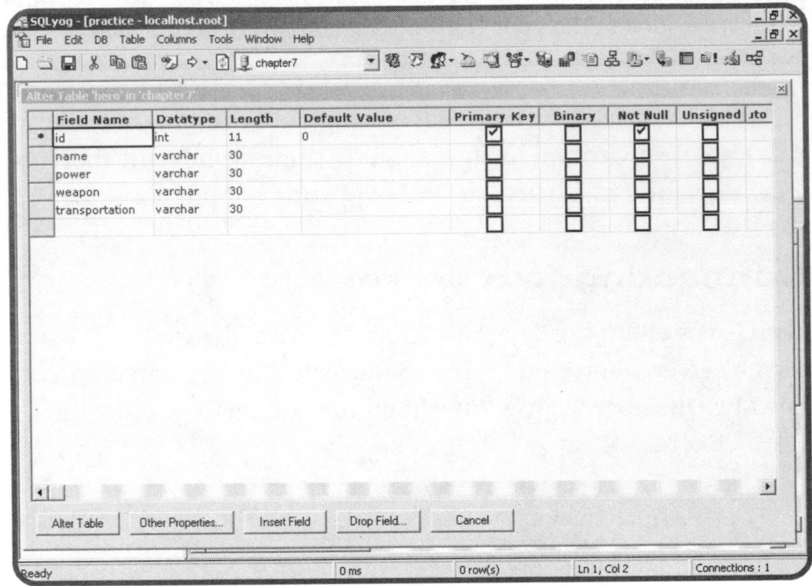

FIGURE 7.11

It's easy to create a table and modify its structure with SQLyog.

With SQLyog you can choose variable types from a drop-down list, and many field properties are available as checkboxes. Most of those options are not important for now. Note that `id` is set up as the primary key. When you are finished creating or modifying the table, the proper SQL code to perform the transaction will be automatically generated and executed for you.

Special thanks to Lee Seitz and his hysterical Super-Hero generator at http://home.hiwaay.net/~lkseitz/comics/herogen/.

Check this site out sometime when you're bored.

Editing Table Data

You can use SQLyog to edit your table in a format much like a spreadsheet. Figure 7.12 illustrates this capability.

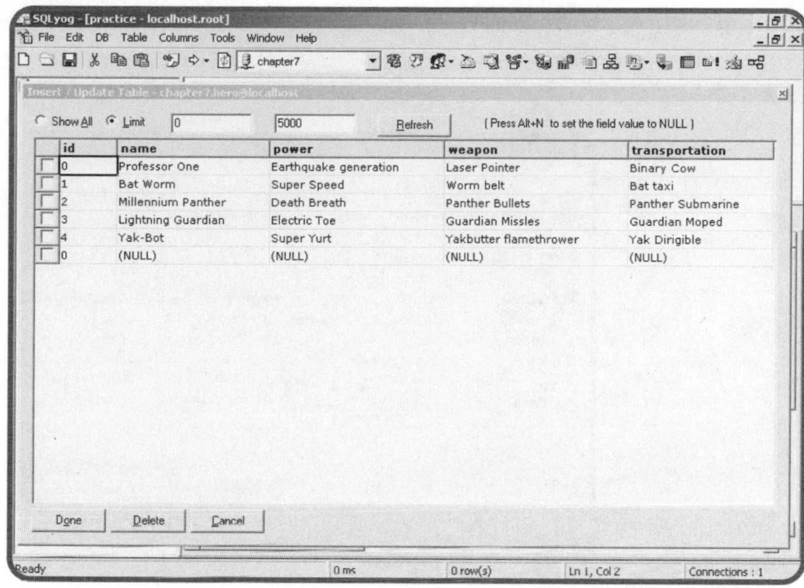

FIGURE 7.12

You can edit a number of records easily in the edit view.

To edit a table in SQLyog, select the table in the table list on the left-hand side of the SQL screen. You can then either press F11 to edit the table, or choose `Insert/Update Data` from the `Table` menu. Once you're done editing the data, you can hit the Done button, and SQLyog automatically creates and runs the SQL code needed to modify the table data. If you type data in the last row, you will get a new record.

Exporting a Table

Some of SQLyog's most interesting features involve ways to export information about your tables. You can generate formats that show the data in a number of formats. Once you've gotten a view of a table (by selecting the table and pressing the Enter key) you can go to the tools menu and select "Export Result Set." You will see a dialog like the one featured in Figure 7.13.

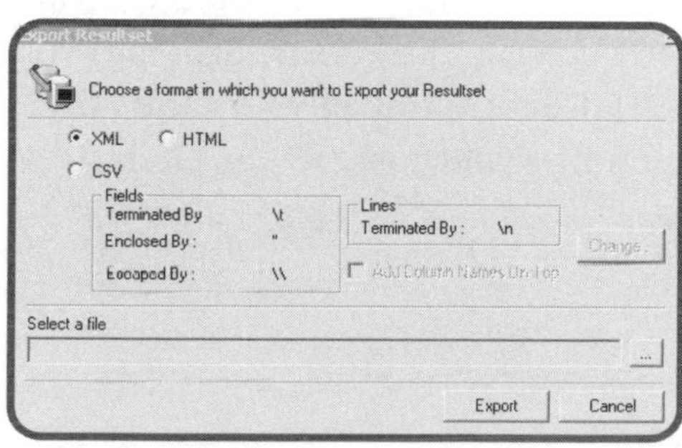

FIGURE 7.13

The export result set dialog allows you to save table data in a number of formats.

You can easily generate an HTML summary of your data by selecting the HTML option and specifying a filename. Figure 7.14 shows the HTML output of the hero data table.

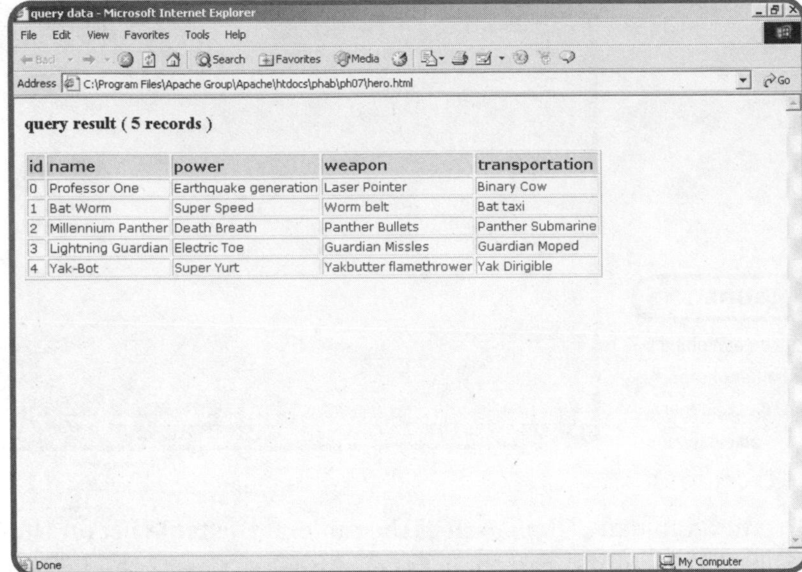

query result (5 records)

id	name	power	weapon	transportation
0	Professor One	Earthquake generation	Laser Pointer	Binary Cow
1	Bat Worm	Super Speed	Worm belt	Bat taxi
2	Millennium Panther	Death Breath	Panther Bullets	Panther Submarine
3	Lightning Guardian	Electric Toe	Guardian Missles	Guardian Moped
4	Yak-Bot	Super Yurt	Yakbutter flamethrower	Yak Dirigible

FIGURE 7.14

You can easily print HTML summaries of your data results.

You might prefer to have your results saved in some sort of delimited format such as those discussed in Chapter 6, "Working with Files." You can easily generate such a format by choosing the CSV (Comma-Separated Value) option, and choosing what your delimiters will be. This is a good choice if you want your data to be readable by a spreadsheet or if you are writing a program that can handle such a format but cannot do direct database access. Figure 7.15 illustrates the CSV version of the hero data set.

You can also set up an XML file to hold the data. As you can see from the illustration in Figure 7.16, XML is much like HTML, and it describes the information in a self-documenting form.

When you start to write more complex databases, you'll quickly learn the value of descriptions of each table. You can use the "Create Schema" command under the "DB" menu to generate an HTML description of your table. This schema can be an important part of your programming and documentation strategy. Figure 7.17 shows the schema of the `hero` table.

	A	B	C	D	E
1	0	Professor One	Earthquak	Laser Pointer	Binary Cow
2	1	Bat Worm	Super Spe	Worm belt	Bat taxi
3	2	Millennium Panther	Death Bre	Panther Bullets	Panther Submarine
4	3	Lightning Guardian	Electric To	Guardian Missles	Guardian Moped
5	4	Yak-Bot	Super Yurt	Yakbutter flamethrower	Yak Dirigible

FIGURE 7.15

I set up the phone list data as a tab delimited file and read it into Excel.

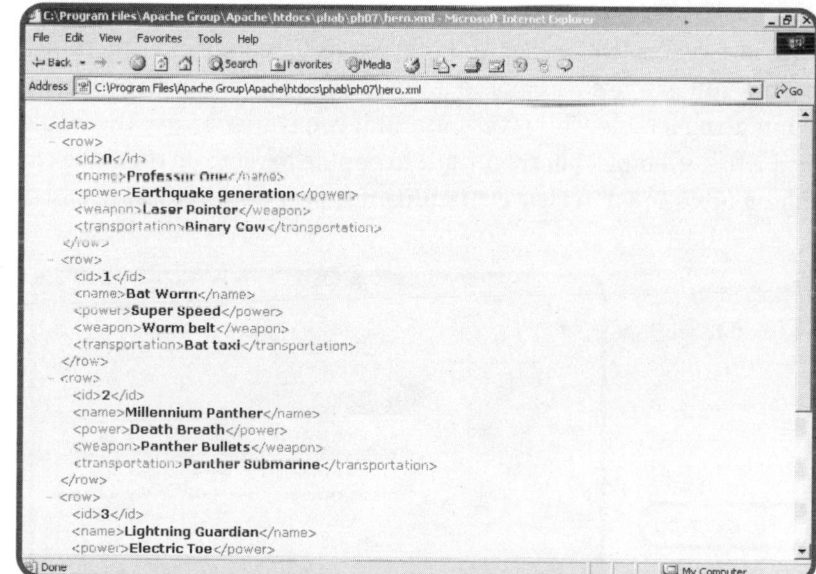

FIGURE 7.16

The XML form of the data generates HTML-like tags to describe the fields in the table.

Schema for database 'chapter7' in 'localhost' - Microsoft Internet Explorer

Address C:\Program Files\Apache Group\Apache\htdocs\phab\ph07\heroSchema.html

chapter7

- hero

hero

Fields

Field	Type	Null	Key	Default	Extra
id	int(11)		PRI	0	
name	varchar(30)	YES		(NULL)	
power	varchar(30)	YES		(NULL)	
weapon	varchar(30)	YES		(NULL)	
transportation	varchar(30)	YES		(NULL)	

Indexes

Table	Non unique	Key name	Seq in index	Column name	Collation	Cardinality	Sub part	Packed	Comment
hero	0	PRIMARY	1	id	A	5	(NULL)	(NULL)	

Back

FIGURE 7.17

The schema for a table describes important information about the table's structure.

One last very useful tool is the "export as batch script" function found on the "DB" menu. You can use this tool to automatically generate an SQL script for creating and populating a table. This is very useful if you choose to use the visual tools for creating and editing a table, but then want to be able to recreate the table through a script. The dialog box shown in Figure 7.18 illustrates the various options for this tool.

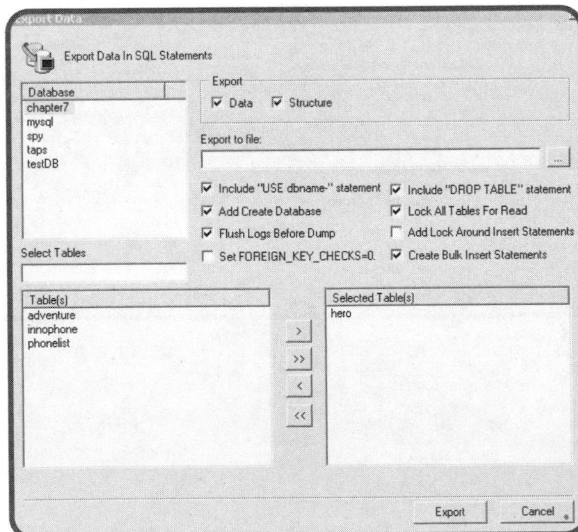

FIGURE 7.18

From this dialog box you can generate code that will manufacture replicas of any database created or viewed with SQLyog.

You can specify whether the resulting script generates the table structure alone or adds the data. You can also specify whether the resulting script contains code to select a database, drop the specified table if it already exists, and the filename of the resulting script.

The ability to automatically generate SQL scripts is incredibly powerful. It can be a great time-saver and you can learn a lot by examining the scripts written with such a feature. However, you are still the programmer, and you are responsible for code in your projects, even if you didn't write it directly. You must still understand what the code being generated does. Most of the code you'll see so far is stuff I've already described, but you may have to look up advanced features. As I've said before, you still have to know how to do this stuff by hand.

Creating More Powerful Queries

So far, the tables you've created haven't really been any more powerful than HTML tables, and they're a lot more trouble. The excitement of databases comes when you use the information to solve problems. Ironically, the most important part of database work isn't usually *getting* the data, but *filtering* the data in order to solve some sort of problem. You might want to get a listing of all heroes in your database who's last name begins with an "E," or perhaps somebody parked a Yak Dirigible in your parking space and you need to know who the driver is. You may also want your list sorted by special power, or you may only want a list of vehicles. All these (admittedly contrived) examples involve grabbing a subset of the original data. The workhorse of SQL is the `SELECT` statement. You've seen the simplest form of this command used to get all the data in a table, like this:

```
SELECT * FROM hero;
```

Figure 7.19 shows this form of the `SELECT` statement operating on the hero table.

SQLyog is a wonderful tool for experimenting with `SELECT` statements because you can write the actual SQL by hand, and then you can see the results immediately in a very clean format. To use SQLyog in this way, type in SQL code in the SQL editor, then press Shift+F5. If you don't want to use SQLyog, you can do the same experiments directly in MySQL. It will still work, but the results will be formatted as text, and not always as easy to see.

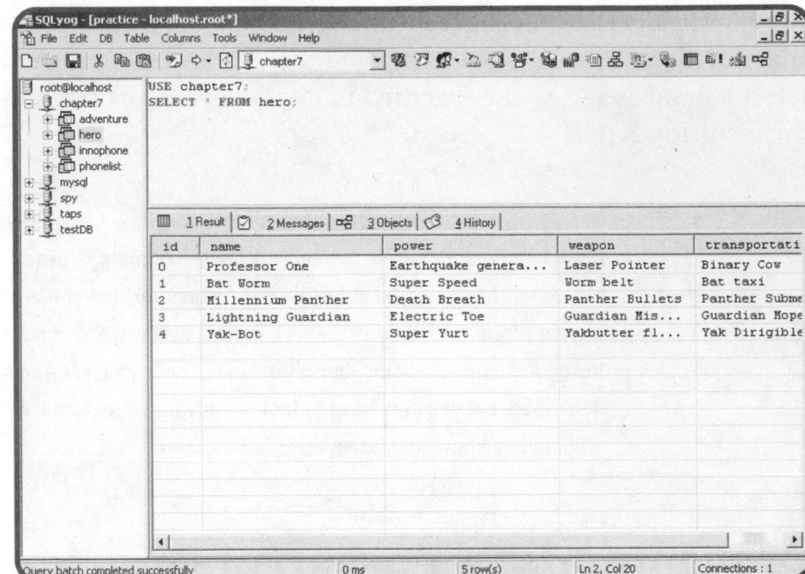

FIGURE 7.19

The SELECT query is in the top right section, and the results are shown underneath.

The SELECT statement is extremely powerful because it can be used to grab a subset of a data set that can return only the requested fields and records. This process of asking questions of the database is commonly called a *query*.

Limiting Columns

There are many times when you might not want all of the fields (or columns) in a table. For example, you might just want a list of the name and weapon of everyone on your list. You can specify this by using the following SELECT statement (illustrated in Figure 7.20).

```
SELECT name, weapon

FROM hero;
```

This may seem like a silly capability for such a simple database as the hero list, but you'll often run into extremely complicated tables with many fields, and you'll need to filter only a few fields. For example, I use a database to track the students I advise. Each student's information contains lots of data, but I might just want a list of names and e-mail addresses. The ability to isolate only the fields I need is one way to get useful information from a database.

The results of a query look a lot like a new table. You can think of a query result as a temporary table.

```
SELECT name, weapon
FROM hero;
```

name	weapon
Professor One	Laser Pointer
Bat Worm	Worm belt
Millennium Panther	Panther Bullets
Lightning Guardian	Guardian Missles
Yak-Bot	Yakbutter flamethrower

FIGURE 7.20

This Query returns only the names and weapons.

Limiting Rows with the WHERE Clause

In addition to limiting the columns returned in a query, you are often interested in limiting the number of rows. For example, you might run across an evil villain who can only be defeated by a laser pointer. The query shown in Figure 7.21 illustrates a query that solves exactly this dilemma.

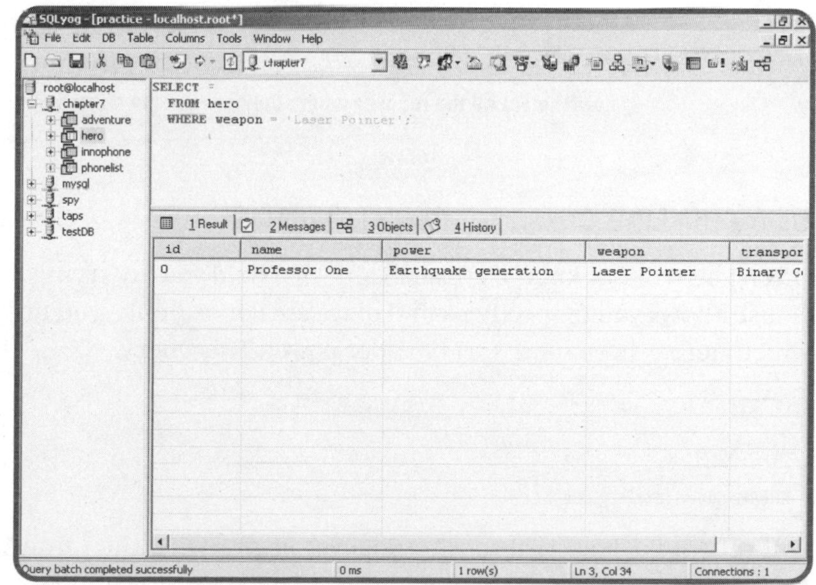

FIGURE 7.21

If you know how to set up the query, you can get very specific results. In this case, the query selects only heroes with a laser pointer.

```
SELECT *
  FROM hero
  WHERE weapon = 'Laser Pointer';
```

returns only the rows matching a specific condition.

Adding a Condition with a WHERE Clause

You can add a WHERE statement to a query to specify which row or rows you want to see. This clause allows you to specify a condition. The database manager will check every record in the table. If the condition is true for that record, it will be included in the result set. The conditions in a `WHERE` clause are similar to those in PHP code, but they are not *exactly* the same. In SQL, the single equal sign (=) is used for equality. Also, text elements are encased in single quotes. ('). You can also use <, >, and <= or >= and != conditions to limit your search.

The usage of comparison operators is pretty easy to understand for numeric data, such as integers and real numbers. It's not quite so obvious how a language will treat text comparisons. SQL has developed some standard rules, but each implementation might be somewhat different. SQL generally works in a case-insensitive way, so "Yak-Bot" would match "yak-bot" or "yAK-bOT." Also, the < and > operators refer to alphabetic order, so

```
SELECT *
  FROM hero
  WHERE name < 'D';
```

will select all the records where the hero's name starts with "A," "B," or "C."

Using the LIKE Clause for Partial Matches

Often you will not know the exact value of a field you are trying to match. The `LIKE` clause allows you to specify partial matches. For example, you might wish to know which heroes have some sort of super power. This query

```
SELECT *
  FROM hero
  WHERE power LIKE 'Super%';
```

will return back each hero whose power begins with the value "Super." The percent sign (%) can be used as a wild card to indicate any number of characters. You can use a variation of the LIKE clause to find information about all heroes with a transportation scheme that starts with the letter "B."

```
SELECT name, transportation
  FROM hero
  WHERE transportation LIKE 'B%';
```

You can also use the underscore character (_) to specify one character.

The simple wildcard character support in SQL is sufficient for many purposes. If you like regular expressions, you can use the REGEXP clause to specify whether a field matches a regular expression. This is a very powerful tool, but it is an extension to the SQL standard. It works fine in MySQL, but it is not supported in all SQL databases.

Generating Multiple Conditions

You can combine conditions with AND, OR, and NOT keywords for more complex expressions. For example,

```
SELECT *
  FROM hero
  WHERE transportation LIKE 'B%'
    AND power LIKE '%super%';
```

selects those heroes whose transportation starts with "B" and who have a power with "super" in its name.

This capability to create compound expressions will be very useful as you build more complex databases with multiple tables.

Using the ORDER BY Clause to Sort Results

One more nifty feature of the SELECT statement is the ability to sort the results by any field. Figures 7.22 and 7.23 illustrate how the ORDER BY clause can determine how tables are sorted.

The ORDER BY clause allows you to determine how the data is sorted. You can specify any field you wish as the sorting field. As you can see in Figure 7.23, the DESC clause specifies that data should be sorted in descending order.

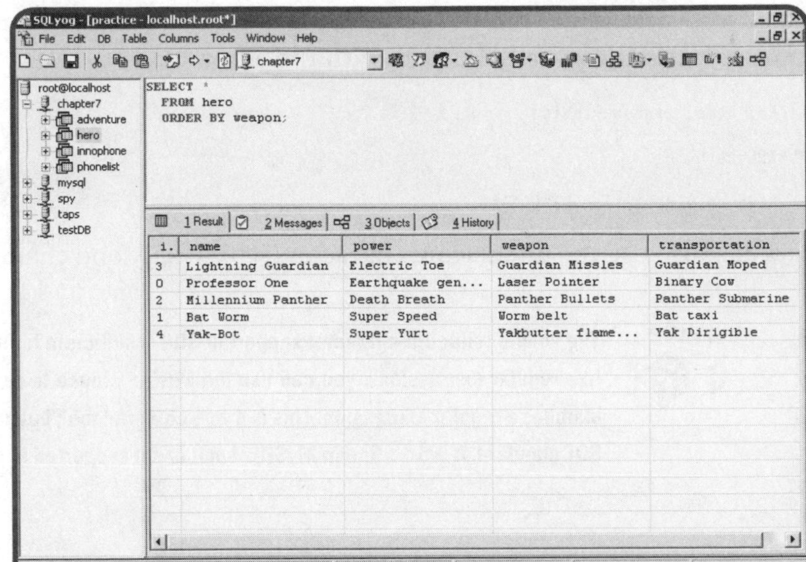

FIGURE 7.22

This query shows the entire database sorted by the weapon name.

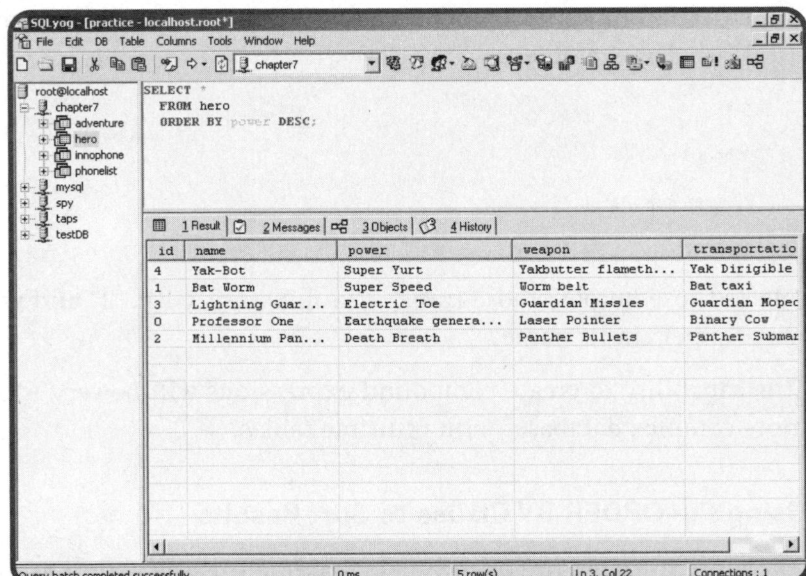

FIGURE 7.23

This query sorts by the power in descending (reverse alphabetical) order.

Changing the Data with the UPDATE Statement

You can also use SQL to modify the data in a database. The key to this behavior is the `UPDATE` statement. An example will help it make sense.

```
UPDATE hero
  SET power = 'Super Electric Toe'
  WHERE name = 'Lightning Guardian';
```

This code upgrades Lightning Guardian's power to the Super Electric Toe (which is presumably a lot better than the ordinary Electric Toe).

Generally, you will want to update only once record at a time. You can use a `WHERE` clause to select which record in the table will be updated.

Returning to the Adventure Game

The adventure generator featured at the beginning of this chapter uses a combination of MySQL and PHP code. You'll learn more about the PHP part in Chapter 8, "Connecting to Databases Within PHP." For now though, you have enough information to start building the data structure that forms the core of the game.

Designing the Data Structure

The adventure game is entirely about data. It has an incredibly repetitive structure. The same code operates over and over, but it operates on different parts of the database. I started the program by sketching out the primary play screen and thinking about what data elements I would need for each screen of the game. I ended up building a table that looks like Table 7.3.

As you examine the chart, you can see that I simplified the game so that each possible choice in the game boils down to seven elements. Each node (or decision point) in the game consists of an id (or room number), a room name, and a description of the current circumstances. Each node also has pointers that describe what happens when the user chooses to go in various directions from that node. For example, if the user is in the warehouse (node 3) and chooses to go east, he will go to node 4, which represents the doorway. Going south from node three takes the user to node 5, which is the box. I carefully thought about the game so the data structure represents all the places the user can go in this game. I chose to think of winning and losing as nodes, so everything in the game can be encapsulated in the table.

It's critical to understand that creating the table on paper is the first step. Once you've decided what kind of data your program needs, you can think about how you will put that data together. As you'll see, choosing a database gives me an incredible amount of control, and makes it pretty easy to work with the data. Perhaps the most amazing thing is this program can handle an entirely different game simply by changing the database. I don't have to change a single line of code to make the game entirely different. All I have to do is point to a different database or change the database.

Table 7.3 Data Structure of Enigma Adventure

id	name	description	north	east	south	west
0	-nothing-	You cannot go that way!	1	0	0	0
1	start over	You are at a submarine yard, looking for the famous Enigma code machine	0	3	0	2
2	sub deck	As you step on the submarine deck, a guard approaches you. Your only choice is to jump off the sub before you are caught.	15	15	15	15
3	warehouse	You wait inside the warehouse. You see a doorway to the east and a box to the south.	0	4	5	0
4	doorway	You walked right into a group of guards. It does not look good...	0	19	0	15
5	box	You crawl inside the box and wait. Suddenly, you feel the box being picked up and carried across the wharf!	6	0	0	7
6	wait	..You wait until the box settles in a dark space. You can move forward or aft...	8	0	9	0
7	jump out	You decide to jump out of the box, but you are cornered at the end of the wharf.	15	19	15	15
8	forward	As you move forward, two rough sailors grab you and hurl you out of the conning tower.	15	15	15	15
9	aft	In a darkened room, you see the enigma device. How will you get it out of the sub?	13	11	10	12
10	signal on enigma	You use the enigma device to send a signal. Allied forces recognize your signal and surround the ship when it surfaces.	14	0	0	0
11	shoot your way out	A gunfight on a submerged sub is a bad idea...	19	0	0	0
12	wait with enigma	You wait, but the sailors discover that enigma is missing and scour the sub for it. You are discovered and cast out in the torpedo tube.	15	0	0	0
13	replace enigma and wait	You put the enigma back in place and wait patiently, but you never get another chance. You are discovered when the sub pulls in to harbor.	19	0	0	0
14	Win	Congratulations! You have captured the device and shortened the war!	1	0	0	0
15	Water	You are in the water. The sub moves away. It looks bad...	19	0	0	0
16			0	0	0	0
17			0	0	0	0
18			0	0	0	0
19	Game Over	The game is over. You lose.	1	0	0	0

Once I decided on the data structure, I built an SQL script to create the first draft of the database. That script is shown here.

```
## build Adventure SQL File
## for MySQL
## Andy Harris

DROP TABLE IF EXISTS adventure;

CREATE TABLE ADVENTURE (
  id int PRIMARY KEY,
  name varchar(20),
  description varchar(200),
  north int,
  east int,
  south int,
  west int
);

INSERT INTO adventure values(
  0, 'lost', 'You cannot go that way!',
  1, 0, 0, 0
);

INSERT INTO adventure values(
  1, 'start', 'You are at a submarine yard, looking for the famous Enigma code machine',
  0, 3, 0, 2
);

INSERT INTO adventure values(
  2, 'sub deck', 'As you step on the submarine deck, a guard approaches you.  Your only choice is
to jump off the sub before you are caught.',
  15, 15, 15, 15
```

```
);

INSERT INTO adventure values(
  3, 'warehouse', 'You wait inside the warehouse.  You see a doorway to the south and a box to
the east.',
  0, 4, 5, 0
);

INSERT INTO adventure values(
  4, 'doorway', 'You walked right into a group of guards. It does not look good...', 0, 19, 0, 15
);

INSERT INTO adventure values(
  5, 'box', 'You crawl inside the box and wait. Suddenly, you feel the box being picked up and
carried across the wharf!', 6, 0, 0, 7
);

INSERT INTO adventure values(
  6, 'wait', '..You wait until the box settles in a dark space. You can move forward or aft...',
8, 0, 9, 0
);

INSERT INTO adventure values(
  7, 'jump out', 'You decide to jump out of the box, but you are cornered at the end of the
wharf.', 15 ,19, 15, 15
);

INSERT INTO adventure values(
  8, 'forward', 'As you move forward, two rough sailors grab you and hurl you out of the conning
tower.', 15 ,15, 15, 15
);

INSERT INTO adventure values(
```

```
  9, 'aft', 'In a darkened room, you see the enigma device. How will you get it out of the sub?',
13 ,11, 10, 12
);

INSERT INTO adventure values(
  10, 'signal on enigma', 'You use the enigma device to send a signal. Allied forces recognize
your signal and surround the ship when it surfaces', 14 ,0, 0, 0
);

INSERT INTO adventure values(
  11, 'shoot your way out', 'A gunfight on a submerged sub is a bad idea...', 19 ,0, 0, 0
);

INSERT INTO adventure values(
  12, 'wait with enigma' ,'You wait, but the sailors discover that enigma is missing and scour
the sub for it. You are discovered and cast out in the torpedo tube.', 15 ,0, 0, 0
);

INSERT INTO adventure values(
  13, 'replace enigma and wait','You put the enigma back in place and wait patiently, but you
never get another chance. You are discovered when the sub pulls in to harbor.', 19 ,0, 0, 0
);

INSERT INTO adventure values(
  14, 'Win', 'Congratulations! You have captured the device and shortened the war!', 1, 0, 0, 0
);

INSERT INTO adventure values(
  15, 'Water', 'You are in the water. The sub moves away. It looks bad...', 19 ,0, 0, 0
);

INSERT INTO adventure values(
  16,'','', 0, 0, 0, 0
```

```
);


INSERT INTO adventure values(
  17,'','', 0, 0, 0, 0
);


INSERT INTO adventure values(
  18,'','', 0, 0, 0, 0
);


INSERT INTO adventure values(
  19, 'Game Over' ,'The game is over. You lose.', 1, 0, 0, 0
);


SELECT id, name, north, east, south, west FROM adventure;
SELECT id, description FROM adventure;
```

I actually wrote this code by hand, but I could have designed it with SQLyog just as well. Note that I created the table, inserted values into it, and wrote a couple of `SELECT` statements to check the values. I like to have a script for creating a database even if I built it in a tool like SQLyog, because I managed to mess up this database several times as I was writing the code for this chapter. It was very handy to have a script that could instantly rebuild the database without any tears.

Summary

Although you didn't write any PHP at all in this chapter, you did learn how to create a basic data structure using the SQL language. You learned how to work with the MySQL console to create, and use databases. You learned how to return data from your database using the `SELECT` statement. You know how to modify the `SELECT` statement to get more specific results. You learned how SQLyog can simplify the creation and manipulation of MySQL databases. You built a data structure for an adventure game.

CHALLENGES

1. Design a basic database. Start with something simple like a phone list.
2. Create your database in SQL.
3. Write a batch program to create and populate your database.
4. Use SQLyog to manipulate your database and view its results in other formats.

Connecting to Databases Within PHP

After all this talk of databases, you might be eager to connect a database to your PHP programs. PHP is well known for its seamless integration of databases, especially MySQL. It's actually quite easy to connect to a MySQL database from within PHP. Once you've established the connection, you'll be able to send SQL commands to the database and receive the results as data you can use in your PHP program. By the end of this chapter, you'll build the adventure game featured at the beginning of Chapter 7, "Using MySQL to Create Databases." As you'll see, if the data is designed well, the programming isn't very hard. Specifically, you'll learn how to:

- Get a connection to a MySQL database from within PHP.
- Use a particular database.
- Send a query to the database.
- Parse the query results.
- Check for data errors.
- Build HTML output from data results.

Connecting to the Hero Database

To show how this works, I'll build a simple PHP program that returns all the values in the hero database you created in Chapter 7. Figure 8.1 illustrates the Show Hero PHP program.

I decided to go back to this simpler database rather than the more complex adventure game. When you're learning new concepts, it's best to work with the simplest environment you can at first, and then move to more complex situations. The adventure database has a lot of information in it, and the way the records point to each other is a little complicated. I wanted to start with a simpler database to be sure I understood the basics of data connection before working with a production database that is bound to have complexities of its own.

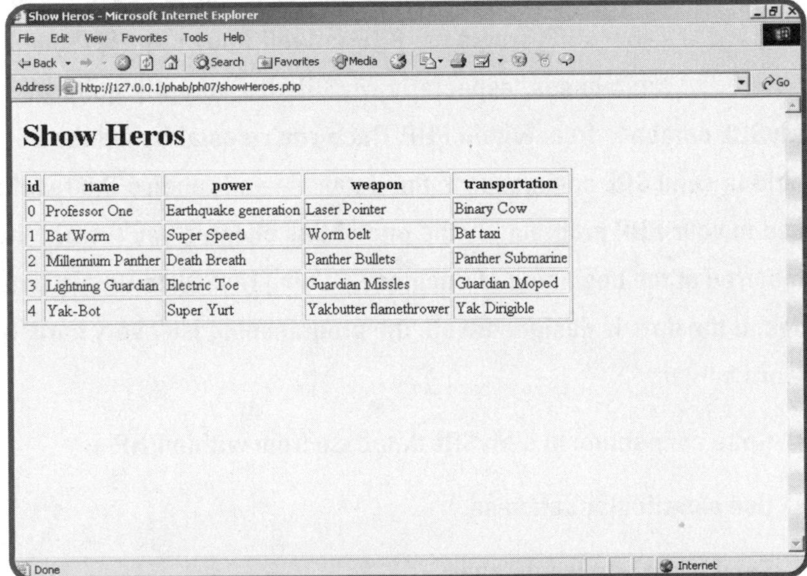

id	name	power	weapon	transportation
0	Professor One	Earthquake generation	Laser Pointer	Binary Cow
1	Bat Worm	Super Speed	Worm belt	Bat taxi
2	Millennium Panther	Death Breath	Panther Bullets	Panther Submarine
3	Lightning Guardian	Electric Toe	Guardian Missles	Guardian Moped
4	Yak-Bot	Super Yurt	Yakbutter flamethrower	Yak Dirigible

FIGURE 8.1

This HTML table is generated by a PHP program reading the database.

The code that generates this page is shown below:

```
<body>
<h1>Show Heros</h1>
<?
```

```
//make the database connection
$conn  = mysql_connect("localhost", "", "");
mysql_select_db("chapter7", $conn);

//create a query
$sql = "SELECT * FROM hero";
$result = mysql_query($sql, $conn);

print "<table border = 1>\n";

//get field names
print "<tr>\n";
while ($field = mysql_fetch_field($result)){
  print "  <th>$field->name</th>\n";
} // end while
print "</tr>\n\n";

//get row data as an associative array
while ($row = mysql_fetch_assoc($result)){
  print "<tr>\n";
  //look at each field
  foreach ($row as $col=>$val){
    print "  <td>$val</td>\n";
  } // end foreach
  print "</tr>\n\n";
}// end while

print "</table>\n";
?>
</body>
</html>
```

Glance over the code, and you'll see it's mostly familiar except for a few new functions that begin with "mysql_" These functions are designed to allow access to MySQL databases. If you look through the PHP documentation, you'll see very similar functions for several other types of databases, including Oracle, Informix, mSQL, and ODBC. You'll find the process for connecting to and using other databases are pretty much the same no matter which database you're using.

Getting a Connection

The first job is to get a connection between your PHP program and your MySQL server. You can connect to any server you have permission to use. The `mysql_connect` function arranges the communication link between MySQL and PHP. Here's the `connect` statement from the `showHero` program:

```
$conn  = mysql_connect("localhost", "", "");
```

The `mysql_connect()` function requires three parameters: server name, username, and password. The server name is the name or URL of the MySQL server you wish to connect to (this will be `localhost` if your PHP and MySQL servers reside on the same machine, which is frequently the case). The username refers to the username in MySQL. Most database packages have user accounts.

You will probably have to change the userName and password fields if you are running this code on a server somewhere. I used default values that work fine on an isolated test server, but you'll need to change to your username and password if you try this code on a production server.

You can use the same username and password you use to log into MySQL, and your program will have all the same access you do. Of course, you may want more restricted access for your programs, so you may want to create a special account, which has only the appropriate permissions, for users of your program.

IN THE REAL WORLD

Database security is an important and challenging issue.

There are a few easy things you can do to protect your data from most hackers. The first thing is to obscure your username and password information whenever you publish your code. I removed my username and password from the code shown here. In a practice environment, you can leave these values blank, but you should ensure you don't have wide open code that allows access to your data. If you need to post your code (for example in a class situation) be sure to change the password to something besides your real password.

The `mysql_connect()` function returns an integer referring to the database connection. You can think of this identifier much like the file pointers you learned in Chapter 6 "Working with Files." The data connection should be stored in a variable (I usually use something like `$conn`) because many of the other database functions will need to access the connection.

Choosing a Database

A data connection can have a number of databases connected to it. The `mysql_set_db()` function lets you choose a database. It works just like the `USE` command inside SQL. The `mysql_set_db()` function requires the name of a database and a data connection. This function returns the value `FALSE` if it was unable to connect to the specified database.

Creating a Query

Creating a query is very easy. The relevant code from `showHero.php` is reproduced here:

```
//create a query
$sql = "SELECT * FROM hero";
$result = mysql_query($sql, $conn);
```

You begin by placing SQL code inside a variable.

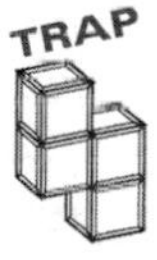

When you entered SQL commands into the SQL console or SQLyog, the commands required a semicolon. When your PHP program sends a command to the DBMS, the semicolon will automatically be added, so you should *not* end your SQL commands with semicolons. Of course, you'll be assigning these commands within a line of PHP code, which still has its own semicolon. (Sheesh!)

The `mysql_query()` function allows you to pass an SQL command through a connection to a database. You can send any SQL command to the database with `mysql_query()`, including table creation statements, updates, and queries. It returns a special element called a *result set*. If the SQL command was a query, the result variable will hold a pointer to the data, which we'll take apart in the next step. If it's a data definition command (the commands used to create, and modify tables) the result object will usually contain the string related to the success or failure of the operation.

Getting the Field Names

I'll be printing the data out in an HTML table. I could create the table headings by hand, because I know what all the fields are, but it's better to get the field information directly from the query, because you won't always know which fields are being returned by a particular query. The next chunk of code manages this task.

```
print "<table border = 1>\n";


//get field names

print "<tr>\n";

while ($field = mysql_fetch_field($result)){

  print "  <th>$field->name</th>\n";

} // end while

print "</tr>\n\n";
```

The `mysql_fetch_field()` function expects a query result as its one parameter. It then fetches the next field and stores it in the `$field` variable. If there are no fields left in the result, the function returns the value `FALSE`. This allows the field function to also be used as a conditional statement.

The `$field` variable is actually an object. You haven't used PHP objects yet, but they're really not too difficult. The `$field` object in this case is much like an associative array. It has a number of properties (which can be thought of as the attributes of the field). The field object has a number of attributes, listed in Table 8.1.

TABLE 8.1 COMMONLY USED PROPERTIES OF THE FIELD OBJECT

Property	Attribute
max_length	How long the field is (Especially important in VARCHAR fields)
name	The name of the field
primary_key	TRUE if the field is a primary key
table	Name of table this field belongs to
type	Data type of this field

By far the most common use of the field object is to determine the names of all the fields in a query. The other attributes can be useful in certain situations. You can see the complete list of attributes in the MySQL online help.

You use a slightly new syntax to refer to the properties of an object. Notice that I printed `$field->name` to the HTML table. This syntax simply refers to the `name` property of the `field` object. For now if you want to think of it as a fancy associative array, that would be reasonably accurate.

Parsing the Result Set

The rest of the code examines the result set. I'll reproduce it here so you can refresh your memory.

```
//get row data as an associative array
while ($row = mysql_fetch_assoc($result)){
  print "<tr>\n";
  //look at each field
  foreach ($row as $col=>$val){
    print "  <td>$val</td>\n";
  } // end foreach
  print "</tr>\n\n";
}// end while
```

The `mysql_fetch_assoc()` function fetches the next row from a result set. It requires a result pointer as its parameter, and it returns an associative array.

There are a number of other related functions for pulling a row from a result set. `mysql_fetch_object()` stores a row as an object much like the `mysql_fetch_fields()` function does. The `mysql_fetch_array()` function fetches an array that can be treated as a normal array, an associative array, or both. I tend to use `mysql_fetch_assoc()` because I think it's the most straightforward approach for those unfamiliar with object-oriented syntax. Of course, you should feel free to investigate these other functions and use them if they make more sense to you.

If there are no rows left in the result set, `mysql_fetch_assoc()` will return the value `FALSE`. It is often used as a condition in a `while` loop as I did here to fetch each row in a result set. Each row will represent a row of the eventual HTML table, so I print the HTML code to start a new row inside the `while` loop.

Once you've gotten a row, it's stored as an associative array. You can parse this array using a standard `foreach` loop. I chose to assign each element to `$col` and `$val` variables. I actually don't need `$col` in this case, but it can be handy to have. Inside the `foreach` loop I placed code to print out the current field in a table cell.

Returning to the Adventure Game Program

Recall at the end of Chapter 7 you created a database for the adventure game. Now that you know how to connect a PHP program to a MySQL database, you're ready to begin writing the game itself.

Connecting to the Adventure Database

Once I had built the database, the first PHP program I wrote tried to do the simplest possible connection to the database. I wanted to ensure I got all the data correctly. Here's the code for that program:

```
<html>
<head>
<title>Show Adventure</title>
</head>
<body>

<?
$conn  = mysql_connect("localhost", "", "");
mysql_select_db("chapter7", $conn);
$sql  = "SELECT * FROM adventure";
$result = mysql_query($sql);
while ($row = mysql_fetch_assoc($result)){

  foreach($row as $key=>$value){
    print "$key: $value<br>\n";
  } // end foreach
```

```
  print "<hr>\n";

} // end while

?>
</body>
</html>
```

This simple program was used to establish the connection and to ensure that everything was stored as I expected. Whenever I write a data program, I usually write something like this that quickly steps through my data to ensure everything is working correctly. There's no point in moving on until you know you have the basic connection.

I did not give you a screenshot of this program because it isn't very pretty, but I did include it on the CD-ROM so you can run it yourself. The point here is to start small and then turn your basic program into something more sophisticated one step at a time.

Displaying One Segment

The actual gameplay consists of repeated calls to the `showSegment.php` program. This program takes a segment id as its one input and then uses that data to build a page based on that record of the database. The only surprise is how simple the code is for this program.

```
<html>
<head>
<title>Show Segment</title>
<style type = "text/css">
body {
  color:red
}
td {
  color: white;
  background-color: blue;
  width: 20%;
```

```
  height: 3em;
  font-size: 20pt
}
</style>
</head>
<body>
<?
if (empty($room)){
  $room = 1;
} // end if

//connect to database
$conn  = mysql_connect("localhost", "", "");
$select = mysql_select_db("chapter7", $conn);
$sql = "SELECT * FROM adventure WHERE id = '$room'";
$result = mysql_query($sql);
$mainRow = mysql_fetch_assoc($result);

$theText = $mainRow["description"];
$northButton = buildButton("north");
$eastButton = buildButton("east");
$westButton = buildButton("west");
$southButton = buildButton("south");
$roomName = $mainRow["name"];

print <<<HERE
<center><h1>$roomName</h1></center>
<form method = "post">
<table border = 1>
<tr>
  <td></td>
  <td>$northButton</td>
```

```
  <td></td>
 </tr>

 <tr>
  <td>$eastButton</td>
  <td>$theText</td>
  <td>$westButton</td>
 </tr>

 <tr>
  <td></td>
  <td>$southButton</td>
  <td></td>
 </tr>

</table>
<center>
<input type = "submit"
       value = "go">
</center>
</form>

HERE;

function buildButton($dir){
  //builds a button for the specified direction
  global $mainRow, $conn;
  $newID = $mainRow[$dir];
  //print "newID is $newID";
  $query = "SELECT name FROM adventure WHERE id = $newID";
  $result = mysql_query($query, $conn);
  $row = mysql_fetch_assoc($result);
```

```
  $roomName = $row["name"];


  $buttonText = <<< HERE
  <input type = "radio"
         name = "room"
         value = "$newID">$roomName


HERE;


  return $buttonText;


} // end build button
?>
</body>
</html>
```

Creating a CSS Style

I began the HTML with a CSS style. My program is visually unappealing, but placing a CSS style here is the answer to my visual design disability. All I need to do is get somebody with an actual sense of style to clean up my CSS and I have a good-looking page.

Making the Data Connection

As usual, the program begins with some housekeeping. If the user hasn't specifically chosen a segment number, I'll start them out in room number 1, which will be the starting room.

```
if (empty($room)){
  $room = 1;
} // end if


//connect to database
$conn  = mysql_connect("localhost", "", "");
$select = mysql_select_db("chapter7", $conn);
```

```
$sql = "SELECT * FROM adventure WHERE id = '$room'";
$result = mysql_query($sql);
$mainRow = mysql_fetch_assoc($result);
$theText = $mainRow["description"];
```

I then make an ordinary connection to the database and choose the record pertaining to the current room number. That query is stored in the `$mainRow` variable as an associative array.

Generating Variables for the Code

Most of the program writes the HTML for the current record to the screen. To make things simple, I decided to create some variables for anything that might be tricky.

```
$theText = $mainRow["description"];
$roomName = $mainRow["name"];
$northButton = buildButton("north");
$eastButton = buildButton("east");
$westButton = buildButton("west");
$southButton = buildButton("south");
```

I stored the description field of the current row into a variable named `$theText`. I made a similar variable for the room name.

> **IN THE REAL WORLD**
>
> **It isn't strictly necessary to store the description field in a variable, but I'll be interpolating this value into HTML code, and I've found that interpolating associative array values can be a little tricky. In general, I like to copy an associative value to some temporary variable if I'm going to interpolate it. It's just a lot easier that way.**

The button variables are a little different. I decided to create an HTML option button to represent each of the places the user could go. I'll use a custom function called `buildButton()` to make each button.

Writing the buildButton() Function

The procedure for building the buttons was repetitive enough to warrant a function. Each button is a radio button corresponding to a direction. The radio button will have a value that comes from the corresponding direction value from the current record. If the `north` field of the current record is 12 (meaning if the user goes North load up the data in record 12), the radio button's value should be 12. The trickier thing is getting the appropriate label. All that's stored in the current record is the id of the next room. If you want to display the room's name, you have to make another query to the database. That's exactly what the `buildButton()` function does.

```
function buildButton($dir){
  //builds a button for the specified direction
  global $mainRow, $conn;
  $newID = $mainRow[$dir];
  //print "newID is $newID";
  $query = "SELECT name FROM adventure WHERE id = $newID";
  $result = mysql_query($query, $conn);
  $row = mysql_fetch_assoc($result);
  $roomName = $row["name"];

  $buttonText = <<< HERE
  <input type = "radio"
         name = "room"
         value = "$newID">$roomName

HERE;

  return $buttonText;

} // end build button
```

The function borrows the `$mainRow` array (which holds the value of the main record this page is about) and the data connection in `$conn`. I pull the ID for this button from the `$mainRow` array and store it in a local variable. The `buildButton()` function requires a direction name sent as a parameter. This direction should be the field name for one of the direction fields.

I repeat the query creation process, building a query that requests only the row associated with the new ID. I then pull the room name from that array. Once that's done, it's easy to build the radio button text. The radio button is called `room`, so the next time this program is called, the `$room` variable will correspond to whichever radio button the user selected.

Finishing the HTML

All that's left is to add a Submit button to the form and close up the form and HTML. The amazing thing is, that's all you need. This code alone is enough to let the user play this game. It takes some effort to set up the data structure, but then all you have to do is provide a link to the first record (by calling `showSegment.php` without any parameters) and the program will keep calling itself.

Viewing and Selecting Records

I suppose you could stop there, because the game is working, but the really great thing about this structure is how flexible it is. It won't take much more work to create an editor that allows you to add and modify records however you wish.

This actually requires a couple of PHP programs. The first (shown in Figure 8.2) prints out a summary of the entire game, and allows the user to edit any node.

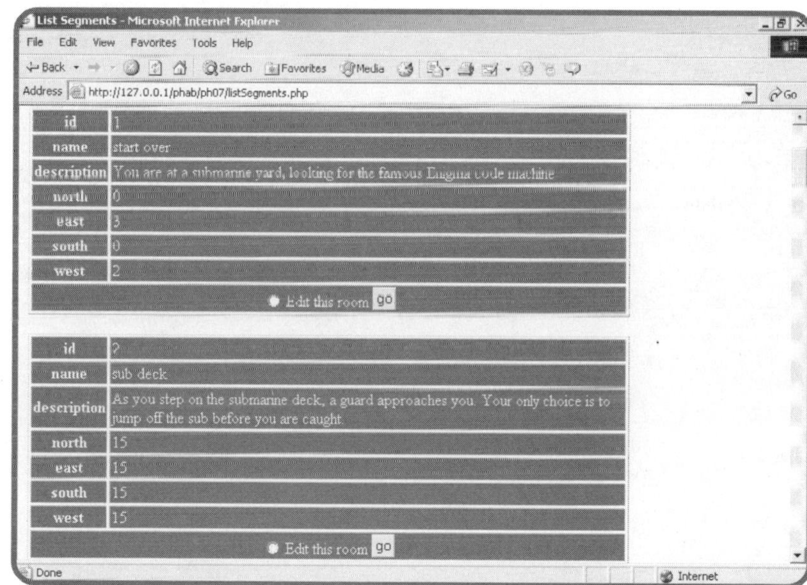

FIGURE 8.2

The listSegments program lists all the data and allows the user to choose a record for editing.

The code for the `listSegments.php` program is actually quite similar to the `showAdventure.php` program you saw before. It's simply cleaned up a bit to put the data in tables, and has a form to call an editor when the user selects a record to modify.

```
<html>

<head>

<title>List Segments</title>
```

```
<style type = "text/css">
body {
  color:red
}
td, th {
  color: white;
  background-color: blue;
}
</style>
</head>
<body>

<?
$conn  = mysql_connect("localhost", "", "");
$select = mysql_select_db("chapter7", $conn);
$sql = "SELECT * FROM adventure";
$result = mysql_query($sql);
print <<<HERE
<form action = "editSegment.php"
      method = "post">

HERE;

while ($row = mysql_fetch_assoc($result)){
  print "<table border = 1 width = 80%>\n";

  foreach($row as $key=>$value){
    //print "$key: $value<br>\n";
    $roomNum = $row["id"];
    print <<<HERE
  <tr>
    <th width = 10%>$key</th>
```

```
    <td>$value</td>
  </tr>

HERE;

  } // end foreach
  print <<<HERE
  <tr>
    <td colspan = 2><center>
      <input type = "radio"
             name = "room"
             value = "$roomNum">
      Edit this room
      <input type = "submit"
             value = "go">
    </center></td>
  </tr>
</table><br>

HERE;

} // end while

?>
<center>
<input type = "submit"
       value = "edit indicated room">
</center>
</form>
</body>
</html>
```

The entire program is contained in a form, which will call `editSegment.php` when activated. The program opens a data connection and pulls all elements from the database. It builds an HTML table for each record. Each table contains a radio button called "room" with the value of the current room number. Each table also has a copy of the Submit button so the user doesn't have to scroll all the way to the bottom of the page to submit the form.

Editing the Record

When the user has chosen a record from `listSegments.php`, the `editSegment.php` program (shown in Figure 8.3) will swing into action.

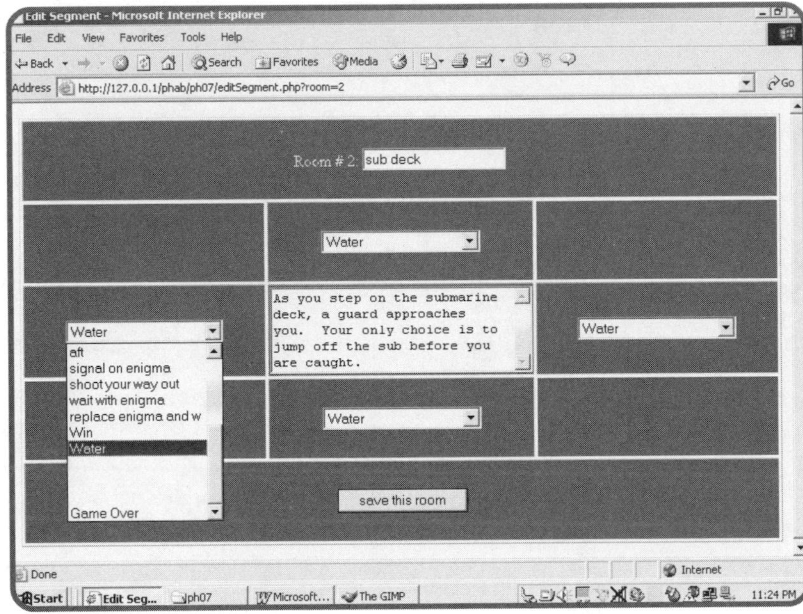

FIGURE 8.3

The edit record program displays data from a requested record and lets the user manipulate that data.

It's important to understand that the `editSegment` program *doesn't* actually change the record in the database. Instead, it pulls up a form containing the requested record's current values and allows the user to determine what the new values should be. The `editSegment` page is another form. When the user submits this form, control is passed to one more program which actually modifies the database. The code for `editSegment` is actually very similar to the code used to display a segment in play mode. The primary difference is that all the record data goes into editable fields.

Take a careful look at how the game developer can select a room to go into for each position. A drop-down list box shows all the existing room names. This device allows the game developer to work directly with room names even though the database will be much more concerned with room numbers.

```
<html>
<head>
<title>Edit Segment</title>
<style type = "text/css">
body {
  color:red
}
td {
  color: white;
  background-color: blue;
  width: 20%;
  height: 5em;
  text-align: center;
}
</style>
</head>
<body>
<?
if (empty($room)){
  $room = 0;
} // end if

//connect to database
$conn  = mysql_connect("localhost", "", "");
$select = mysql_select_db("chapter7", $conn);

$sql = "SELECT * FROM adventure WHERE id = '$room'";
$result = mysql_query($sql);
$mainRow = mysql_fetch_assoc($result);
$theText = $mainRow["description"];
$roomName = $mainRow["name"];
```

```
$northList = makeList("north", $mainRow["north"]);
$westList = makeList("west", $mainRow["west"]);
$eastList = makeList("east", $mainRow["east"]);
$southList = makeList("south", $mainRow["south"]);
$roomNum = $mainRow["id"];

print <<<HERE

<form action = "saveRoom.php"
      method = "post">
<table border = 1>
<tr>
  <td colspan = 3>
    Room # $roomNum:
    <input type = "text"
           name = "name"
           value = "$roomName">
    <input type = "hidden"
           name = "id"
           value = "$roomNum">
  </td>
</tr>

<tr>
  <td></td>
  <td>$northList</td>
  <td></td>
</tr>

<tr>
  <td>$westList</td>
  <td>
    <textarea rows = 5 cols = 30 name = "description">$theText</textarea>
```

```
  </td>
  <td>$eastList</td>
</tr>

<tr>
  <td></td>
  <td>$southList</td>
  <td></td>
</tr>

<tr>
  <td colspan = 3>
    <input type = "submit"
           value = "save this room">
  </td>

</table>


</form>

HERE;

function makeList($dir, $current){
  //make a list of all the places in the system

  global $conn;
  $listCode = "<select name = $dir>\n";
  $sql = "SELECT id, name FROM adventure";
  $result = mysql_query($sql);
  $rowNum = 0;
  while ($row = mysql_fetch_assoc($result)){
    $id = $row["id"];
```

```
    $placeName = $row["name"];
    $listCode .= "  <option value = $id\n";

    //select this option if it's the one indicated
    if ($rowNum == $current){
      $listCode .= "           selected\n";
    } // end if

    $listCode .= ">$placeName</option>\n";
    $rowNum++;
  } // end while
  return $listCode;
} // end makeList

?>

</body>
</html>
```

Generating Variables

After the standard database connection, the code creates a number of variables. Some of these variables (`$theText`, `$roomName`, and `$roomNum`) are simplifications of the associative array. Another set of variables are results of the `makeList()` function. The job of this function is to return an HTML list box containing the room names of every segment in the database. The list box will be set up so that whatever room number is associated with the indicated field will be selected as the default.

Printing the HTML Code

The central part of the program consists of a large print statement that develops the HTML code. The code in this case is a large table enclosed in a form. Every field in the record has a form element associated with it. When the user submits this form, it should have all the data necessary to update a record in the database. The one element the user should not be able to directly edit is the room number. This is stored in a hidden field. The directional room numbers are encoded in the list boxes. All other data is in appropriately named text boxes.

Creating the List Boxes

The list boxes require a little bit of thought to construct.

The `makeList()` function expects two parameters. The `$dir` parameter holds the direction field name of the current list box. The `$current` parameter holds information about which room is currently selected for this particular field of the current record. The data connection handler `$conn` is the only global variable. The variable `$listCode` will hold the actual HTML code of the listbox that will be returned to the main program.

The function makes a query to the database to request all the room names. Each name is added to the list box code at the appropriate time with the corresponding numeric value. Whenever the record number corresponds to the current value of the record, HTML code specifies that this should be the selected item in the list box.

Committing Changes to the Database

One more program is necessary. The `editSegment.php` program allows the user to edit the data, but when the user is finished with this task, he or she will submit the form, which will call the `saveRoom.php` program. I won't repeat the screen shot for this program, because the visuals are unimportant. However, this is the program that actually updates the database with whatever values the user has chosen.

```
<head>
<title>SaveRoom.php</title>
</head>
<body>

<?
//Once a room has been edited by editSegment, this program
//updates the database accordingly.

//connect to database
$conn  = mysql_connect("localhost", "", "");
$select = mysql_select_db("chapter7", $conn);

$sql = <<<HERE
UPDATE adventure
```

```
SET
  name = '$name',
  description = '$description',
  north = $north,
  east = $east,
  south = $south,
  west = $west
WHERE
  id = $id

HERE;

//print $sql;
$result = mysql_query($sql);
if ($result){
  print "<h3>$name room updated successfully</h3>\n";
  print "<a href = \"listSegments.php\">view the rooms</a>\n";
} else {
  print "<h3>There was a problem with the database</h3>\n";
} // end if

?>
</body>
</html>
```

This program begins with standard data connections. It then constructs an `UPDATE` `SQL` statement. The statement is quite simple, because all the work is done in the previous program. I then simply applied the query to the database and checked the result. An `UPDATE` statement won't return a recordset like a `SELECT` statement. Instead, it will return the value `FALSE` if it was unable to process the command. If the update request was successful, I let the user know and provide a link back to the `listSegments` program. If there was a problem, I provide some (not very helpful) feedback to the user.

Summary

In this chapter you began to use external programs to manage data. You learned how MySQL can be used to interpret basic SQL statements for defining and manipulating data. You created a database directly in the MySQL console, and you also learned how to build and manipulate databases with SQLyog. You combined these skills to create an interesting and expandable game.

CHALLENGES

1. Add a 'new room' command to the adventure generator. HINT: Think about how I created a new test in the quiz machine program from Chapter 6.
2. Write PHP programs to view, add, and edit records in the phone list.
3. Write a program that asks a user's name and searches the database for that user.
4. Create a front-end for another simple database.

Data Normalization

In the last two chapters you learned how to create a basic database and connect it to a PHP program. PHP and MySQL are wonderful for working with basic databases. However, most real-world problems involve data that is too complex to fit in one table. Database designers have developed some standard techniques for handling complex data that reduce redundancy, improve efficiency, and provide flexibility. In this chapter you will learn how to use the relational model to build complex databases involving multiple entities. Specifically, you will learn:

- How the relational model works.
- How to build use-case models for predicting data usage.
- How to construct entity-relationship diagrams to model your data.
- How to build multi-table databases.
- How joins are used to connect tables.
- How to build a link table to model many-to-many relationships.
- How to optimize your table design for later programming.

Introducing the Spy Database

In this chapter you will build a database to manage your international spy ring. (You *do* have an international spy ring, don't you?) Saving the world is a complicated task, so you'll need a database to keep track of all your agents. Secret agents are assigned to various operations around the globe, and certain agents have certain skills. The examples in this chapter will take you through the construction of such a database. You'll see how to construct the database in MySQL. In the final chapter, you'll use this database to make a really powerful spymaster application in PHP.

The spy database reflects a few facts about my spy organization (called the Pantheon of Humanitarian Performance, or PHP):

- Each agent has a code name.
- Each agent can have any number of skills.
- More than one agent can have the same skill.
- Each agent is assigned to one operation at a time.
- More than one agent can be assigned to one operation.
- The location of a spy is determined by the operation.
- Each operation has only one location.

This list of rules helps to explain some characteristics of the data. In database parlance, they are called *business rules*. I'll need to design the database so that these rules are enforced.

> **IN THE REAL WORLD**
>
> **I set up this particular set of rules in a somewhat arbitrary way because they help make my database as simple as possible while still illustrating most of the main problems you'll encounter in data design. Usually you don't get to make up business rules. Instead, you'll need to learn them by talking to those who use the data every day.**

The badSpy Database

As you learned in Chapter 7 "Using MySQL to Create Databases," it isn't difficult to build a data table, especially if you have a tool like SQLyog. Figure 9.1 illustrates the schema of my first pass at the spy database.

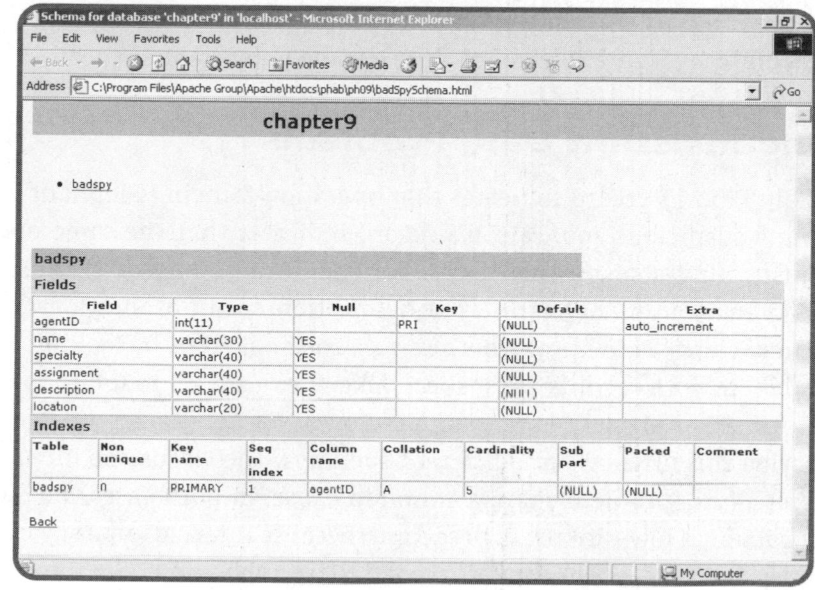

chapter9

- badspy

badspy

Fields

Field	Type	Null	Key	Default	Extra
agentID	int(11)		PRI	(NULL)	auto_increment
name	varchar(30)	YES		(NULL)	
specialty	varchar(40)	YES		(NULL)	
assignment	varchar(40)	YES		(NULL)	
description	varchar(40)	YES		(NULL)	
location	varchar(20)	YES		(NULL)	

Indexes

Table	Non unique	Key name	Seq in index	Column name	Collation	Cardinality	Sub part	Packed	Comment
badspy	0	PRIMARY	1	agentID	A	5	(NULL)	(NULL)	

Back

FIGURE 9.1

The badSpy database schema looks reasonable enough.

At first glance, the design of the `badSpy` database seems like it ought to work, but as soon as you begin adding data to the table, you'll begin to see some problems. Figure 9.2 shows the results of the `badSpy` data after I started entering information about some of my field agents.

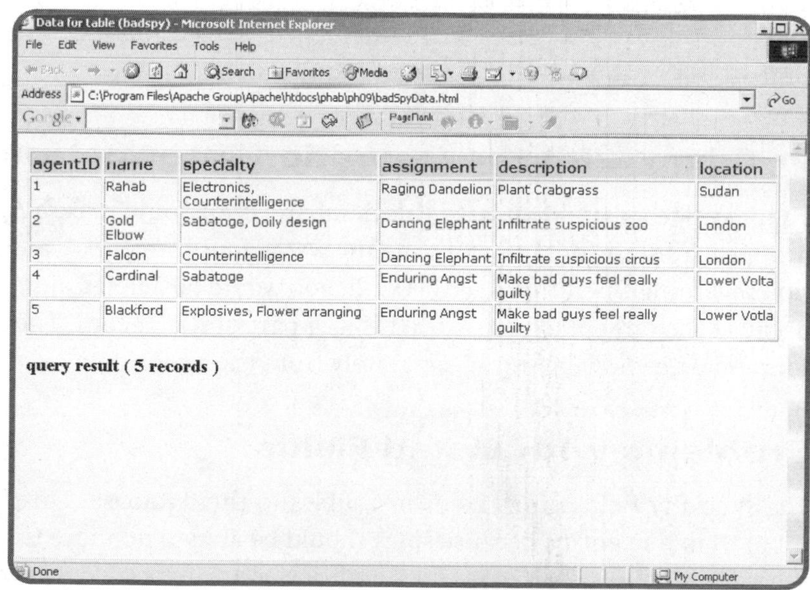

agentID	name	specialty	assignment	description	location
1	Rahab	Electronics, Counterintelligence	Raging Dandelion	Plant Crabgrass	Sudan
2	Gold Elbow	Sabatoge, Doily design	Dancing Elephant	Infiltrate suspicious zoo	London
3	Falcon	Counterintelligence	Dancing Elephant	Infiltrate suspicious circus	London
4	Cardinal	Sabatoge	Enduring Angst	Make bad guys feel really guilty	Lower Volta
5	Blackford	Explosives, Flower arranging	Enduring Angst	Make bad guys feel really guilty	Lower Votla

query result (5 records)

FIGURE 9.2

The badSpy database after I added a few agents.

Once you start entering data into the table, you'll see a few problems crop up. Look carefully at Figure 9.2 and you'll see some potential issues.

Inconsistent Data Problems

Gold Elbow's record indicates that operation Dancing Elephant is about infiltrating a suspicious zoo. Falcon's record indicates that the same operation is about infiltrating a suspicious circus. For the purpose of this example, I'm expecting that an assignment has only one description, so one of these descriptions is wrong. There's no way to know whether it's a zoo or a circus by looking at the data in the table, so both records are suspect. Likewise, it's hard to tell if operation Enduring Angst takes place in Lower Volta or Lower Votla, because the two records that describe this mission have different spellings. The circus/zoo inconsistency and the Volta/Votla problem share a common cause. In both cases the data entry person (probably a low-ranking civil servant, because international spy masters are *far* too busy to do their own data entry) had to type the same data into the database multiple times. This kind of inconsistency causes all kinds of problems. If you require a data entry person to enter the same data repeatedly, you will see inconsistencies in the results. Different people will choose different abbreviations. You may see multiple spellings of the same term. Some people will simply not enter data if it's too difficult. When this happens, you cannot rely on the data (is it a zoo or a circus?). You also can't search the data with confidence. (If I look for all operatives in Lower Volta, I'll miss Blackford, because he's listed as being in Lower *Votla*.) If you look carefully, you'll notice that I misspelled "sabatoge." It will be very difficult to find all places this word is misspelled and fix them all.

Problem with the Operation Information

There's another problem with this database. If for some reason Agent Rahab were dropped from the database (maybe she was a double agent all along), the information regarding Operation Raging Dandelion would be deleted along with her record, because the only place it is stored is as a part of her record. The operation's data somehow needs to be stored separately from the agent data.

Problems with Listed Fields

The specialty field brings its own troubles to the database. This field can contain more than one entity, because spies should be able to do more than one thing. (My favorite combination is explosives and flower arranging.) Fields with lists in them can be problematic. For one thing, it's much harder to figure out what size to make a field that may contain several entities. If your most talented spy has ten different skills, you would need enough room to store all ten skills in every spy's record. It can be difficult to search on fields that contain lists of data. You might be tempted to put several different skill fields (maybe a `skill1`, `skill2`, and `skill3` field, for example) but this doesn't completely solve the problem. It would be better to have a more flexible system that can accommodate any number of skills. The flat file system you've seen in this `badSpy` database is not capable of that kind of versatility.

Designing a Better Data Structure

The spy master database isn't really all that complicated, but the `badSpy` database shows you a number of ways even a simple database can go wrong. This is a pretty important database, because it will be used to save the free world, so it deserves a little more thought. Fortunately, data developers have come up with a number of ways to think about the structure of data. It is usually best to back away from the computer and think carefully about how data is used before you write a single line of code.

Defining Rules for a Good Data Design

Data developers have come up with a list of rules for creating well-behaved databases:

- Break your data into multiple tables.
- No field can have a list of entries.
- Do not duplicate data.
- Make each table describe only one entity.
- Create a single primary key field for each table.

A database that follows all these rules will avoid most of the problems evident in the `badSpy` database. Fortunately, there are some well-known procedures for improving a database so it can follow all these rules.

Normalizing Your Data

Data programmers try to prevent the problems evident in the `badSpy` database through a process called *data normalization*. The basic concept of normalization is to break down a database into a series of tables. If each of these tables is designed correctly, the database will be less likely to have the sorts of problems described so far in this chapter. Entire books have been written about data normalization, but the process breaks down into three major steps, called *normal forms*.

First Normal Form: Eliminate Repetition

The goal of the first normal form (sometimes abbreviated 1NF) is to eliminate repetition in the database. The primary culprit in the `badSpy` database is the `specialty` field. One solution would be to have two different tables, one for agents, and another for specialties.

Data designers seem to play a one-string banjo. The solution to almost every data design problem is to create another table. As you'll see, there still is quite an art form to what should be in that new table.

The two tables would look somewhat like Tables 9.1 and 9.2.

TABLE 9.1 AGENT TABLE IN 1NF

agentID	name	Assignment	Description	Location
1	Rahab	Raging Dandelion	Plant Crabgrass	Sudan
2	Gold Elbow	Dancing Elephant	Infiltrate suspicious zoo	London
3	Falcon	Dancing Elephant	Infiltrate suspicious circus	London

TABLE 9.2 SPECIALTY TABLE IN 1NF

specialtyID	name
1	electronics
2	counterintelligence
3	sabotage

Note that I did not include all data in these example tables, just enough to give you a sense of how these tables would be organized. Also, there isn't really a good way to connect these tables back together yet, but you'll learn that later in this chapter.

Second Normal Form: Eliminate Redundancies

Once all your tables are in the first normal form, the next step is to deal with all the potential redundancy issues. These mainly occur because data is entered more than one time. To fix this, you need to (you guessed it) build new tables. The `agent` table could be further improved by moving all data about operations to another table. Figure 9.3 shows a special diagram called an Entity Relationship diagram, which illustrates the relationships between these tables:

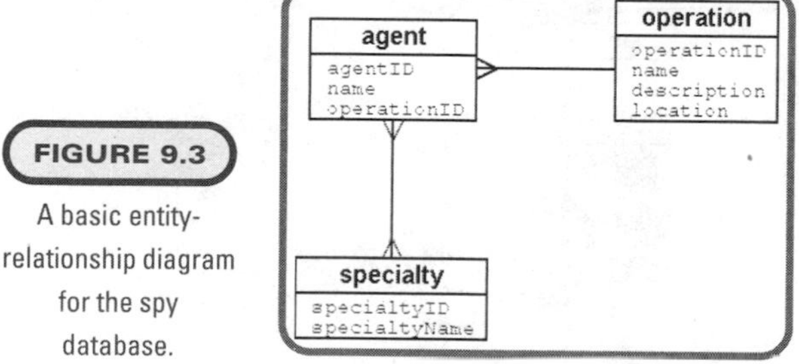

FIGURE 9.3

A basic entity-relationship diagram for the spy database.

An Entity Relationship diagram (ER diagram) is used to diagram the relationships between data elements. In this situation, I thought carefully about the data in the spy database. As I thought about the data, three distinct entities emerged. By separating the `operation` data from the `agent` data, I have removed redundancy, because the user will only enter operational data one time. This will eliminate several of the problems in the original database. It will also fix the situation where an operation's data was lost because a spy turned out to be a double agent. (I'm still bitter about that defection.)

Third Normal Form: Ensure Functional Dependency

The third normal form concentrates on the elements associated with each entity. In order for a table to be in the third normal form, that table must have a single primary key, and every field in the table must relate only to that key. For example, the `description` field is a description of the *operation*, not the *agent*, so it belongs in the `operation` table. In the third phase of normalization, you look through each piece of data in your table and ensure that it directly relates to the table it is placed in. If not, you need to either move it to a more appropriate table or build a new table for it.

IN THE REAL WORLD

You might notice that my database fell into third normal form automatically when I put it in second normal form. This is not unusual for very small databases, but rare with the large complex databases used to describe real-world enterprises. Even if your database seems to be in the third normal form already, go through each field to see if it relates directly to its table.

Defining Types of Relationships

The easiest way to normalize your databases is with a stylized view of them. ER diagrams are commonly used as a data design tool. Take another look at the ER diagram for the spy database in Figure 9.4.

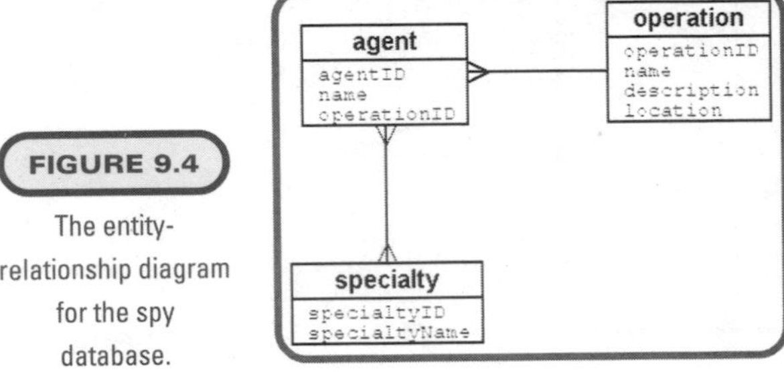

FIGURE 9.4

The entity-relationship diagram for the spy database.

This diagram illustrates the three entities in the spy database (at least up to now) and the relationships between them. Each entity is enclosed in a rectangle, and the lines between the entities represent the relationships between the entities. Take a careful look at the relationship lines. They have crow's-feet on them to indicate some special characteristics of the relationship. There are essentially three kinds of relationships (at least in this simplistic overview of data modeling).

Recognizing One-to-One Relationships

One-to-one relationships happen when each instance of entity A has exactly one instance of entity B. A one-to-one entity is described as a simple line between two entities with no special symbols on either end.

One-to-one relationships are actually rare, because usually if the two entities are that closely related, they can be combined into one table without any penalty. There are no one-to-one relationships in the spy ER diagram shown in Figure 9.4.

Describing Many-to-One Relationships

One-to-many (and many-to-one) relationships happen when one entity can contain more than one instance of the other. For example, each operation can have many spies, but (for the sake of this example) each agent can only be assigned to one mission at a time. Thus the agent-to-operation relationship is considered a many-to-one relationship, because a spy can have only one operation, but one operation can relate to many agents. In this very simplistic version of ER notation, I'm using crow's-feet to indicate the many side of the relationship.

There are actually several different kinds of one-to-many relationships, each with a different use and symbol. For this overview, we'll treat them all the same and use the generic crow's-feet symbol, but once you start writing more involved databases, you'll want to investigate data diagramming more closely by looking into books on data normalization and software engineering. Likewise, data normalization is a far more involved topic than the brief discussion in this introductory book. At some point you'll want to study the topic more carefully.

Recognizing Many-to-Many Relationships

The final type of relationship shown in the spy ER diagram is a many-to-many relationship. This type of relationship occurs when each entity can have many instances of the other. Agents and skills have this type of relationship, because one agent can have any number of skills, and each skill can be used by any number of agents. A many-to-many relationship is usually shown by crow's-feet on each end of the connecting line.

It's important to generate an ER diagram of your data including the relationship types, because there are different strategies for creating each type of relationship. You'll see these strategies emerge as I build the SQL for the improved spy database.

In the Real World

Professional programmers often use expensive software tools to help build data diagrams, but you don't need anything more than paper and pencil to draw ER figures. I do my best data design with a partner drawing on a white board. I like to talk through designs out loud and look at them in a large format. Once I've got a sense of the design, I usually use a vector-based drawing program to produce a more formal version of the diagram. This type of drawing tool is useful because it allows you to connect elements together, already has the crow's-feet lines available, and allows you to move elements around without disrupting the lines between them. Dia is an excellent open-source program for drawing all kinds of diagrams. I used it to produce all the ER figures in this chapter. A copy of Dia is on the CD that accompanies this book.

Building Your Data Tables

Once you have designed the data according to the rules of normalization, you are ready to actually build sample data tables in SQL. It pays to build your tables carefully to avoid problems. I prefer to build all my tables in an SQL script so I can easily rebuild my database if (okay, when) my programs mess up the data structure. Besides, enemy agents are always lurking about preparing to sabotage my operations.

I also add plenty of sample data in the script. You don't want to work with actual data early on, because you are guaranteed to mess up somewhere during the process. However, it is a good idea to work with sample data that is a copied subset of the actual data. Your sample data should anticipate some of the anomalies that might occur in actual data (for example, what if a person doesn't have a middle name?). My entire script for the spy database is available on the CD-Rom as `buildSpy.sql`. All SQL code fragments shown in the rest of this chapter come from that file.

Setting Up the System

I began my SQL script with some comments that describe the database and a few design decisions I made when building the database.

```
######################################
# buildSpy.sql
# builds and populates all databases for spy examples
# uses mysql - should adapt easily to other rdbms
# by Andy Harris for PHP/MySQL for Abs. Beg
######################################

######################################
# conventions
######################################
# primary key = table name . ID
# primary key always first field
# all primary keys autonumbered
# all field names camel-cased
# only link tables use underscore
# foreign keys indicated although mySQL does not enforce
# every table used as foreign reference has a name field
```

```
###########################################

###########################################
#housekeeping
###########################################

use chapter9;
DROP TABLE IF EXISTS badSpy;
DROP TABLE IF EXISTS agent;
DROP TABLE IF EXISTS operation;
DROP TABLE IF EXISTS specialty;
DROP TABLE IF EXISTS agent_specialty;
DROP TABLE IF EXISTS spyFirst;
```

Notice that I specified a series of conventions. These self-imposed rules will help make my database easier to manage when things get complicated. Some of the rules might not make sense yet (because I haven't identified what a foreign key is, for instance), but the important thing is I have clearly identified some rules that will help me later on.

The code then specifies the `chapter9` database, and deletes all tables if they already existed. This behavior ensures I'll start with a fresh version of the data.

Creating the agent Table

The normalized agent table is actually quite simple. The actual table is shown in Table 9.3.

TABLE 9.3 THE AGENT TABLE

agentID	name	operationID
1	Bond	1
2	Falcon	1
3	Cardinal	2
4	Blackford	2

The only data remaining in the agent table is the agent's name and a numerical field for the operation. The `operationID` field is used as the glue that holds together the `agent` and `operation` tables.

I've added a few things to improve the SQL code for creating the `agent` table to ensure that it behaves well.

```
CREATE TABLE agent (
  agentID int(11) NOT NULL AUTO_INCREMENT,
  name varchar(50) default NULL,
  operationID int(11) default NULL,
  PRIMARY KEY  (agentID),
  FOREIGN KEY (operationID) REFERENCES operation (operationID)
);
```

Recall that the first field in a table is usually called the `primary key`. Primary keys must be unique and each record must have one. I've also chosen to name each primary key according to a special convention. Primary key names will always begin with the table name and end with "ID." I added this convention because it will make things easier later on when I write programs to work with this data. The `NOT NULL` modifier ensures that all records of this table must have a primary key. The `AUTO_INCREMENT` identifier is a special tool that allows MySQL to pick a new value for this field if no value is specified. This will ensure that all entries are unique.

Not all databases use the `AUTO_INCREMENT` feature in the same way. You might need to look up some other way to automatically generate key fields if you aren't using MySQL.

I've added an indicator at the end of the `CREATE TABLE` statement to indicate that `agentID` is the primary key of the `agent` table.

Creating a Reference to the operation Table

Take a careful look at the `operationID` field. This field contains an integer, which will be used to refer to a particular operation. I also added an indicator specifying `operationID` as a foreign key reference to the `operation` table. The `operationID` field in the `agent` table will contain a reference to the primary key of the `operation` table. This type of field is referred to as a *foreign key*.

Some DBMS systems require you to specify primary and foreign keys. MySQL currently does not require this, but it's a good idea to do so anyway for two reasons. First, it's likely that future versions of MySQL will require these statements, because they are used to improve the reliability of a database. Second, it's very good to specify in the code when you wish a field to have a special purpose, even if the DBMS doesn't do anything with that information.

Inserting a Value into the agent Table

The `INSERT` statements for the `agent` table have one new trick made possible by the `AUTO_INCREMENT` designation of the primary key.

```
INSERT INTO agent VALUES(
  null, 'Bond', 1
);
```

The primary key is initialized with the value `null`. This might be surprising because primary keys are explicitly designed to never contain a null value. Since the `agentID` field is set to `AUTO_INCREMENT`, the null value is automatically replaced with an unused integer. This trick ensures that each primary key value will be unique.

Building the operation Table

The new `operation` table contains information referring to an operation. (See Table 9.4 for descriptions of some operation IDs.)

Table 9.4 The operation Table

operationID	name	description	location
1	Dancing Elephant	Infiltrate suspicious zoo	London
2	Enduring Angst	Make bad guys feel really guilty	Lower Volta
3	Furious Dandelion	Plant crabgrass in enemy lawns	East Java

Each operation gets its own record in the operation table. All the data corresponding to an operation is stored in the operation record. Each operation's data is stored only one time. This has a number of positive effects:

- It's only necessary to enter operation data once per op, saving time on data entry.
- Since there's no repeated data, you won't have data inconsistency problems (like the circus/zoo problem).
- The new database will take less space, because there's no repeated data.
- The operation is not necessarily tied to an agent, so you won't accidentally delete all references to an operation by deleting the only agent assigned to that mission (remember, this could happen with the original data design).
- If you need to update operation data, you don't need to go through every agent to figure out which ones were assigned to that operation (again, you would have had to do this with the old database design).

The SQL used to create the operation table is much like that used for the agent table:

```
CREATE TABLE operation (
  operationID int(11) NOT NULL AUTO_INCREMENT,
  name varchar(50) default NULL,
  description varchar(50) default NULL,
  location varchar(50) default NULL,
  PRIMARY KEY  ('OperationID')
);

INSERT INTO operation VALUES(
  null, 'Dancing Elephant',
  'Infiltrate suspicious zoo', 'London'
);
```

As you can see, the operation table conforms to the rules of normalization, and it also is much like the agent table. Notice that I'm being very careful about how I name things. SQL is (theoretically) case-insensitive, but I've found that this is not always true (especially in MySQL, where the Windows versions appear not concerned about case, but UNIX versions will treat operationID and OperationID as different field names). I specified that all field names will use 'camel-case' (just like you've been doing with your PHP variables). I have also named the key field according to my own formula (table name followed by "ID").

Using a Join to Connect Tables

The only downside to disconnecting the data tables is the necessity to somehow rejoin the data when needed. The user really doesn't care that the operation and the agent are in different tables, but he or she still will want the data to be visible as if they were on the same table. The secret to re-attaching tables is a tool called the *inner join*. Take a look at the following `SELECT` statement in SQL:

```
SELECT agent.name AS agent, operation.name AS operation
FROM agent, operation
WHERE agent.operationID = operation.operationID
ORDER BY agent.name;
```

At first glance this looks like an ordinary query, but it is a little different because it joins up data from two different tables. Table 9.5 illustrates the results of this query.

TABLE 9.5 COMBINING TWO TABLES

agent	operation
Blackford	Enduring Angst
Bond	Dancing Elephant
Cardinal	Enduring Angst
Falcon	Dancing Elephant
Rahab	Furious Dandelion

Creating Useful Joins

An SQL query can pull data from more than one table. To do this, there a couple of basic rules.

First, you might need to specify the field names more formally. Notice that the `SELECT` statement specifies `agent.name` rather than simply `name`. This is necessary because both tables contain a field called `name`. Using the table.field syntax is much like using a person's first and last name. It's not necessary if there's no chance of confusion, but in a larger environment the more complete naming scheme can avoid confusion.

Also, note the use of the `AS` clause. This provides an alias for the column and provides a nicer output.

The FROM clause up to now has only specified one table. In this example, it's necessary to specify that data will be coming from two different tables.

Examining a Join Without a WHERE Clause

The WHERE clause helps to clarify the relationship between the two tables. As an explanation, consider the following query:

```
SELECT
  agent.name AS 'agent',
  agent.operationID as 'agent opID',
  operation.operationID as 'op opID',
  operation.name AS 'operation'
FROM agent, operation
ORDER BY agent.name;
```

This query is much like the earlier query, except it includes the operationID field from each table and it omits the WHERE clause. You might be surprised by the results.

Adding a WHERE Clause to Make a Proper Join

Without a WHERE clause, all possible combinations are returned. The only records we're concerned with are those where the operationID fields in the agent table and in the operation table have the same value. The WHERE clause returns only these values joined by a common operation ID.

The secret to making this work is the operationID fields in the two tables. You've already learned that each table should have a primary key. The primary key field is used to uniquely identify each record in a database. In the agents table, agentID is the primary key. In operations, operationID is the primary key. (You might note my unimaginative but very useful naming convention here) I was able to take all data that refers to the operation out of the agent table by replacing those fields with a field that points to the primary key of the operations table. A field that references the primary key of another table is called a foreign key. Primary and foreign keys cement the relationships between tables. See Table 9.6.

Table 9.6 Joining agent and operation without a WHERE clause

agent	agent opID	op opID operation
Blackford	1	1 Dancing Elephant
Blackford	1	2 Enduring Angst
Blackford	1	3 Furious Dandelion
Bond	1	1 Dancing Elephant
Bond	1	2 Enduring Angst
Bond	1	3 Furious Dandelion
Cardinal	2	2 Enduring Angst
Cardinal	2	3 Furious Dandelion
Cardinal	2	1 Dancing Elephant
Falcon	1	1 Dancing Elephant
Falcon	1	2 Enduring Angst
Falcon	1	3 Furious Dandelion
Rahab	3	1 Dancing Elephant
Rahab	3	2 Enduring Angst
Rahab	3	3 Furious Dandelion

Adding a Condition to a Joined Query

Of course, you can still use the `WHERE` clause to limit which records are shown. Use the `AND` structure to build compound conditions. For example, this code:

```
SELECT
  agent.name AS 'agent',
  operation.name AS operation
FROM agent, operation
WHERE agent.operationID = operation.operationID
  AND agent.name LIKE 'B%';
```

will return the code name and operation name of every agent whose code name begins with "B."

The Truth about Inner Joins

You should know that the syntax I provided here is a convenient shortcut supported by most DBMS systems. The formal syntax of the inner join looks like this:

```
SELECT agent.name, operation.name
FROM
  agent INNER JOIN operation
  ON agent.OperationID = operation.OperationID
ORDER BY agent.name;
```

Many data programmers prefer to think of the join as part of the `WHERE` clause and use the `WHERE` syntax. A few SQL databases (notably many offerings from Microsoft) do not allow the `WHERE` syntax for inner joins, and require the `INNER JOIN` to be specified as part of the `FROM` clause. When you use this `INNER JOIN` syntax, the `ON` clause indicates how the tables will be joined.

Building a Link Table for Many-Many Relationships

Once you've created an ER diagram, you can create new tables to handle all the one-to-many relationships. It's a little less obvious what to do with many-to-many relationships such as the link between agents and skills. Recall that each agent can have many skills, and several agents can use each skill. The best way to handle this kind of situation is to build a special kind of table.

Enhancing the ER Diagram

Figure 9.5 shows a new version of the ER diagram that eliminates all many-many relationships.

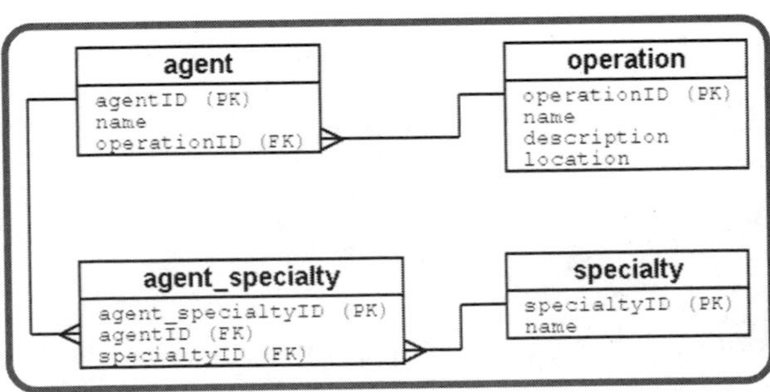

FIGURE 9.5

This newer ER diagram includes a special table to handle the many-many relationship

The ER diagram featured in Figure 9.5 improves on the earlier version in a number of ways. First, I added (PK) to the end of every primary key. I also added (FK) to the end of every foreign key. The placements of the lines in the diagram are now much more important. I now draw a line only between a foreign key reference and the corresponding primary key in the other table. Every relationship should go between a foreign key reference in one table and a primary key in the other. The other main improvement is the addition of the agent_specialty table. This table is interesting because it contains nothing but primary and foreign keys. Each entry in this table represents one link between the agent and specialty tables.

Most tables in a relational database are about entities in the data set, but link tables are about *relationships* between entities.

All the actual data referring to the agent or specialty are encoded in other tables. This arrangement provides a great deal of flexibility.

Creating the specialty Table

The specialty table is actually extremely simple, as shown in Table 9.7.

TABLE 9.7 THE SPECIALTY TABLE

specialtyID	name
0	Electronics
1	Counterintelligence
2	Sabotage
3	Doily Design
4	Explosives
5	Flower Arranging

As you can see, there is nothing in the specialty table that connects it directly with any particular agent. Likewise, you'll find no references to specialties in the agent table. The complex relationship between these two tables is handled by the new agent_specialty table. This special kind of table is called a *link table* because it is used to manage the relationships between other tables. Table 9.8 shows a sample set of data in the agent_specialty table.

TABLE 9.8 THE AGENT_SPECIALTY TABLE

agent_specialty_ID	agentID	specialtyID
1	1	2
2	1	3
3	2	1
4	2	6
5	3	2
6	4	4
7	4	5

Interpreting the agent_specialty Table with a Query

Of course, the agent_specialty table is not directly useful to the user, because it contains nothing but foreign key references. You can translate the data to something more meaningful with an SQL statement:

```
SELECT agent_specialtyID,
       agent.name AS 'agent',
       specialty.name AS 'specialty'
FROM agent_specialty,
     agent,
     specialty
WHERE agent.agentID = agent_specialty.agentID
  AND specialty.specialtyID = agent_specialty.specialtyID;
```

It requires two comparisons to join the three tables. It is necessary to forge the relationship between `agent` and `agent_specialty` by common `agentID` values. It's also necessary to secure the bond between `specialty` and `agent_specialty` by comparing the `specialtyID` fields. The results of such a query show that the correct relationships have indeed been joined, as you can see in Table 9.9.

The link table provides the linkage between tables that have many-many relationships. Each time you want a new relationship between an agent and a specialty, you add a new record to the `agent_specialty` table.

Table 9.9 Query Interpretation of agent_specialty Table

agent_specialtyID	agent	specialty
1	Bond	Sabotage
2	Bond	Doily Design
3	Falcon	Counterintelligence
5	Cardinal	Sabotage
6	Blackford	Explosives
7	Blackford	Flower Arranging

Creating Queries That Use Link Tables

Whenever you want to know about the relationships between agents and specialties, the data is available in the `agent_specialty` table. For example, if you need to know which agents know flower arranging, you can use the following query:

```
SELECT
  agent.name
FROM
  agent,
  specialty,
  agent_specialty
WHERE agent.agentID = agent_specialty.agentID
  AND agent_specialty.specialtyID = specialtiy.specialtyID
  AND specialty.name = 'Flower Arranging';
```

This query looks a little scary, but it really isn't as bad as it looks. This query requires data from three different tables. The output will need the `name` from the `agent` table. I don't want to remember what specialty number is associated with "Flower Arranging," so I'll let the query look that up from the `specialty` table. Since I need to know which agent is associated with a particular specialty, I'll use the `agent_specialty` table to link up the other two tables. The `WHERE` clause simply provides the joins. The phrase

```
agents.agentID = agent_specialty.agentID
```

cements the relationship between `agents` and `agent_specialty`. Likewise,

```
agent_specialty.specialtyID = specialties.specialtyID
```

ensures the connection between `specialties` and `agent_specialty`. The last part of the `WHERE` clause is the actual conditional part of the query that only returns records where the specialty is flower arranging. (You know, flower arrangement can be a deadly art in the hands of a skilled practitioner...)

Summary

In this chapter you have moved beyond programming to an understanding of data, the real fuel of modern applications. You learned how to take a poorly designed table and convert it into a series of well-organized tables that can avoid a lot of data problems. You've learned about three stages of normalization. You've learned how to build an Entity-Relationship diagram. You can recognize three kinds of relationships between entities. You can build normalized tables in SQL, including pointers for primary and foreign keys. You can connect normalized tables with `INNER JOIN SQL` statements. You know how to simulate a many-to-many relationship by building a link table. The civilized world is safer for your efforts.

CHALLENGES

1. **See if you can locate ER diagrams for data you work with every day. (Check with your firm's CIS department.) Examine these documents and see if you can make sense of them.**
2. **Examine a database you use regularly. Determine if it follows the requirements stated in this chapter for a well-designed data structure. If not, explain what might be wrong with the data structure and how it could be corrected.**
3. **Diagram an improved data structure for the database you examined in the last question. Create the required tables in SQL and populate them with sample data.**
4. **Design a database for data you use every day. (Be warned, most data problems are a LOT more complex than they first appear.) Create a data diagram, then build the tables and populate with sample data.**

Building a Three-Tiered Data Application

You began this book looking at HTML pages, which are essentially static documents. You then learned how to generate dynamic pages with the powerful PHP language. In the last few chapters, you learned how to use a database management system such as MySQL to build powerful data structures. This last chapter will tie together the PHP programming and data programming aspects to build a full-blown data management system for the spy database. The system you will learn can easily be expanded to any kind of data project you can think of, including e-commerce applications. Specifically, you will learn how to:

- Design a moderate-to-large data application.
- Build a library of reusable data functions.
- Optimize functions for use across data sets.
- Include library files in your programs.

There isn't really much new PHP or MySQL code to learn in this chapter. The focus is on how to build a larger project with minimum effort.

Introducing the Spy Master Program

The Spy Master program is a suite of PHP programs that allows access to the spy database created in Chapter 9, "Data Normalization." While the database created in that chapter is flexible and powerful, it is *not* easy to use unless you know SQL. Even if your users do understand SQL, you don't want them to have direct control of a database, because too many things can go wrong. You need to build some sort of front-end application to the database. In essence, there are three levels to this system. The client computer handles communication with the user. The database server (MySQL) manages the actual data. The PHP program sits between the client and the database acting as an interpreter. PHP provides the bridge between the HTML language of the client and the SQL language of the database. This kind of arrangement is frequently called a *three-tier-architecture*. As you examine the Spy Master program throughout this chapter you'll learn some of the advantages of this particular approach.

Viewing the Main Screen

Start by looking at the program from the user's point of view as shown in Figure 10.1.

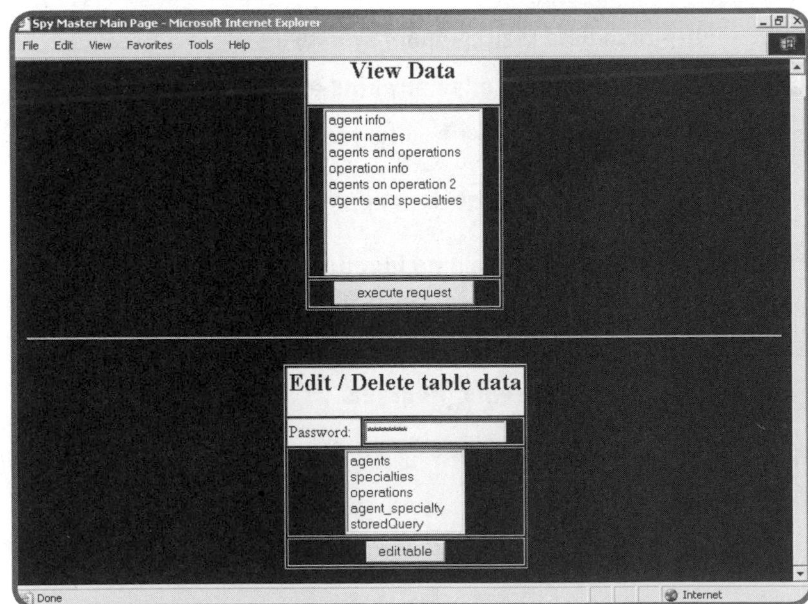

FIGURE 10.1

The entry point to the Spy Master Database is clean and simple.

The main page has two sections. The first is a series of data requests. Each of these requests maps to a query.

Viewing the Results of a Query

When the user selects a query and presses the Submit button, a screen like the one in Figure 10.2 appears.

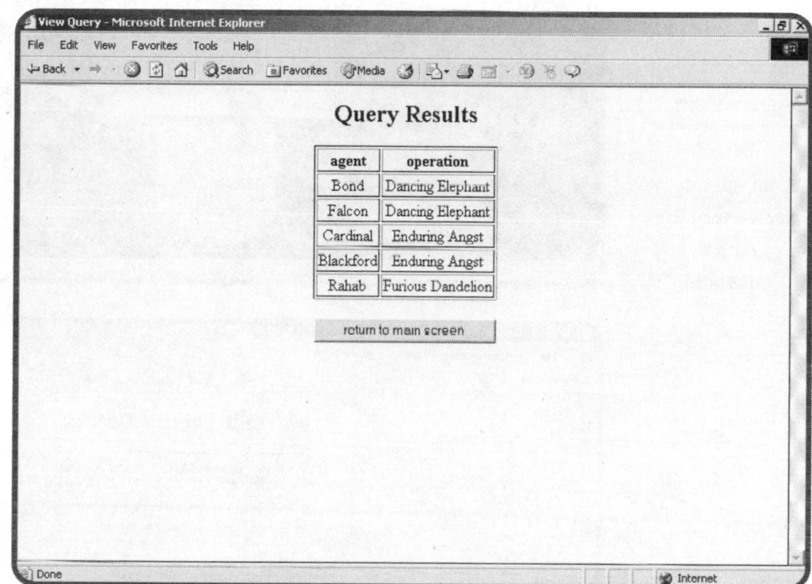

FIGURE 10.2

The results of the query are viewed in an HTML table.

The queries are all pre-built. This means the user cannot make a mistake by typing in inappropriate SQL code, but it also limits the usefulness of the database. Fortunately, there is a system for adding new queries, as you will see.

Viewing Table Data

The other part of the main screen (shown again in Figure 10.3) allows the user to directly manipulate data in the tables. Since this is a more powerful (and thus dangerous) enterprise, access to this part of the system is controlled by a password.

As an example, if I select the `agent` table, I'll see a screen like Figure 10.4.

From this screen, the user can see all the data in the chosen table. The page also gives the user links to add, edit, or delete records from the table.

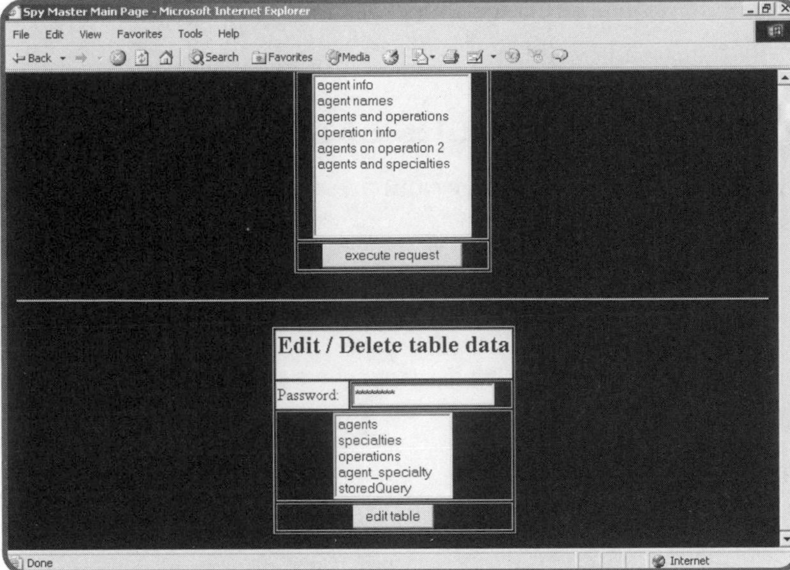

FIGURE 10.3

From the main screen you can also access the table data with a password.

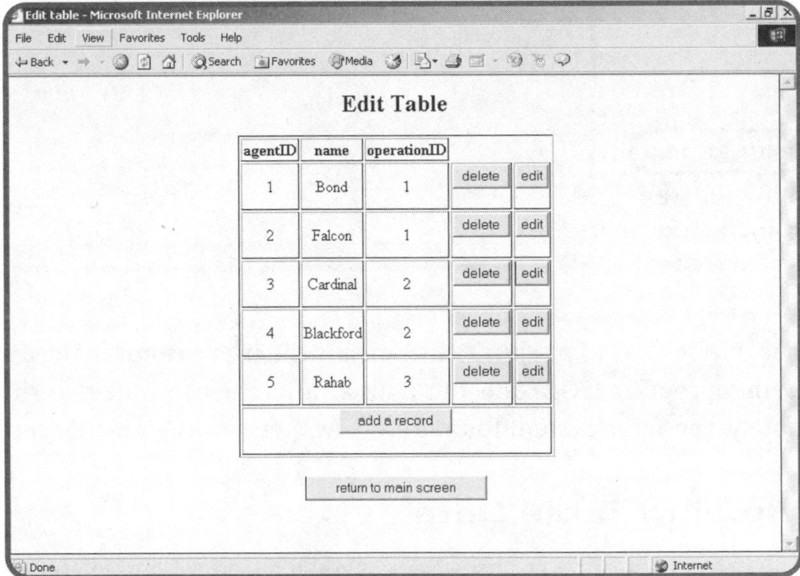

FIGURE 10.4

The `editTable` screen displays all the information in a table.

Editing a Record

If the user chooses to edit a record, a screen similar to Figure 10.5 will appear.

The "Edit Record" page has some important features. First, the user cannot directly change the primary key. If the user could do so, it would have profound

FIGURE 10.5

The user is editing a record in the `agent` table.

destabilizing consequences on the database. Also note the way the `operationID` field is presented. The field itself is a primary key with an integer value, but it would be very difficult for a user to manipulate the integer values directly. Instead, the program provides a drop-down list of operations. When the user chooses from this list, the appropriate numerical index will be sent to the next page.

Confirming the Record Update

When the user clicks the button, a new screen appears and announces the successful update as in Figure 10.6.

Deleting a Record

The user can also choose to delete a record from the "Edit Table" page. This action results in the basic screen shown in Figure 10.7.

You can tell from this example why it's so important to have a script for generating sample data. I had to delete and modify records several times when I was testing the system. After each test I easily restored the database to a stable condition by reloading the `buildSpy.sql` file with the MySQL `SOURCE` command.

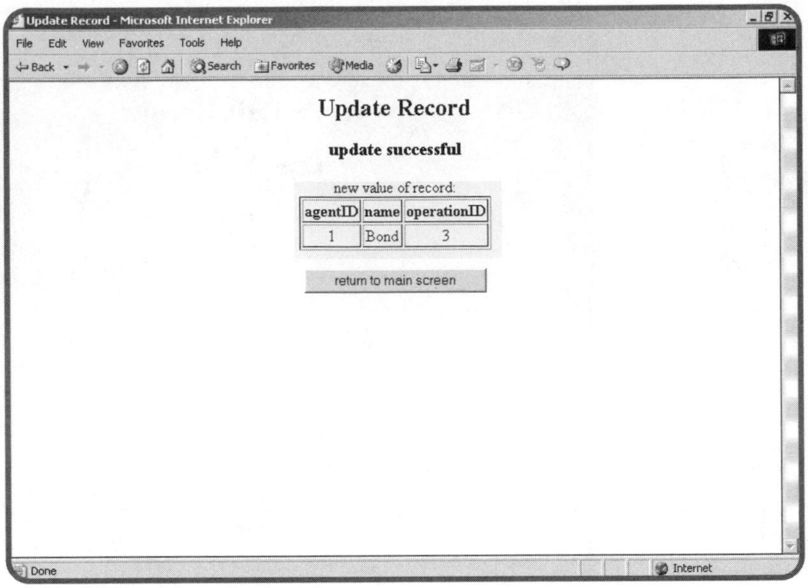

FIGURE 10.6

The user can see the newly updated record.

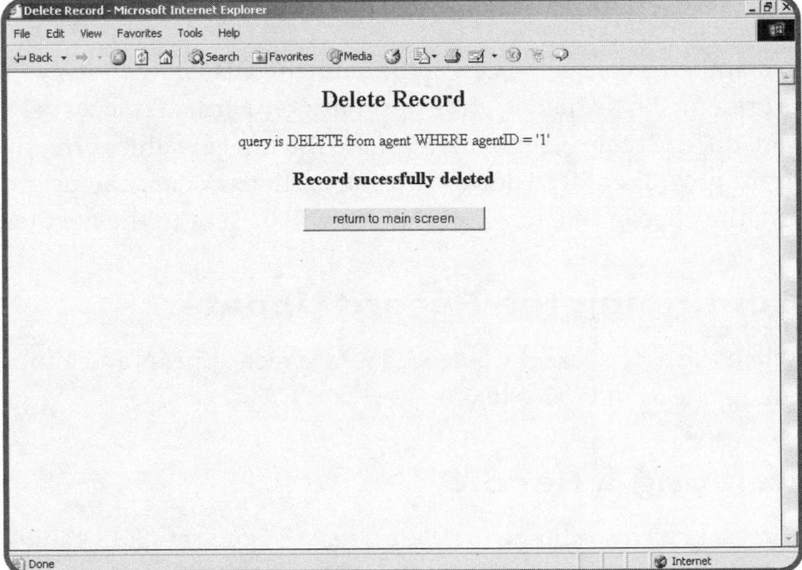

FIGURE 10.7

It's very easy to delete a record.

Adding a Record

Adding a record to the table is a multi-step process much like editing a record. The first page (shown in Figure 10.8) allows you to enter data in all the appropriate fields.

Like the "Edit Record" screen, the "Add Record" page does not allow the user to enter a primary key directly. This page also automatically generates drop-down SELECT boxes for foreign key fields like `operationID`.

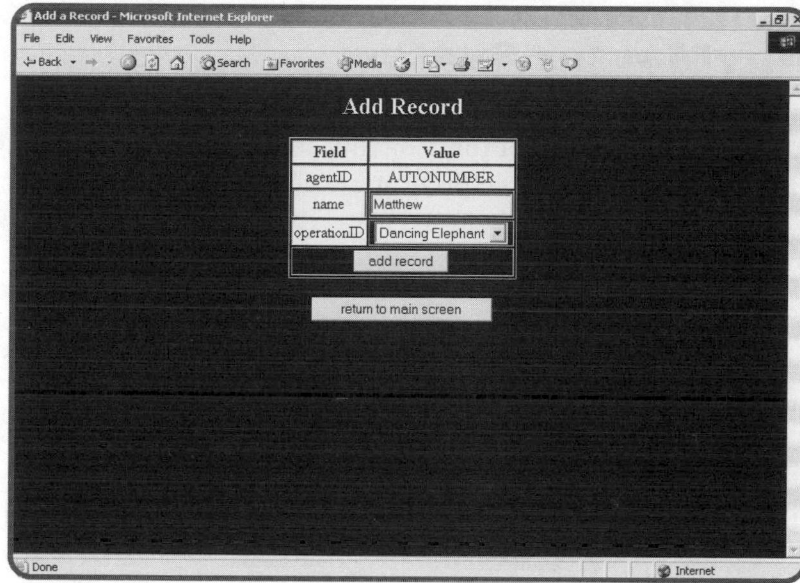

FIGURE 10.8

The add screen includes list boxes for foreign key references.

Processing the Add

When the user chooses to process the add, another page appears confirming the add (or of course describing the failure if it cannot add the record for some reason). This page is shown in Figure 10.9.

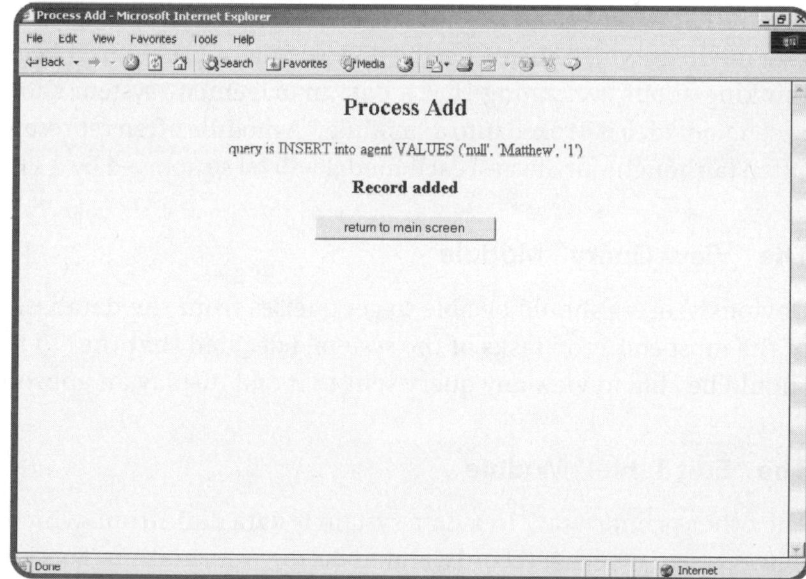

FIGURE 10.9

The user has successfully added an agent.

Building the Design of the SpyMaster System

It can be intimidating to think of all the operations in the "Spy Master" system. The program has a lot of functionality. It could be overwhelming to start coding this system without some sort of strategic plan.

Creating a State Diagram

There are many approaches to complex programming problems. For this particular problem I decided to concentrate on the flow of data through a series of modules. Figure 10.10 shows my overall strategy for the program.

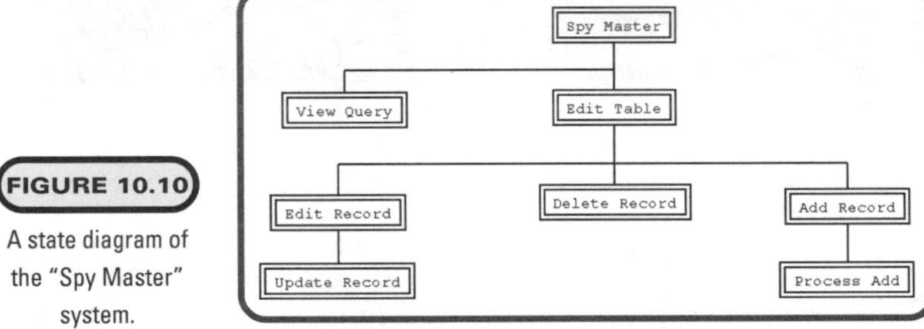

FIGURE 10.10

A state diagram of the "Spy Master" system.

The illustration in Figure 10.10 is sometimes called a *state diagram.* This kind of illustration is used to identify what particular problems need to be solved and indicate modules which might be able to solve these problems. I began the process by thinking about everything that a data management system should be able to do. Each major idea is broken into a "module." A module often represents a single screen. Often (although not always) each model will be supported by a PHP program.

The "View Query" Module

Obviously, users should be able to get queries from the database. This will be one of the most common tasks of the system. I decided that the "View Query" module should be able to view any query sent to it and display an appropriate result.

The "Edit Table" Module

The other primary task in a data system is data definition, which includes adding new records, deleting records, and updating information. This kind of activity can be destructive, so it should be controlled using some kind of access system. All data definition is based on the underlying table structure of the database, so it is important to allow the three main kinds of data definition (editing, deletion, and updating) on each table. The "Edit Table" module provides the interface to these behaviors. It shows all the current records in a table and lets the user edit or delete any particular record. It also has a button that allows the user to add a new record to this table. It's important to see that "Edit Table" doesn't actually cause anything to change in the database. Instead, it serves as a gateway to several other editing modules.

The "Edit Record" and "Update Record" Modules

If you look back at the state diagram, you'll see the "Edit Table" module leads to three other modules. The "Edit Record" module shows one record and allows the user to edit the data in the record. However, the database isn't actually updated until the user submits changes, so editing a record actually requires a two-step process. After the user determines changes in the "Edit Record" module, program control moves on to the "Update Record" module, which actually processes the request and makes the change to the database.

The "Add Record" and "Process Add" Modules

Adding a record is similar to editing, as it requires two passes. The first module ("Add Record") generates a form that allows the user to input the details of the new record. Once the user has determined the record data, the "Process Add" module does the actual SQL necessary to incorporate the new record in the table.

The "Delete Record" Module

Deleting a record is actually a simple process. There's no need for any other user input, so it requires only one module to process a deletion request.

Designing the System

The state diagram is very helpful, because it allows you to see an overview of the entire process. More planning is still necessary, however, because the basic state diagram leaves a lot of questions unanswered. For example:

- Will the "Edit Table" module have to be repeated for each table?
- If so, will we also need copies of all other editing modules?
- Is there a way to automate the process?
- What if the underlying data structure is changed?
- What if I want to apply a similar structure to another database?
- How can I allow queries to be added to the system?

It is tempting to write a system specifically to manage the spy database. The advantage of such a system is it will know exactly how to handle issues relevant to the spy system. For example, `operationID` is a foreign key reference in the `agent` table, so it should be selected by a drop-down list whenever possible. If you build a specific module to handle editing the `agent` table, you can make this happen. However, this process will quickly become unwieldy if you have several tables. It would be better to have a "smart" procedure that can build an edit screen for any table in the database. It would be even better if your program could automatically detect foreign key fields and produce the appropriate user interface element (an HTML `SELECT` clause) when needed. In fact, you could build an entire library of generic routines that could work with any database. That's exactly the approach I chose.

Building a Library of Functions

Although the "Spy Master" program is the longest in this book, you'll find that most of it is surprisingly simple. The centerpiece of the system is a file called "spyLib.php." This file is not meant to run in the user's browser at all. Instead, it contains a library of functions that simplify coding of any database. I stored as much of the PHP code as I could in this library. All the other PHP programs in the system make use of the various functions in the library. This approach has a number of advantages:

- The overall code size is smaller since code does not need to be repeated.
- If I want to improve a module, I do it once in the library rather than in several places.
- It is extremely simple to modify the code library so it works with another database.
- The details of each particular module are hidden in a module so I can focus on the bigger picture when writing each PHP page.
- The routines can be re-used to work with any table in the database.
- The routines can automatically adjust to changes in the data structure.
- The library can be readily re-used for another project.

Figure 10.11 shows a more detailed state diagram.

As you will see when you begin looking at actual code, most of the PHP programs are extremely simple. They usually just collect data for a library function and send program control off to that function, then print any output produced by the function.

Writing the Non-Library Code

I'll begin by describing all the parts of this project except the library. The library module is driven by the needs of the other PHP programs, so it actually makes sense to look at the other programs first.

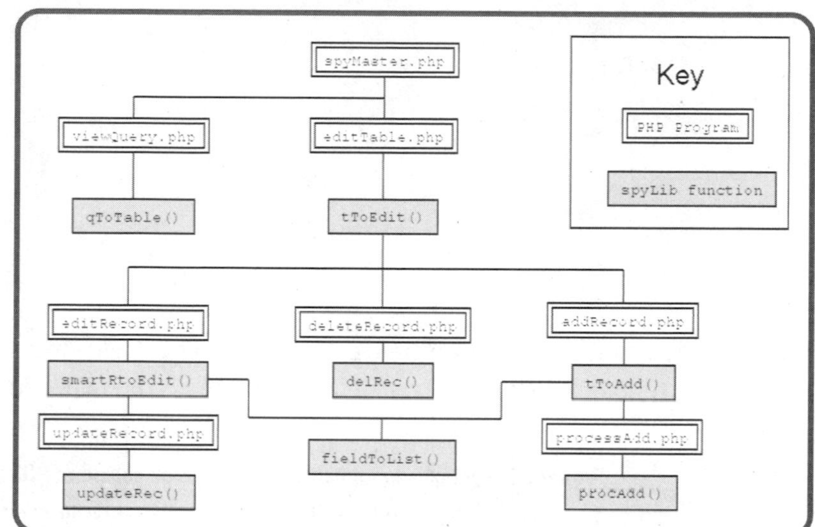

FIGURE 10.11

This state diagram illustrates the relationship between PHP programs and functions in the `spyLib` code library.

Preparing the Database

The database for this segment is almost the same as the one used in Chapter 9 "Data Normalization." I added one table to store queries. All other tables are the same as those in Chapter 9. The SQL script to create this new version of the spy database is available on the CD-ROM as "buildSpy.sql." Note this version is slightly different than the version in Chapter 9, because it includes several queries as part of the data! In order to make the program reasonably secure, I didn't want typical users to be able to make queries. I also don't want users to be limited to the few queries I thought of when building this system. One solution is to store a set of queries in the database and let appropriate users modify the queries. I called my new table the `storedQuery` table. It can be manipulated in the system just like the other tables, so a user with password access can add, edit, and delete queries. Here is the additional code used to build the `storedQuery` table:

```
######################################
# build storedQuery table
######################################

CREATE TABLE storedQuery (
  storedQueryID int(11) NOT NULL AUTO_INCREMENT,
  description varchar(30),
  text varchar(255),
  PRIMARY KEY (storedQueryID)
```

```
);

INSERT INTO storedQuery VALUES (
  null,
  'agent info',
  'SELECT * FROM agent'
);
```

The `storedQuery` table has three fields. The `description` field holds a short English description of each query. The `text` field holds the actual SQL code of the query.

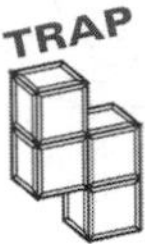

Proper SQL syntax is extremely important when you store SQL syntax inside an SQL database as I'm doing here. It's especially important to keep track of single and double quotes. To include the single quotes that some queries require, you'll need to precede the quote with a backslash character. For example, if I want to store the following query:

```
SELECT * FROM agent WHERE agent.name = 'Bond',
```

I would actually store this text instead:

```
SELECT * FROM agent WHERE agent.name = \'Bond\'
```

This is necessary in order to store the single quote characters. Otherwise they will be interpreted incorrectly. I'll show you how to remove the backslash characters at the appropriate time.

Examining the spyMaster.php Program

The `sypMaster.php` program is the entry point into the system. All access to the system comes from this page. It has two main parts. Each segment encapsulates an HTML form that will send a request to a particular PHP program. The first segment has a small amount of PHP code that sets up the query list box.

Creating the Query Form

```
<html>
<head>
<title>Spy Master Main Page</title>
<?
```

```
  include "spyLib.php";
?>

</head>
<body>
<form action = "viewQuery.php"
      method = "post">

<table border = 1
       width = 200>
<tr>
  <td><center><h2>View Data</h2></center></td>
</tr>

<tr>
  <td><center>
    <select name = "theQuery" size = 10>
<?
//get queries from storedQuery table

$dbConn = connectToSpy();
$query = "SELECT * from storedQuery";
$result = mysql_query($query, $dbConn);
while($row = mysql_fetch_assoc($result)){
  $currentQuery = $row['text'];
  $theDescription = $row['description'];
  print <<<HERE
      <option value = "$currentQuery">$theDescription</option>

HERE;
  } // end while

?>
```

```
    </select>
  </center>
</tr>


<tr>
  <td><center>
    <input type = "submit"
       value = "execute request" >
  </center></td>
</tr>
</table>


</form>
```

Most of the code is ordinary HTML. The HTML code establishes a form that will call `viewQuery.php` when the user presses the Submit button. I added some PHP code here as well. The PHP generates a special input box based on the entries in the `storedQuery` table.

Including the spyLib Library

The first thing to notice is the `include()` statement. This command allows you to import another file. PHP will read that file and interpret it as HTML. An included file can contain HTML, CSS, or PHP code. Most of the functionality for the spy data program is stored in the `spyLib.php` library program. All the other PHP programs in the system begin by including `spyLib.php`. Once this is done, every function in the library can be accessed as if it were a locally defined function. As you will see, this provides tremendous power and flexibility to a programming system.

Connecting to the Spy Database

The utility of the `spyLib` library becomes immediately apparent as I connect to the spy database. Rather than worrying about exactly what database I'm connecting to, I simply defer to the `connectToSpy()` function in `spyLib()`. In the current code I don't need to worry about the details of connecting to the database. With a library I can write the connecting code one time and re-use that function as needed.

There's another advantage to using a library when connecting to a database. It's quite likely that if you move this code to another system you'll have a different way to log in to the data server. If the code for connecting to the server is centralized, it only needs to be changed in one place when you want to update the code. This is far more efficient than searching through dozens of programs to find every reference to the `mysql_connect()` function.

Notice the `connectToSpy()` function returns a data connection pointer I can use for other database activities.

Retrieving the Queries

I decided to encode a series of pre-packaged queries into a table. I'll explain more about my reasons for this in the section on the `viewQuery` program. The main form needs to present a list of query descriptions and let the user select one of these queries. I use an SQL `SELECT` statement to extract everything from the `storedQuery` table. I then use the description and text fields from `storedQuery` to build a multi-line list box.

Creating the Edit Table Form

The second half of the `spyMaster` program presents all the tables in the database and allows the user to choose a table for later editing. Most of the functionality in the system comes through this section. Surprisingly, there is no PHP code at all in this particular part of the page. An HTML form will send the user to the `editTable.php` program.

```
<hr>
<form action = "editTable.php"
      method = "post">

<table border = 1>
<tr>
  <td colspan = 2><center>
    <h2>Edit / Delete table data</h2>
  </center></td>
</tr>

<tr>
```

```
  <td>Password:</td>
  <td>
    <input type = "password"
        name = "pwd"
        value = "absolute"><br>
  </td>
</tr>

<tr>
  <td colspan = 2><center>
    <select name = "tableName"
        size = 5>
      <option value = "agent">agents</option>
      <option value = "specialty">specialties</option>
      <option value = "operation">operations</option>
      <option value = "agent_specialty">agent_specialty</option>
      <option value = "storedQuery">storedQuery</option>
    </select>
  </center></td>
</tr>

<tr>
  <td colspan = 2><center>
    <input type = "submit"
        value = "edit table">
  </center></td>
</tr>
</table>

</form>

</body>
</html>
```

To make debugging easier, I pre-loaded the password field with the appropriate password so I don't have to type it in each time. In a production environment, you should of course leave the password field blank so the user cannot get into the system without the password.

Building the viewQuery.php Program

When the user chooses a query, program control is sent to the `viewQuery.php` program. This program does surprisingly little on its own.

```
<html>
<head>
<title>View Query</title>
</head>
<body>

<center>
<h2>Query Results</h2>
</center>
<?
include "spyLib.php";

$dbConn = connectToSpy();

//take out escape characters...
$theQuery = str_replace("\'", "'", $theQuery);

print qToTable($theQuery);

print mainButton();

?>

</body>
</html>
```

Once viewQuery.php connects to the library, it uses functions in the library to connect to the database and print out desired results. The qToTable() function does most of the actual work. It will take whatever query is passed to it and generate a table with add, delete, and edit buttons.

Why Did I Store Queries in the Database?

You might wonder why I chose this approach to queries. After all, I could have let the user type in a query directly or provided some sort of form that allows the user to search for certain values. Either of these approaches has advantages, but they also pose some risks. It's very dangerous to allow direct access to your data from a Web form. Malicious users can introduce Trojan Horse commands that can snoop on your data, change data, or even delete information from the database. I sometimes build a form that has enough information to create an SQL query and then build that query in a client-side form (sounds like a good end-of-chapter exercise). In this case, I stored queries in another table. People with administrative access have the ability to add new queries to the database, but ordinary users do not. I pre-loaded the storedQuery **database with a number of useful queries, then added the capacity to add new queries whenever the situation demands it. There are still some drawbacks to this system (primarily that ordinary users cannot build custom queries), but it is far more secure than a system that builds a query based on user input.**

The str_replace() function is necessary because SQL queries contain single quote (') characters. When I store a query as a VARCHAR entity, the single quotes embedded in the query cause problems. The normal solution to this problem is to use a backslash, which indicates that the quote should not be immediately interpreted, but should be considered a part of the data. The problem with this is the backslash is still in the string when I try to execute the query. The str_replace() function replaces all instances of "\'" with a simple single quote (').

Note that the qToTable() function doesn't actually print anything to the screen. All it does is build a complex string of HTML code. The viewQuery.php program prints the code to the screen.

If you are using a library, it's best if the library code does not print anything directly to the screen. Instead, it should simply return a value to whatever program called it. This will allow multiple uses for the data. For example, if the qToTable() **function printed directly to the screen, you could not use it to generate a file. Since the library code returns a value but doesn't actually do anything with that value, the code that calls the function has the freedom to use the results in multiple ways.**

The mainButton() function produces a simple HTML form that directs the user back to the spyMaster.php page. Even though the code for this is relatively simple, it is repeated so often that it makes sense to store it in a function rather than copying and pasting it in every page of the system.

Viewing the editTable.php Program

The editTable.php follows a familiar pattern. It has a small amount of PHP code, but most of the real work is sent off to a library function. The main job of this module is to check for an administrative password. If the user does not have the appropriate password, further access to the system is blocked. If the user does have the correct password, the very powerful tToEdit() function provides access to the add, edit, and delete functions.

```
<html>
<head>
<title>Edit table</title>
</head>
<body>
<h2>Edit Table</h2>
<?
include "spyLib.php";

//check password

if ($pwd == $adminPassword){
  $dbConn = connectToSpy();
  print tToEdit("$tableName");
} else {
  print "<h3>You must have administrative access to proceed</h3>\n";
} // end if
print mainButton();

?>
</body>
</html>
```

The $pwd value comes from a field in the spyMaster.php page. The $adminPassword value is stored in spyLibrary.php. (The default admin password is "absolute," but you can change it to whatever you want by editing spyLib.php.)

Viewing the editRecord.php Program

The editRecord.php program is called from a form generated by editTable.php. (Actually, the tToEdit() function generates the form, but tToEdit() is called from editTable.php.) This program expects variables called $tableName, $keyName, and $keyVal. These variables (provided by tToEdit() automatically) help editRecord build a query that will return whatever record the user selects. (You'll need to trust me for now on how the appropriate record data is sent. You can read ahead to the description of tToEdit() for details on how this exactly works.)

```
<html>
<head>
<title>Edit Record</title>
</head>
<body>
<h1>Edit Record</h1>
<?

// expects $tableName, $keyName, $keyVal
include "spyLib.php";

$dbConn = connectToSpy();


$query = "SELECT * FROM $tableName WHERE $keyName = $keyVal";
print smartRToEdit($query);


print mainButton();


?>
</body>
</html>
```

The `editRecord.php` program prints out the results of the `smartRToEdit()` library function. This function takes the single-record query and prints HTML code that lets the user update the record appropriately.

Viewing the updateRecord.php Program

The `smartRToEdit()` function calls another PHP program called `updateRecord.php`. This program calls a library function that actually commits the user's changes to the database.

```
<html>
<head>
<title>Update Record</title>
</head>
<body>

<h2>Update Record</h2>
<?

include "spyLib.php";

$dbConn = connectToSpy();

$fieldNames = "";
$fieldValues = "";

foreach ($_REQUEST as $fieldName => $value){
  if ($fieldName == "tableName"){
    $theTable = $value;
  } else {

    $fields[] = $fieldName;
    $values[] = $value;
  } // end if
```

```
} // end foreach

print updateRec($theTable, $fields, $values);

print mainButton();

?>
</body>
</html>
```

It is more convenient for the `updateRec()` function if the field names and values are sent as arrays, so the PHP code in `updateRecord.php` converts the `$_REQUEST` array to an array of fields and another array of values. These two arrays are passed to the `updateRec()` function, which will process them.

Viewing the deleteRecord.php Program

The `deleteRecord.php` program acts in a now-familiar manner. It mainly serves as a wrapper for a function in the `spyLib` library. In this particular case, the program simply sends the name of the current table, the name of the key field, and the value of the current record's key to the `delRec()` function. That function will delete the record and return a message regarding the success or failure of the operation.

```
<html>
<head>
<title>Delete Record</title>
</head>
<body>
<h2>Delete Record</h2>
<?

include "spyLib.php";

$dbConn = connectToSpy();
print delRec($tableName, $keyName, $keyVal);
print mainButton();
```

```
?>

</body>
</html>
```

Viewing the addRecord.php Program

Adding a record is actually much like editing a record. It actually requires two distinctive steps. The `addRecord.php` program calls the `tToAdd()` function, which builds a form allowing the user to add data to whichever table is currently selected. It isn't necessary to send any information to this function except the name of the table, because the key value will be automatically generated by `tToAdd()`.

```
<html>
<head>
<title>Add a Record</title>
</head>
<body>
<h2>Add Record</h2>
<?
include "spyLib.php";

$dbConn = connectToSpy();

print tToAdd($tableName);
print mainButton();

?>

</body>
</html>
```

Viewing the processAdd.php Program

The `tToAdd()` function called by the `addRecord.php` program doesn't actually add a record. Instead, it places an HTML form on the screen that allows the user to enter the data for a new record. When the user submits this form, he or she is passed to the `processAdd.php` program, which calls `procAdd()` in the library code. The `procAdd()` function generates the appropriate SQL code to actually add the new record to the table. In order to do this, `procAdd()` needs to know the field names and values. These are passed to the function in arrays just like in `updateRecord.php`.

```
<html>
<head>
      <title>Process Add</title>
</head>
<body>
<h2>Process Add</h2>
<?
include "spyLib.php";

$dbConn = connectToSpy();

$fieldNames = "";
$fieldValues = "";

foreach ($_REQUEST as $fieldName => $value){
  if ($fieldName == "tableName"){
    $theTable = $value;
  } else {
    $fields[] = $fieldName;
    $values[] = $value;
  } // end if
} // end foreach

print procAdd($theTable, $fields, $values);

print mainButton();


?>
</body>
</html>
```

Creating the spyLib Library Module

Although I have described several PHP programs in this chapter, most of them are extremely simple. Most of the heavy lifting is done by the `spyLib` library code. Having a library like `spyLib` makes data programming pretty easy, because you don't have to know all the details of `spyLib` in order to make it work. All you need to have is a basic understanding of the functions in the library, what each function expects as input, and what it will produce as output. Although there is a good amount of code in this library (over 500 lines, in fact), there is almost nothing in the code you haven't seen before. It's worth it to look carefully at this code because it can give you a good idea of how to create your own libraries. You'll also find there's no better way to understand the library than to dig around under the hood.

Setting a CSS style

Some of the simplest elements can have profound effects. One example of this maxim is the storage of a CSS style in the library code. Each program in the system will operate using the style specified in the library. This means you can easily change the look and feel of the entire system by manipulating one `<style></style>` block.

```
<style type = "text/css">

body{

  background-color: black;

  color: white;

  text-align:center

}


</style>
```

Remember, when you include a file, it is interpreted as *HTML*, not PHP. This means you can place any HTML code you wish in an `include` file and it will be automatically inserted in your output wherever the `include` function occurred. I took advantage of this fact to include a CSS block in the library. If you want PHP code in your library file, you'll need to surround your code with PHP tags (<? ?>) in the library file.

Setting System-Wide Variables

Another huge advantage of a library file is the ability to set and use variables that will have meaning throughout the entire system. Since each PHP program in the system includes the library, all will have access to any variables declared in the main section of the library file. Of course, you will still need to use the `global` keyword to access a global variable from within a function.

```
<?
//spyLib.php
//holds utilities for spy database


//variables
$userName = "";
$password = "";
$serverName = "localhost";
$dbName = "chapter10";
$dbConn = "";
$adminPassword = "absolute";
$mainProgram = "spyMaster.php";
```

I stored a few key data points in the system-wide variables. The `$userName`, `$password`, and `$serverName` variables are used to set up the data connection. I did this because I expect people to re-use my library for their own databases. They will definitely need to change this information to connect to their own copy of MySQL. It's much safer for them to change this data in variables than in actual program code. If you're writing code for re-use, you might consider moving anything the code adopter might change into variables as I have done here.

The `$adminPassword` variable will hold the password used to edit data in the system. Again, I want anybody re-using this library (including me) to change this value without having to dig through the code.

The `$mainProgram` variable holds the URL of the "control pad" program of the system. In the spy system, I want to provide access back to `spyMaster.php` in every screen. The `mainButton()` function uses the value of `$mainProgram` to build a link back to the primary screen in every other document produced by the system.

Connecting to the Database

The `connectToSpy()` function is fundamental to the spy system. It uses system-level variables to generate a connection to the database. It returns an error message if it is unable to connect to the database. The `mysql_error()` function prints an SQL error message if the data connection was unsuccessful. This information may not be helpful to the end user, but it might give you some insight as you are debugging the system.

```
function connectToSpy(){
  //connects to the spy DB
  global $serverName, $userName, $password;
  $dbConn = mysql_connect($serverName, $userName, $password);
  if (!$dbConn){
   print "<h3>problem connecting to database...</h3>\n";
  } // end if

  $select = mysql_select_db("chapter10");
  if (!$select){
    print mysql_error() . "<br>\n";
  } // end if
  return $dbConn;
} // end connectToSpy
```

The `connectToSpy()` function returns a connection to the database that will be subsequently used in the many queries passed to the database throughout the life span of the system.

Creating a Quick List from a Query

I created a few functions in the `spyMaster` library that didn't get used in the final version of the project. The `qToList()` function is a good example. This program takes any SQL query and returns a simply formatted HTML segment describing the data. I find this format useful when debugging because no complex formatting gets in the way.

```
function qToList($query){
  //given a query, makes a quick list of data
  global $dbConn;
  $output = "";
  $result = mysql_query($query, $dbConn);

  //print "dbConn is $dbConn<br>";
```

```
  //print "result is $result<br>";

  while ($row = mysql_fetch_assoc($result)){
    foreach ($row as $col=>$val){
      $output .= "$col: $val<br>\n";
    } // end foreach
    $output .= "<hr>\n" ;
  } // end while
  return $output;
} // end qToList
```

Building an HTML Table from a Query

The `qToTable()` function is a little more powerful than `qToList()`. It can take any valid SQL `SELECT` statement and build an HTML table from it. The code uses the `mysql_fetch_field()` function to determine field names from the query result. It also steps through each row of the result printing out an HTML row corresponding to the record.

```
function qToTable($query){
  //given a query, automatically creates an HTML table output
  global $dbConn;
  $output = "";
  $result = mysql_query($query, $dbConn);

  $output .= "<table border = 1>\n";
  //get column headings

  //get field names
  $output .= "<tr>\n";
  while ($field = mysql_fetch_field($result)){
    $output .= "  <th>$field->name</th>\n";
  } // end while
  $output .= "</tr>\n\n";

  //get row data as an associative array
```

```
    while ($row = mysql_fetch_assoc($result)){
      $output .= "<tr>\n";
      //look at each field
      foreach ($row as $col=>$val){
        $output .= "  <td>$val</td>\n";
      } // end foreach
      $output .= "</tr>\n\n";
    }// end while

    $output .= "</table>\n";
    return $output;
  } // end qToTable
```

The `qToTable()` function is called by the `viewQuery.php` program, but it could be used any time you want an SQL query formatted as an HTML table (which turns out to be quite often).

Building an HTML Table for Editing an SQL Table

If the user has appropriate access, he or she should be allowed to add, edit, or delete records in any table of the database. While `qToTable()` is suitable for viewing the results of any SQL query, it does not provide any of these features. The `tToEdit()` function is based on `qToTable()` with a few differences. First, `tToEdit()` does not accept a query, but the name of a table. You cannot edit joined queries directly, only tables, so this limitation is sensible. `tToEdit()` creates a query that will return all records in the specified table. In addition to printing the table data, `tToEdit()` adds two forms to each record. One form contains all the data needed by the `editRecord.php` program to begin the record-editing process. The other form added to each record sends all data necessary for deleting a record and calls the `deleteRecord.php` program. One more form at the bottom of the HTML table allows the user to add a record to this table. This form contains information needed by the `addRecord.php` program.

```
function tToEdit($tableName){
  //given a table name, generates HTML table including
  //add, delete and edit buttons

  global $dbConn;
  $output = "";
```

```
$query = "SELECT * FROM $tableName";

$result = mysql_query($query, $dbConn);

$output .= "<table border = 1>\n";
//get column headings

//get field names
$output .= "<tr>\n";
while ($field = mysql_fetch_field($result)){
  $output .= "  <th>$field->name</th>\n";
} // end while

//get name of index field (presuming it's first field)
$keyField = mysql_fetch_field($result, 0);
$keyName = $keyField->name;

//add empty columns for add, edit, and delete
$output .= "<th></th><th></th>\n";
$output .= "</tr>\n\n";

//get row data as an associative array
while ($row = mysql_fetch_assoc($result)){
  $output .= "<tr>\n";
  //look at each field
  foreach ($row as $col=>$val){
    $output .= "  <td>$val</td>\n";
  } // end foreach
  //build little forms for add, delete and edit

  //delete = DELETE FROM <table> WHERE <key> = <keyval>
  $keyVal = $row["$keyName"];
```

```
      $output .= <<< HERE

    <td>
      <form action = "deleteRecord.php">
      <input type = "hidden"
             name = "tableName"
             value = "$tableName">
      <input type= "hidden"
             name = "keyName"
             value = "$keyName">
      <input type = "hidden"
             name = "keyVal"
             value = "$keyVal">
      <input type = "submit"
             value = "delete"></form>
    </td>

HERE;
      //update: won't update yet, but set up edit form
      $output .= <<< HERE
    <td>
      <form action = "editRecord.php"
            method = "post">
      <input type = "hidden"
             name = "tableName"
             value = "$tableName">
      <input type= "hidden"
             name = "keyName"
             value = "$keyName">
      <input type = "hidden"
             name = "keyVal"
             value = "$keyVal">
```

```
    <input type = "submit"
           value = "edit"></form>
  </td>

HERE;

    $output .= "</tr>\n\n";

  }// end while

    //add = INSERT INTO <table> {values}
    //set up insert form send table name
    $keyVal = $row["$keyName"];
    $output .= <<< HERE

  <td colspan = "5">
    <center>
    <form action = "addRecord.php">
    <input type = "hidden"
           name = "tableName"
           value = "$tableName">
    <input type = "submit"
           value = "add a record"></form>
    </center>
  </td>

HERE;

  $output .= "</table>\n";
  return $output;
} // end tToEdit
```

Look carefully at the forms for editing and deleting records. These forms contain hidden fields with the table name, key field name, and record number. This information will be used by subsequent functions to build a query specific to the record associated with that particular table row.

Creating a Generic Form to Edit a Record

The table created in `tToEdit()` calls a program called `editRecord.php`. This program accepts a one-record query. It prints out an HTML table based on the results of that query. The output of `rToEdit()` is shown in Figure 10.12.

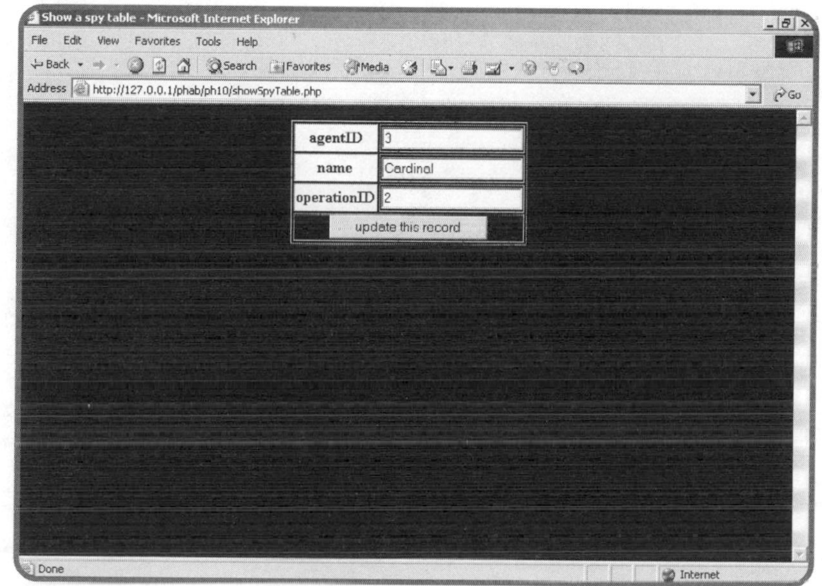

FIGURE 10.12

The `rToEdit` function is simple, but produces dangerous output.

The `rToEdit` function produces a very simple HTML table. Every field has a corresponding text box. The advantage of this approach is it works with any table. However, the use of this form is quite risky. First, the user should not be allowed to change the primary key, because that would in effect edit some other record, which could have disastrous results. Second, the `operationID` field is a foreign key reference. The only valid entries to this field are integers corresponding to records in the `operation` table. There's no way for the user to know what operation a particular integer is related to. Worse, he or she could enter any number (or for that matter any text) into the field. The results would be unpredictable, but almost certainly bad. I'll fix these defects in the `smartRToEdit()` function coming up next, but begin by studying this simpler function, because `smartRToEdit()` is build on `rToEdit()`.

```
function rToEdit ($query){
  //given a one-record query, creates a form to edit that record
  //works on any table, but allows direct editing of keys
  //use smartRToEdit instead if you can

  global $dbConn;
  $output = "";
  $result = mysql_query($query, $dbConn);
  $row = mysql_fetch_assoc($result);

  //get table name from field object
  $fieldObj = mysql_fetch_field($result, 0);
  $tableName = $fieldObj->table;

  $output .= <<< HERE
<form action = "updateRecord.php"
      method = "post">

<input type = "hidden"
       name = "tableName"
       value = "$tableName">

<table border = 1>

HERE;

   foreach ($row as $col=>$val){
     $output .= <<<HERE
   <tr>
     <th>$col</th>
     <td>
       <input type = "text"
              name = "$col"
```

```
              value = "$val">
    </td>
  </tr>

HERE;
  } // end foreach
  $output .= <<< HERE
  <tr>
    <td colspan = 2>
      <center>
      <input type = "submit"
              value = "update this record">
      </center>
    </td>
  </tr>
</table>

HERE;
  return $output;
} // end rToEdit
```

Building a Smarter Edit Form

The `smartRToEdit()` function builds on the basic design of `rToEdit()` but compensates for a couple of major flaws in the `rToEdit()` design. Take a look at the smarter code below and I'll explain why it's better.

```
function smartRToEdit ($query){
  //given a one-record query, creates a form to edit that record
  //Doesn't let user edit first (primary key) field
  //generates dropdown list for foreign keys
  //MUCH safer than ordinary rToEdit function

  // --restrictions on table design--
  //foreign keys MUST be named tableID where 'table' is table name
```

```
 //  (because mySQL doesn't recognize foreign key indicators)
 // I also expect a 'name' field in any table used as a foreign key
 //   (for same reason)

 global $dbConn;
 $output = "";
 $result = mysql_query($query, $dbConn);
 $row = mysql_fetch_assoc($result);

 //get table name from field object
 $fieldObj = mysql_fetch_field($result, 0);
 $tableName = $fieldObj->table;

 $output .= <<< HERE
<form action = "updateRecord.php"
      method = "post">

<input type = "hidden"
       name = "tableName"
       value = "$tableName">

<table border = 1>

HERE;
  $fieldNum = 0;
  foreach ($row as $col=>$val){
    if ($fieldNum == 0){
      //it's primary key. don't make textbox,
      //but store value in hidden field instead
      //user shouldn't be able to edit primary keys
      $output .= <<<HERE
  <tr>
```

```
    <th>$col</th>
    <td>$val
      <input type = "hidden"
             name = "$col"
             value = "$val">
    </td>
  </tr>

HERE;
    } else if (preg_match("/(.*)ID$/", $col, $match)) {
      //it's a foreign key reference
      // get table name (match[1])
      //create a listbox based on table name and its name field
      $valList = fieldToList($match[1],$col, $fieldNum, "name");

      $output .= <<<HERE
  <tr>
    <th>$col</th>
    <td>$valList</td>
  </tr>

HERE;

    } else {
      $output .= <<<HERE
  <tr>
    <th>$col</th>
    <td>
      <input type = "text"
             name = "$col"
             value = "$val">
    </td>
```

```
    </tr>


HERE;
      } // end if
      $fieldNum++;
    } // end foreach
    $output .= <<< HERE
    <tr>
      <td colspan = 2>
        <center>
        <input type = "submit"
               value = "update this record">
        </center>
      </td>
    </tr>
  </table>
  </form>


HERE;
    return $output;
  } // end smartRToEdit
```

What makes this function "smart" is the ability to examine each field in the record and make a guess about what sort of field it is. Figure 10.13 shows the result of the `smartRToEdit()` program so you can compare it to the "not so clever" function in Figure 10.12.

Determining the Field Type

As far as this function is concerned, there are three types of fields in a record that need to be handled differently.

First is the primary key. If a field is the primary key, its value needs to be passed on to the next program, but the user should not be able to edit it.

If a field is a foreign key reference to another table, the user should only be able to edit the value indirectly. The best approach is to have a drop-down list box that shows values the user will recognize. Each of these values corresponds to a key in

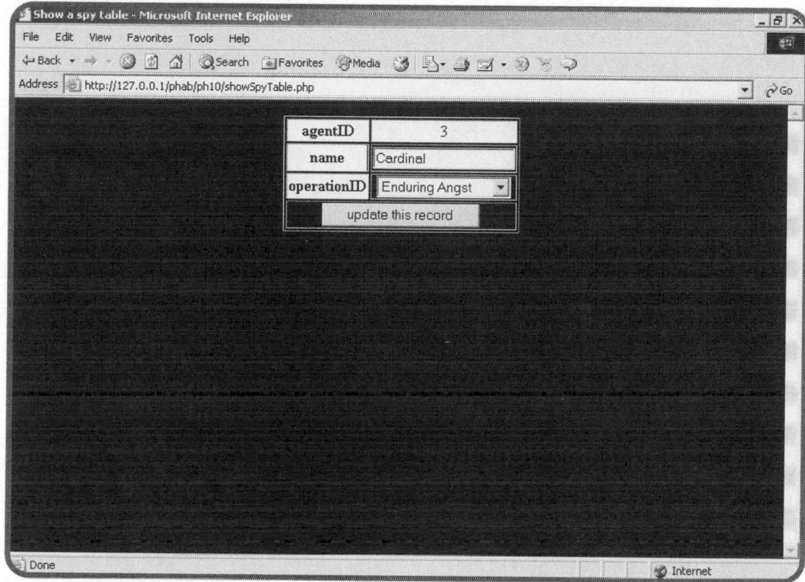

FIGURE 10.13

The smarter function doesn't let the user edit the primary key and provides a drop-down list for all foreign key references.

that secondary record. For example, in Figure 10.13 there is a list box for the `operationID` field. The `operationID` field is a foreign key reference in the `agent` table. The ordinary `rToEdit()` function allowed the user to type any index number into the textbox without any real indication what data correlates to that index. This version builds a drop-down list showing operation names. The key value associated with those names is stored in the value attribute of each option (details to follow in the `fieldToList()` function). The user doesn't have to know anything about foreign key references or relational structures. He or she simply chooses an operation from a list. That list is dynamically generated each time the user chooses to add a record, so it always reflects all the operations in the agency.

The last possibility is a field is neither a primary or secondary key. In this case, I will print a simple text box so the user can input the value of the field. In all cases, the output will reflect the current value of the field.

Working with the Primary Key

The primary key value is much more important to the program than it is to the user. I decided to display it, but not to make it editable in any way. Primary keys should not be edited. They should only be changed by adding or deleting records.

I decided to rely upon some conventions to determine whether a field is a primary key or not. I assumed that the first field of the record (field number 0) is the primary key. This is a very common convention, but it is not universal. Since I created the data design in this case, I can be sure that the number 0 field in every table is the primary key. For that field, I simply printed the field name and value in an ordinary HTML table row. I added the key's value in a hidden field so the next program will have access to it.

Recognizing Foreign Keys

Unfortunately, there is no way (at least in MySQL) to determine if a field is a foreign key reference. I had to rely on a naming convention to make sure my program recognizes a field as a foreign key reference. I decided that all foreign key fields in my database will have the foreign table's name followed by the value `ID`. For example, a foreign key reference to the `operation` table will always be called `operationID` in my database. This is a smart convention to follow anyway, as it makes your field names easy to remember. It becomes critical in `smartRToEdit()` because it's the only way to tell whether a field is a foreign key reference. I used an `else if` clause to check the name of any field that is not the primary key (which was checked in the `if` clause). The `preg_match()` function lets me use a powerful regular expression match to determine the field's name.

Examining the Regular Expression: The statement I used to determine whether a field is a foreign key looks like this:

```
} else if (preg_match("/(.*)ID$/", $col, $match)) {
```

It uses a simple but powerful regular expression: `/(.*)ID$/`. This expression looks for any line that ends with `ID`. (recall that the `$` indicates the end of a string.) The.*indicates any number of characters. The parentheses around `.*` tell PHP to store all the characters before `ID` into a special array, called `$match`. Since there's only one pattern to match in this expression, all the characters before `ID` will contain the name of the table. So, this regular expression takes the name of a field and determines if it ends with `ID`. If so, the beginning part of the field name (everything but `ID`) is stored to `$match[1]`. If `$col` contains `operationID`, this line will return `TRUE` (because `operationID` ends with `ID`) - and the table name (`operation`) will be stored in `$match[1]`.

Building the Foreign Key List Box

If a field is a foreign key reference, it is necessary to build a list box containing some sort of meaningful value the user can read. Since I'll need this capability in a couple of places (and `smartRToEdit()` is already pretty complex), I build a new function called `fieldToList()`. This function (explained in detail later in this chapter) builds a drop-down HTML list based on a table and field name. Rather than worrying about the details of the `fieldToList()` function here, I simply figured out what parameters it would need and printed out the results of that function.

Working with Regular Fields

Any field that is not a primary or foreign key is handled by the `else` clause, which prints out an `rToEdit()`-style text box for user input. This will handle all fields that allow ordinary user input, but it will not trap for certain errors such as string data being placed in numeric fields or data longer than the underlying field will accept. These would be good improvements to the code. If the data designer did not name foreign key references according to my convention, those fields will still be editable with a text box, but the errors that could happen with `rToEdit()` are still concerns.

Committing a Record Update

The end result of either `rToEdit()` or `smartRToEdit()` is an HTML form containing a table name, and a bunch of field names and values. The `updateRecord.php` takes these values and converts them into arrays before calling the `updateRec()` function. It's much easier to work with the fields and values as arrays than in the somewhat amorphous context they embody after `smartRToEdit()` or `rToEdit()`.

```
function updateRec($tableName, $fields, $vals){
  //expects name of a record, fields array values array
  //updates database with new values

  global $dbConn;

  $output = "";
  $keyName = $fields[0];
  $keyVal = $vals[0];
  $query = "";

  $query .= "UPDATE $tableName SET \n";
  for ($i = 1; $i < count($fields); $i++){
    $query .= $fields[$i];
    $query .= " = '";
    $query .= $vals[$i];
    $query .= "',\n";
```

```
} // end for loop

//remove last comma from output
$query = substr($query, 0, strlen($query) - 2);

$query .= "\nWHERE $keyName = '$keyVal'";

$result = mysql_query($query, $dbConn);
if ($result){
  $query = "SELECT * FROM $tableName WHERE $keyName = '$keyVal'";
  $output .= "<h3>update successful</h3>\n";
  $output .= "new value of record:<br>";
  $output .= qToTable($query);
} else {
  $output .= "<h3>there was a problem...</h3><pre>$query</pre>\n";
} // end if
return $output;
} // end updateRec
```

The primary job of `updateRec()` is to build an SQL `UPDATE` statement based on the parameters passed to it. It is expecting a table name, an array containing field names, and another array containing field values. The `UPDATE` statement is primarily a list of field names and values, which can be easily obtained with a `for` loop stepping through the `$fields` and `$vals` arrays.

Once the query has been created, it is submitted to the database. The success or failure of the update is reported back to the user.

Deleting a Record

Deleting a record is actually pretty easy compared to adding or updating. All that's necessary is the table name, key field name, and key field value. The `deleteRec()` function accepts these parameters and uses them to build an SQL `DELETE` statement. As usual, the success or failure of the operation is returned as part of the output string.

```
function delRec ($table, $keyName, $keyVal){
  //deletes $keyVal record from $table
  global $dbConn;
```

```
  $output = "";
  $query = "DELETE from $table WHERE $keyName = '$keyVal'";
  print "query is $query<br>\n";
  $result = mysql_query($query, $dbConn);
  if ($result){
    $output = "<h3>Record successfully deleted</h3>\n";
  } else {
    $output = "<h3>Error deleting record</h3>\n";
  } //end if
  return $output;
} // end delRec
```

Adding a Record

Adding a new record is much like editing a record. It is a two-step process. The first screen builds a page to add a record much like the edit record screen. I used techniques from the `smartRToEdit()` function to ensure the primary and foreign key references are edited appropriately.

```
function tToAdd($tableName){
  //given table name, generates HTML form to add an entry to the
  //table. Works like smartRToEdit in recognizing foreign keys

  global $dbConn;
  $output = "";

  //process a query just to get field names
  $query = "SELECT * FROM $tableName";
  $result = mysql_query($query, $dbConn);

  $output .= <<<HERE
  <form action = "processAdd.php"
        method = "post">
  <table border = "1">
    <tr>
      <th>Field</th>
```

```
      <th>Value</th>
    </tr>

HERE;

  $fieldNum = 0;
  while ($theField = mysql_fetch_field($result)){
    $fieldName = $theField->name;
    if ($fieldNum == 0){
      //it's the primary key field. It'll be autoNumber
      $output .= <<<HERE
      <tr>
        <td>$fieldName</td>
        <td>AUTONUMBER
          <input type = "hidden"
                 name = "$fieldName"
                 value = "null">
        </td>
      </tr>

HERE;
    } else if (preg_match("/(.*)ID$/", $fieldName, $match)) {
      //it's a foreign key reference. Use fieldToList to get
      //a select object for this field

      $valList = fieldToList($match[1],$fieldName, 0, "name");
      $output .= <<<HERE
      <tr>
        <td>$fieldName</td>
        <td>$valList</td>
      </tr>

HERE;
```

```
      } else {
      //it's an ordinary field. Print a text box
      $output .= <<<HERE
        <tr>
          <td>$fieldName</td>
          <td><input type = "text"
                     name = "$fieldName"
                     value = "">
          </td>
        </tr>

HERE;
      } // end if
      $fieldNum++;
    } // end while
    $output .= <<<HERE
      <tr>
        <td colspan = 2>
          <input type = "hidden"
                 name = "tableName"
                 value = "$tableName">
          <input type = "submit"
                 value = "add record">
        </td>
      </tr>
    </table>
    </form>

HERE;

  return $output;

} // end tToAdd
```

The INSERT statement created by this function will use NULL as the primary key value, because all tables in the system are set to AUTO_INCREMENT. I used the same regular expression trick as in smartRToEdit() to recognize foreign key references. If they exist, I built a drop-down list with fieldToList() to display all possible values for that field and send an appropriate key. Any field not recognized as a primary or foreign key will have an ordinary text box.

Processing an Added Record

The tToAdd() function sends its results to processAdd.php, which reorganizes the data much like updateRecord.php. The field names and values are converted to arrays, which are passed to the procAdd() function.

```
function procAdd($tableName, $fields, $vals){
  //generates INSERT query, applies to database
  global $dbConn;

  $output = "";
  $query = "INSERT into $tableName VALUES (";
  foreach ($vals as $theValue){
    $query .= "'$theValue', ";
  } // end foreach

  //trim off trailing space and comma
  $query = substr($query, 0, strlen($query) - 2);

  $query .= ")";
  $output = "query is $query<br>\n";

  $result = mysql_query($query, $dbConn);
  if ($result){
    $output .= "<h3>Record added</h3>\n";
  } else {
    $output .= "<h3>There was an error</h3>\n";
  } // end if
  return $output;
} // end procAdd
```

The main job of `procAdd()` is to build an SQL `INSERT` statement using the results of `tToAdd()`. This insert is passed to the database, and the outcome off the insertion attempt is reported to the user.

Building a List Box from a Field

Both `smartRToEdit()` and `tToAdd()` need drop-down HTML lists following a specific pattern. In both cases, I needed to build a list that allows the user to select a key value based on some other field in the record. This list should be set so any value in the list can be set as selected. The `fieldToList()` function takes four parameters and uses them to build exactly such a list.

```
function fieldToList($tableName, $keyName, $keyVal, $fieldName){
  //given table and field, generates an HTML select structure
  //named $keyName. values will be key field of table, but
  //text will come from the $fieldName value.
  //keyVal indicates which element is currently selected

  global $dbConn;
  $output = "";
  $query = "SELECT $keyName, $fieldName FROM $tableName";
  $result = mysql_query($query, $dbConn);
  $output .= "<select name = $keyName>\n";
  $recNum = 1;
  while ($row = mysql_fetch_assoc($result)){
    $theIndex = $row["$keyName"];
    $theValue = $row["$fieldName"];
    $output .= <<<HERE
    right now, theIndex is $theIndex and keyVal is $keyVal
  <option value = "$theIndex"
HERE;

    //make it currently selected item
    if ($theIndex == $keyVal){
      $output .= " selected";
    } // end if
```

```
    $output .= ">$theValue</option>\n";
    $recNum++;
  } // end while
  $output .= "</select>\n";
  return $output;
} // end fieldToList
```

The `fieldToList()` function begins by generating a query that will return all records in the foreign table. I build an HTML `SELECT` object based on the results of this query. As I step through all records, I check to see if the current record corresponds to the `$keyVal` parameter. If so, that element is selected in the HTML.

Creating a Button That Returns to the Main Page

To simplify navigation, I added a button at the end of each PHP program that returns the user to the program's primary page. The `mainButton()` program creates a very simple form calling whatever program is named in the `$mainProgram` variable indicated at the top of the library.

```
function mainButton(){
  // creates a button to return to the main program

  global $mainProgram;

  $output .= <<<HERE
<form action = "$mainProgram"
      method = "get">
<input type = "submit"
       value = "return to main screen">
</form>

HERE;
  return $output;
} // end mainButton
```

Summary

The details of the Spy Master system can be dizzying, but the overall effect is a flexible design that can be easily updated and modified. This system can accept modifications to the underlying database, and can be adapted to an entirely different data set with relatively little effort. Although you didn't learn any new PHP syntax in this chapter, you saw an example of coding for re-use and flexibility. You learned how to use `include` files to simplify coding of complex systems. You learned how to build a library file with utility routines. You learned how to write code that can be adapted to multiple data sets. You learned how to write code that prevents certain kinds of user errors by limiting choices to legal values. You learned how to build programs that help tie together relational data structures. The things you have learned in this chapter form the foundation of all data-enabled Web programming, which in turn form the backbone of e-commerce and content management systems.

CHALLENGES

1. **Add a module that lets the user interactively query the database. Begin with a page that allows the user to type in an agent's name and returns data based on that agent.**
2. **Once the basic functionality of an "agent search" program is done, add checkboxes that allow certain aspects of the agent to be displayed (operation and skills).**
3. **Build programs that allow searching on other aspects of the data, including skills and operations.**
4. **Modify the spy master database to support another data set.**

Index

Symbols

A

B

C

D

E

F

I

J-K

L

M

N

O

P

T

U

V

W-Z

License Agreement/Notice of Limited Warranty

By opening the sealed disc container in this book, you agree to the following terms and conditions. If, upon reading the following license agreement and notice of limited warranty, you cannot agree to the terms and conditions set forth, return the unused book with unopened disc to the place where you purchased it for a refund.

License:

The enclosed software is copyrighted by the copyright holder(s) indicated on the software disc. You are licensed to copy the software onto a single computer for use by a single user and to a backup disc. You may not reproduce, make copies, or distribute copies or rent or lease the software in whole or in part, except with written permission of the copyright holder(s). You may transfer the enclosed disc only together with this license, and only if you destroy all other copies of the software and the transferee agrees to the terms of the license. You may not decompile, reverse assemble, or reverse engineer the software.

Notice of Limited Warranty:

The enclosed disc is warranted by Premier Press to be free of physical defects in materials and workmanship for a period of sixty (60) days from end user's purchase of the book/disc combination. During the sixty-day term of the limited warranty, Premier Press will provide a replacement disc upon the return of a defective disc.

Limited Liability:

THE SOLE REMEDY FOR BREACH OF THIS LIMITED WARRANTY SHALL CONSIST ENTIRELY OF REPLACEMENT OF THE DEFECTIVE DISC. IN NO EVENT SHALL PREMIER PRESS OR THE AUTHORS BE LIABLE FOR ANY OTHER DAMAGES, INCLUDING LOSS OR CORRUPTION OF DATA, CHANGES IN THE FUNCTIONAL CHARACTERISTICS OF THE HARDWARE OR OPERATING SYSTEM, DELETERIOUS INTERACTION WITH OTHER SOFTWARE, OR ANY OTHER SPECIAL, INCIDENTAL, OR CONSEQUENTIAL DAMAGES THAT MAY ARISE, EVEN IF PREMIER AND/OR THE AUTHORS HAVE PREVIOUSLY BEEN NOTIFIED THAT THE POSSIBILITY OF SUCH DAMAGES EXISTS.

Disclaimer of Warranties:

PREMIER AND THE AUTHORS SPECIFICALLY DISCLAIM ANY AND ALL OTHER WARRANTIES, EITHER EXPRESS OR IMPLIED, INCLUDING WARRANTIES OF MERCHANTABILITY, SUITABILITY TO A PARTICULAR TASK OR PURPOSE, OR FREEDOM FROM ERRORS. SOME STATES DO NOT ALLOW FOR EXCLUSION OF IMPLIED WARRANTIES OR LIMITATION OF INCIDENTAL OR CONSEQUENTIAL DAMAGES, SO THESE LIMITATIONS MIGHT NOT APPLY TO YOU.

Other:

This Agreement is governed by the laws of the State of Indiana without regard to choice of law principles. The United Convention of Contracts for the International Sale of Goods is specifically disclaimed. This Agreement constitutes the entire agreement between you and Premier Press regarding use of the software.